THE DIVINE IMAGE

THE DIVINE IMAGE

Envisioning the Invisible God

Ian A. McFarland

Fortress Press
Minneapolis

THE DIVINE IMAGE
Envisioning the Invisible God

An earlier version of chapter 3 appeared in *Theology Today* 60 (2003): 200–14 and appears here by permission.

Cover image: © Pete Atkinson/The Image Bank/Getty Images. Used by permission.
Cover and book design: James Korsmo

Library of Congress Cataloging-in-Publication Data

McFarland, Ian A. (Ian Alexander), 1963–
The divine image : envisioning the invisible God / Ian A. McFarland.
p. cm.
Includes index.
ISBN 0-8006-3762-3 (alk. paper)
1. Image of God. I. Title.
BT103.M34 2005
233'.5—dc22
2005024277

The paper used in this publication meets the minimum requirements of American National Standard for Information Sciences — Permanence of Paper for Printed Library Materials, ANSI Z329.48-1984.

Manufactured in the U.S.A.

09 08 07 06 05 1 2 3 4 5 6 7 8 9 10

for Maggie and Livvie

Contents

Preface

The Bible says that Jesus Christ is "the image of the invisible God" (Col. 1:15). This confession appears to entail a contradiction, for it asserts that the God who is inherently invisible has a visible form. The aim of this book is to make sense of this paradoxical claim. My thesis is that there is no contradiction here, because though in Christ nothing less than God is seen (John 14:9), this visibility does not in any way compromise God's essential invisibility as the transcendent Creator. Indeed, I will argue that the character of God's visibility in Christ actually serves as a persistent reminder of divine transcendence in the face of fallen humanity's ever-present urge to contain God within the limits of the visible.

The relation between God's inherent invisibility and God's visibility in Christ is complicated by the Bible's description of human beings as creatures made "in the image of God" (Gen. 1:27). Interpreting this claim in the light of the New Testament's identification of Jesus with the divine image, I will argue that it is significant not because it tells us what human beings *are*, but because it indicates the kinds of things they need to *do* if they would know God. Knowing God requires attending to God in a way that deconstructs all false images and idols, or, more to the point, all confusion of God with ourselves. I maintain that the category of the divine image provides resources for this ongoing task by suggesting how the church, as the body of Christ, can be conceived in terms of an interlocking set of practices that serve both to critique and to refashion our vision of the divine so that we may come to know God more fully and more truly.

The idea that human beings were created in God's image (*imago dei* in Latin) has always fascinated theologians. Throughout most of Christian history, this phrase has been interpreted as hinting at some quality or property of human beings by virtue of which they resemble God. Yet insofar as an image is the visible representation of something, the real significance of this passage arguably lies in its implicit claim that God can be seen in creation. Because Genesis 1 does not say that human beings *are* God's image, however, it follows that they cannot be said to represent God as such. That distinction belongs to Jesus alone. Because he *is* the "image of God," to see him is to see God (John 14:9). Yet because Jesus, as the Christ, is the head of a body that includes an indeterminate number of other human members, seeing him requires looking at the rest of the human family with whom his own life is bound up through the incarnation. Jesus' identity as the image of God is thus inseparable from the identities of all those who, having been called to be members of his body, bring the contours of that image into relief. So if we want to know who Jesus—and thus who God—is, we need to look at them.

Defending this thesis requires paying careful attention to the way the concept of image is used in the Bible. The results of this analysis, in turn, set the terms for further reflection on what it means to see and know God, with special attention to the relationship between established Christian convictions regarding God's presence in the world and no less well established beliefs regarding God's transcendence of it. Finally and most importantly, it demands a systematic account of the ways in which knowledge of human beings in general is related to the knowledge of Christ in particular. And at every point it will be necessary to show that the epistemological implications of our having been made in God's image do not simply provide a smokescreen for an idolatrous reversal of roles, in which we make God in ours.

In addition to avoiding a number of problems associated with traditional attempts to interpret the *imago dei* in narrowly anthropological terms, this epistemological interpretation of the divine image provides a basis for understanding the church as a community whose life in all its dimensions serves to test, chasten, and enhance its members' knowledge of God. As the divine image, Jesus remains the touchstone for all Christian talk about God; but because his status as the image through whom God is known is inseparable from his identity as a body whose contours are still being quite literally fleshed out, the church's understanding of God remains very much under construction. To the extent that the church is mindful of this fact, it will strive against the temptation to use its confession of Jesus as the one true *imago dei* as the basis for theological presumption. On the contrary, it will be both ready and eager to acknowledge that in the mystery of its own life as the body of Christ, shaped and reshaped in ever new and unexpected ways by the power of Christ's Spirit, no human person will fail to illumine—even as she or he is illumined by—the glory of the Word made flesh.

I am grateful to many people for their contributions to this project. It was David Kelsey who persuaded me of the problems with traditional attempts to make the *imago dei* the linchpin of theological anthropology. My thinking was deepened through conversations with members of the Workgroup for Constructive Theology at our annual meetings in Nashville, as well as through more informal exchanges with my former colleagues in the School of Divinity, History and Philosophy at the University of Aberdeen. Special thanks go to John Thiel and John Webster, whose comments on earlier versions of the text were invaluable not only in identifying the many areas in need of improvement, but also in providing concrete suggestions for how they might be improved. And I am equally grateful to Michael West and James Korsmo at Fortress Press for supporting this project through to publication. As always, my wife, Ann, has been an unfailing source of patient encouragement and support. My warmest expressions of appreciation, however, are reserved for our two daughters, Magdalena and Olivia, who have been (and, God willing, will continue to be) the most persistent in reminding me of the always surprising ways in which the divine image confronts me in the lives of others. I dedicate this book to them.

chapter 1 The Image of God as a Theological Problem

The Place of the *Imago Dei* in Theology

The category of the divine image has occupied an important place in theological anthropology from the second century and continues to serve as the framework for a good deal of contemporary Christian reflection on human being.[1] While the content of the divine image remains a matter of debate, its significance as a marker for human distinctiveness within creation is a matter of broad theological consensus. The problem is that such an assessment of the *imago dei* seems altogether out of keeping with its place in the Bible. The key text is, of course, Gen. 1:26-27:

> Then God said, "Let us make humankind in our image, according to our likeness; and let them have dominion over the fish of the sea, and over the birds of the air, and over the cattle, and over all the wild animals of the earth, and over every creeping thing that creeps upon the earth." So God created humankind in his image, in the image of God he created them; male and female he created them.[2]

Some form of the phrase is applied to humankind two further times at the beginning of the Hebrew Bible (Gen. 5:1; 9:6) and is thereafter dropped.[3] Though it recurs occasionally in intertestamental literature (for instance, Wisd. 2:23; Sir. 17:3), in the New Testament it is applied to human beings as such only twice and more or less in passing (1 Cor. 11:7; James 3:9).[4] Though the phrase is certainly evocative, such a sporadic pattern of use would seem to suggest caution in according it excessive anthropological weight.

Be that as it may, the lack of attention to the *imago dei* in the Old Testament has not prevented theologians from the time of Irenaeus of Lyons onward from viewing it as the key to formulating the Christian doctrine of human being. Irenaeus's own interpretation of the phrase is remarkably holistic. He explicitly includes the body in the divine image on the grounds that the phrase cannot be restricted to a particular aspect of human being such as the soul or spirit.[5] More often, however, the *imago* has been understood in primarily cognitive terms as referring to a particular created capacity, whether that be reason,[6] freedom,[7] the capacity for self-transcendence,[8] or even an intrinsic orientation to God.[9] But as Karl Barth was quick to point out, none of these suggestions has the least grounding in the Genesis texts, which make no mention of any such capacity in connection with humanity's creation in the image of God.[10]

A functional interpretation of the phrase, according to which the *imago dei* is understood to refer to human dominion over other creatures, appears more promising. The fact that the concepts of image and dominion are clearly correlated in Gen. 1:26 gives this viewpoint a prima facie plausibility that commended it to John Chrysostom as well as to some contemporary thinkers.[11] Unfortunately, two problems attend this interpretation. First, the close correlation of the two ideas does not necessarily imply that dominion is to be understood as the content of the divine image. Their juxtaposition could just as plausibly be explained as a matter of cause and effect, with the *imago dei* being understood as the basis for humanity being assigned a place of preeminence in the created sphere.[12] That this latter explanation is more likely gains support from the fact that none of the subsequent references to the *imago dei* in Genesis make any mention of human dominion.[13]

A third option involves interpreting the *imago dei* in terms of human relationality. According to this line of interpretation, human beings image God insofar as their existence as persons in relation (paradigmatically as male and female) is a creaturely analogue to the relationships among the three persons of the Trinity. Barth commends this interpretation as fitting best with the parallelism between "image/likeness of God" and "male and female" found in both Gen. 1:27 and Gen. 5:1-2,[14] and his view finds powerful contemporary endorsement in the work of biblical scholar Phyllis Trible, among others.[15] Here, too, however, the balance of image language in Genesis renders this interpretation problematic: when murder is prohibited in Gen. 9:6 on the grounds that "God made the human being in his own image," there is no suggestion that the image in the individual human being is only partial.[16] In this context, Aquinas seems justified in concluding that Gen. 1:27 (and, by implication, Gen. 5:1-2) is best interpreted as affirming that "the image of God is common to both sexes" rather than defined in terms of sexual distinction.[17]

At the end of his own wide-ranging review of the history of exposition of the phrase, Claus Westermann argues persuasively that the desire to interpret "image of God" as a statement about human nature is exegetically without foundation. According to Westermann, the key to understanding the significance of Gen. 1:26-27 is context, and attention to context shows that the subject matter of the passage is the process whereby human beings are created and not the character of human nature as such.[18] Thus, while he accepts the view that the phrase "image of God" points to a relationship between the human creature and its Creator, he maintains that the truth of this insight has been vitiated because theologians like Barth place it within the wrong conceptual framework:

> It is not one of many possible answers to the question: "What is the image and likeness of God or in what does it consist?," but an answer to the question: "What is the meaning of this further determination in the account of the creation of human beings?" It consists in determining further the nature of the act of creation which enables an event to take place between God and humans; it is not a quality of human beings.[19]

For Westermann the assertion that human beings are made in God's image has the purely narrative function of setting the stage for further interaction between God and humankind. It does not imply any sort of ontological correspondence between divine and human being, but merely establishes the narrative preconditions for the story that follows. From this perspective, speculation about its material content is simply beside the point.

The attempt to interpret the *imago dei* as a specifiable quality of human nature might also be criticized on more general theological (versus specifically exegetical) grounds for suggesting that some aspect of human creation is ontologically more proximate to God than another. While the dominant strands of the Christian theological tradition have consistently balked at claiming that any part of human being is divine, the suggestion that certain "spiritual" attributes (for instance, reason) are somehow closer to divinity than material ones risks just such an ontological confusion. The tendency, long identified by feminist theologians, to elevate some categories of people over others on the grounds that they embody these attributes to a greater extent makes this clear.[20] If God creates the whole world *ex nihilo*, however, then it is the case that not only all creatures but also all features of creaturely existence are equally distant from God: insofar as all are created, they are *eo ipso* absolutely and without qualification other than the Creator.

Of course, this brief review of attempts to interpret the *imago dei* in anthropological terms has ignored the decisive factor in Christian appropriation of the phrase, which is its application in the New Testament to Jesus Christ as the incarnate Son of God (2 Cor. 4:4; Col. 1:15; compare Heb. 1:3). As the prototype of human existence, Jesus is the image into which believers are to be transformed (Rom. 8:29; 1 Cor. 15:49; compare

Phil. 3:21). According to Paul, he is the second Adam of whom the first was only a reflection or type (Rom. 5:14; 1 Cor. 15:45). In short, Christ alone is truly the image of God. The rest of humanity shares that status derivatively, as creatures made "in" or "according to" this primordial image.[21] When this point is taken into account, it becomes possible to explain in christological terms the lack of attention the concept of the divine image receives in the Old Testament (as well as in later rabbinical sources): prior to Jesus' advent, we simply lack the reference point necessary to make sense of the phrase. Only with the incarnation do we acquire the tools to reflect meaningfully on what it means to be made in the image of God.

Refocusing attention on Jesus as the image of God can help to displace more traditional efforts to interpret the divine image in terms of some intrinsic characteristic of human being. But while the importance of the concept of the divine image for New Testament Christology (at least in its Pauline form) is undeniable, it is not immediately clear that shifting the ground of discussion to Christology establishes the *imago dei* as a fundamental category for Christian understanding of human being. As already noted, the use of the phrase in Genesis (as well as in later Wisdom literature) sheds little light on the distinctiveness of the human creature. What more do we learn about what it means to be human from the fact that the image of God is predicated of Jesus? It is, of course, a commonplace of Christian belief that in Jesus we see the true and proper form of humanity, but it does not immediately follow that this point allows us to unpack the content of the divine image as it applies to human beings. Granted that Jesus reveals that "we are God's children now" and gives us the assurance that "we will be like him," the fact that he himself has still to be revealed in glory means that the content of this knowledge is open-ended, since we do not yet "see him as he is" (1 John 3:2).

By contrast, we seem on much firmer ground when we claim to learn from Jesus something new about God. Jesus shows us that God so loved the world as to send the only-begotten Son to save it (John 3:16), that in this act of salvation God did not spare this Son but gave him up for us all (Rom. 8:32), thereby receiving the destructive force of sin and death (2 Cor. 5:21; compare Gal. 3:13). More generally, through this narrative of self-giving love, we learn that the one God of Israel—the God of Abraham, Isaac, and Jacob—is not an undifferentiated unity but a Trinity of Father, Son, and Spirit who is free to relate to us as one of us as while yet remaining both over us and other than us as sovereign Lord.

Here, too, of course, caution needs to be exercised. The divine essence—the ontological content of God's triunity—remains beyond the grasp of creaturely knowledge even in glory, let alone under the conditions of fallen historical existence. All the same, there is a genuine difference between Jesus' significance for our understanding of God on the one hand and his role in revealing to us the nature of humanity on the other. The evidence suggests that it was from the very beginning clear to Christians and non-Christians alike that the confession of Jesus as Lord had profound effect on how God was identified and understood. The claim that Christians "ought so to think of Jesus Christ as of God" (2 Clem. 1:1) finds contemporary confirmation as a fact of Christian practice in the observations of those outside, such as Pliny the Younger, who reports the Christian practice of "singing a hymn to Christ as though to God."[22] This distinctive feature of Christian worship quickly set the church apart even from the synagogue, with which it shared the same Scriptures. And though it took the better part of four centuries to work out the dogmatic details, the Christian worship of Jesus issued in a radically new way of speaking and thinking about God that differed from the philosophical monotheism of classical antiquity no less than from Jewish and (later) Muslim confession of one God.[23]

Where human beings are concerned, however, the effects of Christian confession were not quite so clear-cut. This is not to deny that Christian anthropology was from the start marked by features that set it apart from alternative ways of thinking about human being. Two such features in particular stand out. First, the narratives of Genesis 1–2 implied a clear and absolute distinction between God the Creator and the human creature that contrasts sharply with various accounts (found in different forms among the Greeks, Babylonians, and other ancient Mediterranean peoples) which understood human beings to be at least partly composed of divine material.[24] Second, the orthodox Christian insistence on human freedom represented a direct challenge to the fatalism characteristic of other religious systems of antiquity. Crucial though these aspects of Christian belief were, however, both were inherited from Judaism and not developments uniquely associated with the confession of Jesus as Lord.

To be sure, the New Testament bears ample witness that the confession of Jesus as Lord was also the source of conflict with certain features of Jewish practice that were clearly rooted in a particular anthropological vision. Paul and Luke both testify to the depth of the challenge posed to established Jewish perceptions by the idea that uncircumcised Gentiles—widely regarded as an inherently depraved category of humanity (see, for instance, Rom. 1:19-32)[25]—were to be accepted as full members of the covenant community (Romans 1–2; Gal. 2:11-14; Acts 15:1-29; compare Acts 10:27—11:18). But as significant as these developments undoubtedly were, they do not appear to have been connected with a radically new understanding of human being. The question seems to be less that of a new vision of the human as such than the demand that views already current in the synagogue be applied more inclusively. Thus, Luke portrays Peter defending his conduct in baptizing the household of the Gentile Cornelius on the grounds that "God gave them the same gift [of the Spirit] that [God] gave us when we believed in the Lord Jesus Christ" and thus "has made no distinction between them and us" (Acts 11:17; 15:9; compare Paul's discussion of the grafting of Gentiles into Israel in Rom. 11:17-24).

At no point is there any suggestion that the equality of Jew and Gentile is grounded in all human beings having been created in the image of God, notwithstanding the fact that the point would presumably have been acknowledged by even the most traditional-minded Jewish Christians. Instead (and in line with the arguments of Peter recorded in Acts), Paul claims that the abolition of the distinctions between Jew and Greek, slave and free, male and female (Gal. 3:28; compare Col. 3:11) is based on the extrinsic reality of Christ rather than on any intrinsic qualities possessed by all human beings in virtue of their common descent from Adam. Moreover, Paul's insistence that believers need to be transformed into Christ's image (Rom. 8:28-29; 2 Cor. 3:18; Col. 3:10) implies that they do not possess this image in themselves. Thus, if they are one in him, it is because he has made them one (Eph. 2:14), not because they share some prior unity apart from him.[26] In this way, the effect of the Christian confession of Jesus as the image of God is not to focus attention on humankind, but to prod people to look away from themselves to God as the source and guarantor of their identity.

The Anthropological Limits of the *Imago Dei*

Over against this anthropological minimalism, however, there stands the basic fact that the flesh and blood of Jesus, "who *is* the image of God" (2 Cor. 4:4), were human. It would seem to follow that our distinctive character as creatures made *in* that image can be determined by reference to him. This is the position of Francis Watson, who argues in his book *Text and Truth* that "we learn from Jesus what it is to be human."[27] In line with many of the considerations already mentioned, however, Watson's anthropological conclusions are limited to the following claims:

1. Because the human Jesus is like God, other humans are like God in that they are like Jesus;
2. Through the Holy Spirit there occurs in the Christian community "a human being and action corresponding to Jesus' and therefore participating directly in the image of God";

3. Jesus' resurrection points to the fact that all human beings are destined to overcome death.[28]

All three points are thoroughly consistent with the tenor of the New Testament witness to Jesus' significance for the human family. Underlying each of them is the contention that we can distinguish what is true and lasting in human being from the false and ephemeral only by reference to Jesus. While this use of Jesus as the touchstone against which all claims about the human must be tested is certainly consistent with the thesis that we learn our anthropology from Jesus, Watson's own very modest and rather broadly sketched conclusions suggest that even in the light of Christ our understanding of what it means to be human remains fairly vague.

The limits on the anthropological detail we can derive from Jesus come to the fore in Watson's treatment of Jesus' particularity. In response to feminist concerns about the ontological and soteriological significance of Jesus' maleness, he avers that Jesus' teaching us what it means to be human needs to be distinguished from his teaching us what it is to be male or female. At most, he argues, men may learn from Jesus "to see through certain characteristically male illusions (about power and status, for example)"; but, he contends, "they learn this from Jesus and not from Jesus' maleness."[29]

There are two points to make here. First, it does not seem to me that the distinction Watson makes here between Jesus and Jesus' maleness is altogether persuasive. Although it is an important corollary of Chalcedonian Christology that Jesus' being male both can and must be distinguished from his being human, his maleness is nevertheless an inalienable aspect of his own particular human identity.[30] In this context, I doubt we can separate what we learn from Jesus from Jesus' being male, even if we (rightly) refrain from hypostasizing his maleness as a quasi-independent source of anthropological knowledge. Feminist theologians have argued quite persuasively that it is precisely Jesus' maleness that gives force to his explicit and implicit indictments of those modes of power socially coded as "male." Put simply, Jesus' teaching and practice (for example, the foot-washing episode recorded in John 13) would acquire an altogether different significance if he had been a woman.[31]

If this first point is granted, then our inability neatly to distinguish Jesus' particularity as a man (as well as a Jew, an artisan, and so forth) from his identity as a human being raises significant problems for any attempt to characterize other human beings' likeness to him. How do we extract the shared qualities of human being as *imago dei* from the uniqueness of his story? If our interpretation of his life as a whole cannot be separated from his being a male, Galilean Jew of the first century (even if such features as these cannot be considered sources of revelation in isolation from their instantiation in this particular life), then our ability to generalize from Jesus to ourselves would appear to be limited in the extreme.

This suspicion is verified by the second point to be observed about Watson's argument here, which is that his appeal to Jesus functions only to rule out a certain false interpretation of human being (namely, that humanity is ideally male, or that it is most authentically manifest through patterns of behavior socially coded as male). To be sure, later on Watson cites Rom. 12:1-2 in support of the contention that Jesus illustrates a twofold process, encompassing both "negatively, a refusal to be 'conformed to this world' . . . and, positively, a being 'transformed by the renewal of the mind.'"[32] In practice, however, it would seem much easier to provide definite content to the former, negative dimension of theological anthropology than to the latter, positive one. Because "the world" is marked by established behaviors and norms, the fact of nonconformity is comparatively easy to identify, even if the range of practices to be opposed may be a matter of debate. By contrast, the unrepeatable particularity of Jesus' story makes it much harder to specify the content of positive transformation according to his image. What exactly is specifically new about Jesus, and how can we abstract it from his own particular temporal and cultural location? Things are complicated still further by the fact that his story is not yet over: not until he returns will we "see him as he is"—and thus finally come to understand who we are (1 John 3:2).

This is not to say that the open-endedness of Jesus' story forces us into a position of complete anthropological agnosticism. Because Christians trust that the Lord who will return at the end time is none other than the Jesus who was crucified, they can be confident that nothing yet to be revealed of Jesus in the future will contradict what has already been revealed in the past. The three conclusions Watson himself draws from his reflection on the *imago dei* reflect this confidence and are justified by reference to it. Nevertheless, Watson's own results suggest that an anthropology developed on this basis will prove far better at describing what human being is *not* than what it is. For example, though there seems good theological reason to affirm with Watson that human existence transcends death (and thus to rule out the view that human mortality precludes the possibility of a future with God), Jesus' story provides only the vaguest suggestions about what existence will be like on the far side of death.[33]

Nor is this anthropological indeterminacy restricted to the life of the world to come. Even if we restrict our gaze to the present world of time and space, it is far from self-evident what constitutes "a human being and action corresponding to Jesus." Jesus lived in a particular time and place, and his actions acquire their significance in relation to the circumstances of his own existence. Christians may and should trust that the gift of the Spirit will continue to show them how to instantiate Jesus' practice in other situations, but Scripture itself warns that claims to have the Spirit of the Lord need to be tested (1 John 4:1). Even the claim that we are all like God insofar as we are like Jesus begs the question of exactly how we are like Jesus (that is, what it means to be human). Here, too, the sharpness of division within the Christian community over questions like abortion and euthanasia (not to mention a historical record that shows European Christians all too ready to question the degree to which non-Europeans are truly "like Jesus") suggests that the content of our likeness remains a pressing and by no means easily resolved problem.

The upshot of this discussion is not to question Watson's basic claim that Christology should govern theological anthropology. It is not even to critique the basic content of his own claims regarding the basic features of human being that can be derived from disciplined christological reflection. It is, however, to ask whether the results obtained do not suggest that the venerable tradition of interpreting the *imago dei* as the key to theological anthropology is perhaps wrongly conceived. To be sure, it is no small thing if we learn from Jesus that human being is not definable in terms of some clearly identifiable set of qualities or properties. Yet the value of this conclusion would seem to be the fairly limited one of reminding us that we are better equipped to say what the image of God in us is *not* than to describe what it is. Jesus may be the measure of talk about humankind, but the fact that he has yet to be fully revealed only highlights the fact that for the time being the precise content of our humanity "is *hidden* with Christ in God" (Col. 3:3).

The "negative metaphysics" (to borrow a phrase from Rowan Williams) that lies just beneath the surface of Watson's analysis comes to the fore in feminist analysis of the *imago dei* presented by Mary McClintock Fulkerson in her essay "Contesting the Gendered Subject."[34] More suspicious than Watson of the ways in which Jesus' particularity may distort the anthropological appropriation of the *imago dei*, Fulkerson employs poststructuralist analysis to argue that even attempts to formulate more inclusive understandings of the divine image rest on the implicit exclusion of some human beings. For example, while she appreciates the ways in which white feminists like Rosemary Ruether have deployed the category of the *imago dei* to argue that (white) women are made in God's image no less than (white) men, Fulkerson notes that this strategy implicitly leaves out whole categories of people (including people of color and homosexuals, not to mention androgynes) who are not included in the discursive regime that defines humanity as (white, heterosexual) men and women.[35]

Fulkerson's point is that no amount of tinkering with the terminology of the *imago dei* will address this problem. Because our ability to find meaning in language rests on the mutual opposition of terms that define a particular discursive space, no proposed definition of the *imago dei* can succeed in being fully inclusive of all human beings. To be sure, she shares with Watson the conviction that the story of Jesus provides the framework within which the linguistic exclusion of the "unsaid" other can be challenged.[36] But she is far more reluctant than Watson to extract from Jesus' story any positive content about what it means to be human. For Fulkerson, Jesus' significance lies not in giving us information about the true nature of humanity but in problematizing existing understandings of human being.

Rather than providing a fixed touchstone against which claims about the human can be tested and stored up for future use, Fulkerson is inclined to see in the telling of Jesus' story a means of orienting the reader to an alternate discursive regime that provides the impetus for calling established practice into question. It therefore provides the kind of framework that is necessary if the process of unearthing concrete practices of exclusion is to function as part of a program for social change. She contends that the story of Jesus is particularly suited to this end because it is an open-ended story that is characterized by "a sense for the outside."[37]

Within this broader perspective, the concept of the *imago dei* plays an important but restricted role. The open-ended character of Jesus' story suggests that the divine image he instantiates has a purely negative anthropological function. Fulkerson's remarks here are worth quoting at some length:

> A narrative of th[e] God-creation relation cannot use *imago Dei* to add women to the class of human creatures. Poststructuralism reminds us that there must be a purely negative function for the claim that woman is created *imago* and the story that tries to match it. The work of Ruether's principle [of promoting the full humanity of women] should be that "men are not" *imago Dei* because the need to affirm *women* is constructed out of a pernicious system of significations that constitute *men*. This is not to say that woman is the real image of God; it is not even to say that both are. It is only to say that in this particular set of discursive arrangements, what the reigning discursive system means by *man* is not the *imago Dei*.[38]

Once again, it turns out that the *imago dei* is better at telling us what the human is not than what it is.

Fulkerson's perspective has the merit of preserving the otherness of the divine image in Jesus over against our own constructions of the human. At the same time, however, in her thinking the *imago dei* seems to be reduced to something like a Derridean trace: an absence that is not representable within any system of signification. As attractive as this notion may be as a means of challenging socially entrenched views of the normatively human, it seems to cut against the grain of the biblical depiction of "the image of the invisible God" (Col. 1:15) as a concrete and identifiable person. In light of these considerations, it may be worth considering that the limits on the anthropological application of the *imago dei* identified in different ways by Watson and Fulkerson may be a clue that the central theological significance of the phrase lies elsewhere. The language of Colossians 1 in particular raises the possibility that the biblical identification of Jesus as the image of God may be important less for what it tells us about humankind (including Jesus as a human being) than for what it tells us about God.[39]

The *Imago Dei* and Knowledge of God

Putting theological and hermeneutical considerations to one side for a moment, it might seem appropriate to begin an investigation into the theological significance of the *imago dei* by examining the grammar of the term *image* itself. An image conveys knowledge of the thing imaged.[40] It would therefore seem to follow that the point of describing some entity as the image of God would be to convey knowledge of God. Yet this line of interpretation is not as straightforward a solution to the theological problems associated with the *imago dei* as it may first appear. To be sure, if someone were to hand me a piece of paper with a drawing on it and say, "This is the image of Abraham Lincoln," I would assume that her intent was to tell me something about Lincoln (namely, what he looked like). Yet I am able to appropriate this information as knowledge only if I have been able previously to compare drawings and their subjects directly in such a way as to understand how such two-dimensional depictions relate to their corresponding three-dimensional originals. In the case of a God who is inherently invisible (Col. 1:15; 1 Tim. 1:17; compare John 1:18), however, such experience is unavailable: because I have no proper analogue between the Creator and any reality of which I have seen an image, I lack the conceptual framework I need in order to know how to move from the image to a true understanding of the prototype.

Nor do things improve if the divine image is conceived on analogy with the person who is said to be the "spittin' image" of a parent (in line with the biblical characterization of Jesus' relationship to God as that of the Son to the Father in, for instance, John 1:14, 18). As opposed to a deliberately manufactured artistic or photographic reproduction, image here refers to a kind of organic recapitulation, in which a person resembles her mother or father with respect to certain specifiable features—the eyes, the nose, the shape of the mouth. If I do not already know what the parent looks like, however, I will need to ask in which of her features the person is like her parent in order to be able to understand the resemblance. Here, too, then, interpreting the image presupposes some independently derived knowledge of the prototype as a basis for comparison—a knowledge that is lacking where God is concerned.

Now it might be objected that in contrast to the case of an earthly parent and child, in which similarity is always matched by some degree of dissimilarity, Jesus is said to be "the exact imprint of God's very being" (Heb. 1:3) in whom "the whole fullness of deity dwells bodily" (Col. 2:9). Where the correspondence between image and prototype is so exact, it might be supposed, no independent knowledge of the latter is needed to interpret the former: as the one, true image of God, Jesus' relationship with God is marked by no dissimilarity and thus both can and does serve as the only necessary referent for knowledge of God. An explanation along these lines was developed in the third century by Origen of Alexandria, who provides perhaps the most christologically focused discussion of the *imago Dei* in antiquity. He proposed the following analogy:

> Suppose that there were a statue of so enormous a size as to fill the whole world, and which on that account could be seen by no one; and that another statue were formed altogether resembling it in the shape of the limbs, and in the features of the countenance, and in form and material, but without the same immensity of size, so that those who were unable to behold the one of enormous proportions, should, on seeing the latter, acknowledge that they had seen the former, because it preserved all the features of its limbs and countenance, and even the very form and material, so closely, as to be altogether undistinguishable from it; by some such similitude . . . we . . . obtain the means of beholding the divine light by looking upon the brightness.[41]

Suggestive though this illustration is, it remains problematic given that the distinction between Jesus and the God he images is according to Scripture qualitative and not (as in Origen's simile) merely quantitative. The Bible specifies that Jesus is the image of the invisible God precisely in his embodied visibility (Col. 1:15); moreover, it turns out that in this visibility he is like *human beings* "in every respect" (Heb. 2:17), even though the Scriptures elsewhere take great pains to rule out any possible identification between God and human beings (see, for instance, Num. 23:19; Isa. 55:8-9; Hos. 11:9).[42]

It would seem to follow that what we can know of Jesus can give us no knowledge of God, because to the extent that we focus on Christ's humanity (which is all we can know as human beings limited by sensory experience), we will inevitably be led down the path of idolatry and exchange "the glory of the immortal God for images resembling a mortal human being" (Rom. 1:23). It would be foolish to deny that Christians have shown themselves all too susceptible to this temptation whenever they have made Christ stand proxy for the ambitions and pretensions of civilization or race or nation or church. And yet the experience of those who first confessed Jesus as Lord was that it was precisely in Christ's humanity—in what can be "heard," "seen," "looked at," and "touched with . . . hands" (1 John 1:1; compare 2 Peter 1:16-18)—that God is manifest as the Creator whose rule dictates that we "keep [our]selves from idols" (1 John 5:21). From this perspective, it would seem to follow that the manifold forms of idolatry by which subsequent generations of Christians have shown themselves so easily beguiled follows not from focusing too intently on the particularity of Jesus, but rather from a failure to attend to that particularity, from the attempt to look beyond or behind it to some allegedly deeper or higher reality as the image of God in him.

If idolatry (that is, the failure to know God aright) is in this way connected with a failure to look at Jesus, the central question posed by the category of the image of God is thus how we look at the finite humanity of Jesus in such a way as to obtain genuine knowledge of the infinite God. This question needs to be distinguished from the very different one of how such knowledge is *possible*. From a human perspective, there is no possibility that the invisible God should be known in the visible humanity of Jesus of Nazareth for the reasons outlined above: according to the grammar of the word *image*, the interpretation of an image (in other words, the ability to recognize it as the image *of* something) calls for some independent knowledge of the prototype, and for Christians such knowledge is simply not available where God is concerned (indeed, that unavailability is precisely why the sending of Christ is necessary if human beings are to come to a true knowledge of God). The possibility of such knowledge lies entirely with God, who wills to make the humanity of Jesus the visible, material locus of a divinity whose majesty is inherently invisible and immaterial.

If the epistemological basis of our seeing and knowing God in Jesus remains a mystery, however, the question of how concretely we come to see and know God in Jesus is not. We see and know God when and as we look at Jesus as the one, true image of God. As the myriad images of Jesus that mark Christian literature and iconography show, however, there is no shortage of mutually inconsistent pictures of Jesus to choose from; and the fact that Jesus himself is now confessed to have ascended to heaven does not help matters. But even if Jesus were available in the way he was in first-century Palestine, would this make a difference? Would our understanding of Jesus as the divine image be enhanced by even the most precise holographic image, or the most detailed chronicle of his words and deeds? Would not all such artifacts quickly be transformed into so much more fodder for humanity's idolatrous inclinations? Or is there some other means of getting at Jesus' particularity that takes a different perspective on what it means to behold in him the divine image? As a first step toward exploring the possibility of an affirmative answer to this last question, we will in the next chapter take a closer look at what it means to encounter an image in biblical perspective.

chapter 2 The Ambiguity of Images

The Problem of Images in Christian Perspective

Although the phrase "image of God" is introduced in the very first chapter of Genesis, the Hebrew Scriptures are in general characterized by a reluctance to associate images with God, and this reluctance is carried over into all the religions that draw upon them. A very early manifestation of this perspective is preserved in the curse against "anyone who makes an idol or casts an image . . . the work of an artisan, and sets it up in secret" (Deut. 27:15), but Israel's iconoclastic sensibility receives classic form in the Ten Commandments:

> You shall not make for yourself an idol, whether in the form of anything that is in heaven above, or that is on the earth beneath, or that is in the water under the earth. You shall not bow down to them or worship them; for I the LORD your God am a jealous God, punishing children for the iniquity of their parents, to the third and fourth generation of those who reject me, but showing steadfast love to the thousandth generation of those who love me and keep my commandments. (Exod. 20:4-6; Deut. 5:8-10)

While tradition later derived this prohibition from the belief that God did not take visible form at Sinai (Deut. 4:15-16), the reference to divine jealousy suggests that the fundamental rationale behind the commandment is that to worship an image is necessarily to worship some being other than the God of Israel.[1] Thus, even though the Israelites explicitly identify Aaron's golden calf as "your God [*eloheka*] . . . who brought you up out of the land of Egypt," and Aaron himself describes their worship as "a festival to the LORD [*YHWH*]" (Exod. 32:4-5), their action is condemned as sin (v. 21; compare v. 7).

Given the Christian conviction that the God of Jesus Christ is the same God of Abraham, Isaac, and Jacob who spoke to Moses on Sinai, it should come as no surprise that the rejection of idolatry carries over into Christianity. The ridicule of idols, characteristic of postexilic Judaism (see, for instance, Ps. 115:3-8; Isa. 44:9-20; Wis. 13:10-19) and which later became a staple of early Christian apologetics, is also clearly visible in the writings of the New Testament. Alongside more routine denunciations of idolatry, Paul explicitly connects the sad state of the Gentile world with its willingness to exchange the "glory of the immortal God for images resembling a mortal human being or birds or four-footed animals or reptiles" (Rom. 1:23).

Here, of course, Paul is simply echoing the Torah's rejection of every attempt to fashion an image of God to worship. And yet the fact that Paul also claims that Jesus, though quite definitely a human being "born of a woman, born under the law" (Gal. 4:4), is also the one at whose name "every knee should bend, in heaven and on earth and under the earth" (Phil. 2:10) forces the question of whether he is altogether consistent on this point. Certainly the fact that Christians not only worship Jesus but also have seen fit to shape images of him (and others) for liturgical use strikes Jews and Muslims as idolatrous. In response to this challenge, Christian iconodules (those who do not reject the liturgical use of images) have drawn a distinction between the veneration or reverence (*proskynesis* or *dulia*) paid to images and the adoration (*latria*) reserved for God alone,[2] but the point remains that material forms are regarded as having a legitimate and productive role to play in the believer's relationship to God. In this context, even Christian iconoclasts appear to run afoul of the Decalogue, so long as they join Paul in making Jesus of Nazareth an object of worship.

Some light is shed on the logic of this Christian divergence from Jewish and Muslim practice by the early Christian characterization of Jesus as "image of God" (2 Cor. 4:4; Col. 1:15; compare Heb. 1:3). It was a commonplace of ancient thought that an image mediated the power and presence of the one represented.[3] To speak of Jesus as God's image was thus implicitly to affirm that he was divine as well as human. To be sure, the writers of the New Testament nowhere invoke Jesus' status as God's image as grounds for the human manufacture of images for liturgical use, but later generations of Christians have seen the latter as a natural outgrowth of the former. Because the God who had refused to be *given* an image *by* human beings has in Christ now *taken* one *for* them, it is argued, the manufacture of liturgical images can no longer be rejected out of hand as human presumption.[4] Indeed, for iconodules that charge can be redirected against those whose disdain of images constitutes a refusal to recognize Christ's divine status and thus a blasphemous rejection of God's gracious initiative in taking creaturely form.[5]

The Biblical Suspicion of Images

I will examine more closely the merits of this line of reasoning later in the chapter. At the very least, however, it seems clear that the desire to combine worship of Jesus with the claim to be the faithful followers of Israel's God raises important theological questions that can only be resolved by closer analysis both of the biblical texts themselves and of subsequent Christian reflection on them. One possible line of approach is to note the conceptual parallel between the prohibition against the manufacture of images in the Second Commandment (Exod. 20:4; Deut. 5:8) and that against the misuse of God's name in the Third (Exod. 20:7; Deut. 5:11).[6] Just as the Third Commandment appears designed to block any attempt to conjure God through the speaking of the divine name, so the Second is arguably aimed at the kind of identification of God with an image that might be thought to allow the possibility of controlling or manipulating the deity through some form of sympathetic magic.[7] According to this interpretation of the Decalogue, the prohibition of images blocks any confusion between the world that humanity has been authorized to subdue (Gen. 1:28) and the Creator who remains always humanity's Lord, but it does not necessarily bespeak a wholesale rejection of sacred iconography.[8]

At first glance, this line of argument appears to receive support from the fact that the same God who in Exodus 20 appears to prohibit all images just a few chapters later gives very precise instructions regarding the manufacture of images for use in worship (see, for instance, Exod. 25:18-20; 26:1). This point has long been noted by Christian supporters of sacred images, most recently in the *Catechism of the Catholic Church*, which cites "the bronze serpent, the ark of the covenant, and the cherubim" as examples within the Old Testament of "ordained or permitted . . . images that pointed symbolically toward salvation."[9] Yet the force of these examples as providing positive support for the use of images as a means of securing knowledge of God would seem ambiguous at best. It is certainly the case that Christians have from the earliest times viewed the bronze serpent of Moses as a type of the crucified (John 3:14), but this retrospective reading in no way implies that the serpent had any sort of positive iconic significance in Old Testament times. The Bible clearly records that its original purpose was the purely pragmatic one of stemming a plague of real snakes (Num. 21:8-9). We are told that it did later become a cultic object, but only in the context of the writer describing (with evident satisfaction) how it was destroyed by King Hezekiah as part of a general assault on pagan religious practices (2 Kings 18:4).[10]

There are no similar reports of idolatry with respect to the cherubim on the ark, but neither is there any indication that these figures were understood to mediate knowledge of God. The ark seems to have been conceived as a kind of throne, on which God was invisibly seated "between the two cherubim" (Exod. 25:22; compare Num. 7:89). In this respect, the cherubim, far from providing a basis for the imaging of the divine, merely highlight the unrepresentable character of Israel's God. Moreover, the fact that these "authorized" images were hidden away in the innermost part of the temple (1 Kings 8:6-8; compare 6:19, 23), to be viewed only on the Day of Atonement, and then only by the high priest (Lev. 16:2-5, 29-34), further erodes the idea that they foreshadow the advent of some more concrete, publicly available representation of Israel's God. Inasmuch as the biblical exposition of the Second Commandment makes it clear that liturgical images excite the divine jealousy (Exod. 20:5; Deut. 5:9; compare Ezek. 8:5-12), the conclusion seems unavoidable that, from the perspective of the Old Testament, such images invariably distance the worshiper from God.

This is not to deny that worries regarding the manipulation of God by means of images may have been the original stimulus behind the codification of the Second Commandment, but it is to point out that such practical concerns were open to being developed in a more purely theoretical direction. Thus, one way of explaining why images of God *may* not be constructed is that they *cannot* be, since no fixed, material image can possibly depict the One whose name is (in the opinion of many Old Testament scholars) "I will be what I will be" (Exod. 3:14; compare 33:19). Even Moses, whose intimacy with God is unparalleled in the biblical tradition (Deut. 34:10), is incapable of seeing God's face (Exod. 33:20).[11] And though the prophet Isaiah apparently claims to have seen "the Lord sitting on a throne" (Isa. 6:1), a closer look at his account suggests that his gaze scarcely got above the hemline before it was obscured by smoke (vv. 4-5). In a similar context, Ezekiel reports a vision of "something that seemed like a human form" seated on the divine throne (Ezek. 1:26), but the prophet immediately distinguishes his vision from the experience of direct visual contact with God by claiming only to have seen "the appearance of the likeness of the glory of the LORD" (Ezek. 1:28).[12]

And yet it would be a mistake to interpret this evidence as showing that the biblical suspicion of images is rooted in a belief that God is so transcendent as to be incapable of being identified with any created thing. There are two problems with such a conclusion. First, the Old Testament shows no interest in denying that created things really can signal God's presence: if Elijah did not encounter God in the earthquake, wind, or fire, Moses evidently did in the burning bush. Second (and with particular reference to the problem of manufactured images), it is open to question whether or not the worship of images is inconsistent with a belief that God transcends all physical representation. While the enormous variety of religious practices associated with images makes generalization difficult, it is certainly possible to make the logical point that even when worshipers say of an image, "This is our god," it does not follow that they intend to affirm that the image exhausts the divinity in question. An image may be understood as a locus of divine power and presence, but the frequency with which multiple images of the same divinity may be encountered within a given religious tradition implies that there is more to the divinity than the image.[13] Indeed, one might argue that a proliferation of images is every bit as capable of reminding the worshiper of divine transcendence as a thoroughgoing iconoclasm, on the grounds that a god who can be depicted through a wide variety of images evidently cannot be identified directly or exhaustively with any one of them.

At this point, the straightforward interpretation of the biblical prohibition against images as a defense of divine transcendence requires further elaboration. Without question the Second Commandment serves as a powerful reminder of divine transcendence, but in one important respect this way of interpreting it is only partially correct. Divine transcendence was a commonplace of the ancient Mediterranean world and in no way limited to the highfalutin speculations of philosophers. One has only to call to mind the Athenians' altar "To an unknown god" (Acts 17:23) to be reminded that the person in the street was capable of recognizing that the divine was not exhausted by her own local pantheon.[14] Yet Paul's reaction to this artifact of local piety demonstrates the distinctiveness of the Jewish position. Whereas the Athenian altar was presumably constructed in the belief that the fullness of the divine transcends any particular deity, Paul rather perversely suggests that the perennial (for pagans) problem of the "unknown god" is permanently resolved where the God of Israel is proclaimed:

> What therefore you worship as unknown, this I proclaim to you. The God who made the world and everything in it, [the one] who is Lord of heaven and earth, does not live in shrines made by human hands, . . . as though he needed anything, since he himself gives to all mortals life and breath and all things. From one ancestor he made all nations to inhabit the whole earth, and he allotted the times of their existence and the boundaries of the places where they would live, so that they would search for God . . . though indeed he is not far from each one of us. For "In him we live and move and have our being." (Acts 17:23-28)

Israel's God is certainly transcendent but is not for this reason to be identified with transcendence in the abstract or interpreted as an anonymous and unknowable "wholly other." If it is true that human beings "ought not to think that the deity is like gold, or silver, or stone, an image formed by the art of mortals" (Acts 17:29), they should nevertheless recognize that God is a particular, self-identified "I": the God of Abraham, Isaac, and Jacob.

The stance assumed by Paul on the Areopagus highlights the relationship between particular conceptions of divine transcendence and the possibility of images (and thus human knowledge) of God. If divinity simply and straightforwardly transcends the world, then it follows that no worldly reality more closely corresponds to or is any more suited to divinity than any other. Efforts to refer to divinity—especially by way of negative formulations designed to mark off divine from worldly reality—may be ventured, but the very choice of negations used will itself serve to construct a picture of God that reflects the theological prejudices of the speaker. In this way, the effort to construct an image of God only results in an image of oneself; and honesty will demand that this image be shadowed by a parallel altar "to an unknown god." Theological claims turn out to be nothing more than the arbitrary products of individual or corporate projection, with the wise recognizing that the divine must be as unknown as it is unknowable.

Viewed from this perspective, putative images of God will certainly be judged inaccurate, but they will probably not be taken as seriously as the Second Commandment seems to do. Inasmuch as the presence of an image will be no more misleading than its absence, each is equally far from the divine, with the result that neither is to be more feared or desired than the other. By contrast, Paul's insistence on naming the "unknown God" of the Athenians is consistent with the vehemence of the Decalogue on the question of images, inasmuch as it reflects an understanding of divine transcendence in which talk about God is neither impossible nor arbitrary. God is certainly unknowable, in the sense of transcending all finite, creaturely capacity; but God is not for that reason unknown. After all, the Second Commandment is not the product of Moses' autonomous speculation on the character of a Wholly Other who lies beyond all creaturely experience, but the direct command of "the God of your father, the God of Abraham, the God of Isaac, and the God of Jacob" (Exod. 3:6; compare 3:15; 4:5), who summons Moses from tending his father-in-law's flock and promises to be "with" him as he confronts the power of Pharaoh (Exod. 3:12). In the same way, God's later declaration that "as the heavens are higher than the earth, so are my ways higher than your ways and my thoughts than your thoughts" (Isa. 55:9) is not offered as a rationale for pious agnosticism, but as a reminder of how important it is for human beings to "seek the Lord while he may be found" (v. 6) and not in objects of their own making. Far from being a corollary of divine remoteness, then, the Decalogue's prohibition of images would appear to be rooted in the fact that God has been made known to Israel in the most intimate fashion possible (Deut. 4:7-19). In short, idols are forbidden not because God is unknown, but because knowing God depends on God alone. And this, in turn, means that the question of images may not be as easily resolved as a cursory reading of the Second Commandment might otherwise suggest.

The Biblical Affirmation of Images

In support of this last point, it is important to note that as emphatically as the Old Testament decries the attempt to make a physical representation of God, close examination of its language shows that it would be overhasty to read this prohibition as implying that God is without form. To be sure, the mass of Israelites saw no form (*t^{e}munah*) when God appeared to them in the wilderness (Deut. 4:12, 15), but the seventy elders who represented them with Moses on Sinai "beheld God" (Exod. 24:11), and we are elsewhere told that Moses "beholds the form (*t^{e}munah*) of the LORD" (Num. 12:8; compare Heb. 11:27), even if it is understood that these visions fell short of the divine face (Exod. 33:20). In this context, it is important to note that the focus of the Second Commandment is specifically the human manufacture of images for worship (compare Lev. 26:1; Deut. 27:15), not the possibility of divine self-manifestation in and through creation (see, for instance, Pss. 19:1; 97:6). Moreover, central to the Old Testament witness is the promise that the glory of God shall in the end time be visible to all (see, for instance, Isa. 35:2; 40:5; Ezek. 39:21).[15]

In both canonical versions of the Decalogue, the word used for those images of God that are prohibited is *pesel* (LXX *eidolon*), which refers to an idol (that is, the image of a false god) and carries correspondingly negative connotations wherever it appears (compare Deut. 4:16, 23, 25; 2 Kings 21:7; 2 Chron. 33:7; Isa. 40:19-20; 42:17; 44:9-20; 48:5; Jer. 10:14; 51:17; Nah. 1:14; Hab. 2:18). But not all images are *peselim*. For example, while the Hebrew word *tselem* (LXX *eikon*) sometimes refers to idols (see, for example, Num. 33:52; 2 Kings 11:18; Ezek. 7:20), it can also be used neutrally to characterize Seth's resemblance to Adam (Gen. 5:3). Moreover, in its first and most well-known appearance, it has a thoroughly positive connotation, with humankind distinguished from all other creatures precisely in having been created "in the image [*b^{e}tselem*] of God" (Gen. 1:27; compare 9:6).

In short, the fact that God cannot be represented by an idol does not mean that God lacks an image. Though the worship of images made by human beings is fundamentally alien to the Hebrew conception of God, Genesis confronts us with God fashioning a creature in the divine image, and thus with the claim that such an image exists. Needless to say, this aspect of the biblical narrative does nothing to mitigate God's transcendence of the created order, but it does indicate that the identity of this God must be used to interpret the category of transcendence and not the other way round. Unlike the unmoved mover of Aristotle, the transcendence of Israel's God is not an ontological straitjacket that keeps the divine permanently closed in on itself. Quite the contrary, in the Bible God's transcendence is a function of God's freedom as the one who "will be what I will be" (Exod. 3:14). In the work of creation this freedom is realized in constituting, sustaining, and relating to a pluriform reality that is not divine, and it is fully consistent with such freedom that among the beings God creates there should be one made in God's own image.

When it comes to understanding the significance of a being made in God's image, however, things become more difficult. Images generally function to convey information. It was common practice in the ancient world no less than in the modern for rulers to set up their images throughout their realm as a sign of their sovereignty, and some commentators are inclined to interpret the language of Gen. 1:26-27 in these terms, with human beings fashioned as living images, through whose dominion God may be known in creation as creation's Lord.[16] Yet there is no suggestion in the Old Testament that human beings' creation in the image of God makes them a reliable source for knowledge of God. Quite the contrary, considerable stress is laid on the fact that Israel's decisive encounter with God involved no images (Deut. 4:15-18), and on the radical contrast between God and human beings (see, for instance, Num. 23:19; 1 Sam. 15:29; Job 4:17; compare Mark 10:18).[17] Here the biblical evidence seems to confirm Calvin's judgment that "however much the knowledge of God and ourselves may be mutually connected, the order of right teaching requires that we discuss the former first, then proceed afterward to treat the latter."[18]

It is therefore difficult to know what, if any, conclusions may be drawn from the handful of biblical references to humankind's having been created in God's image. As noted in the previous chapter, no explanation of the phrase is given in Genesis, and the idea is not picked up anywhere else in the Hebrew Bible. When the phrase does reemerge in Jewish writings of the intertestamental period, the focus is less on humankind than on the quasi-personal figure of divine Wisdom. In the Book of Proverbs Wisdom had already been depicted as God's companion in the work of creation (8:22-31). This theme is developed and amplified in the Wisdom of Solomon, where this proximity to God is developed using the language of the divine image (*eikon*):

> For wisdom is more mobile than any motion;
> because of her pureness she pervades and penetrates all things.
> For she is a breath of the power of God,
> and a pure emanation of the glory of the Almighty. . . .
> For she is a reflection of eternal light,
> a spotless mirror of the working of God,
> and an image of [God's] goodness. . . .
> Compared with the light she is found to be superior,
> for it is succeeded by the night,
> but against wisdom evil does not prevail. (Wisd. 7:24-26, 29b-30)

The writer of this text is certainly not oblivious to the tradition of humanity's creation in the divine image (see Wisd. 2:23; compare 9:2), but he makes it clear that Wisdom shares God's attributes in a way quite beyond the capacity of human beings.[19] In addition to possessing an omnipresence that allows her to infuse all things, she is explicitly distinguished from created being as proof against the power of evil. As a reflection (*apaugasma*) of the divine light, Wisdom can be characterized as a flawless mirror (*esoptron akelidoton*) in which the goodness of God's working may be perceived.[20] In filling out this claim, the writer goes on to specify Wisdom as the agent of those great works of salvation history, from the preservation of Abraham (10:5) to the Exodus (10:15-19), through which God has been made known to Israel. From this intertestamental perspective, it is therefore the figure of Wisdom rather than the lives of human beings that we find an image of God through whom God is known.

The terms in which Wisdom is praised would appear to resolve the problem of knowledge of God once and for all, and yet the author is confronted with the fact that the majority of people do not know God. Instead, they seek to know God through creatures who have no claim to be God's image: "the circle of stars, or turbulent water, or the luminaries of heaven" (Wisd. 13:2). Incomprehensible though such behavior might seem, the writer is initially inclined to view it with some sympathy:

> Yet these people are little to be blamed,
> for perhaps they go astray
> while seeking God and desiring to find him.
> For while they live among his works, they keep searching,
> and they trust in what they see, because the things that are seen are beautiful.
> (Wisd. 13:6-7)

Ultimately, however, the heathen are without excuse, "for if they had the power to know so much that they could investigate the world, how did they fail to find sooner the Lord of these things?" (v. 9). In attempting to account for this fact, the writer, following on from the idea that people naturally "trust in what they see," focuses on the visibility of idols as the source of their allure (Wisd. 14:19-20; 15:4-5). In so doing, however, he inadvertently highlights the fact that however much Wisdom, the only true image of God, may be "radiant," "unfading," "easily discerned by those who love her," and "found by those who seek her" (Wisd. 6:12), she does not herself take physical form.

How then is she known? The answer is not altogether clear. It is stressed that Wisdom is not something human beings can acquire by their own efforts (Wisd. 8:21); she must be sent by God (9:10). Yet while in Proverbs God's giving of Wisdom evidently requires the mediation of parents and teachers who provide formal instruction (see, for instance, Prov. 1:8; 2:1; 3:1; 4:1, 10; 5:1, 7; 10:1), the language of the later text is more suggestive of internal inspiration unmediated by any external, creaturely agent. Thus, in Wisd. 7:27 we read that Wisdom "passes into holy souls and makes them friends of God, and prophets," and in 9:17 that this happens by the sending of God's "holy spirit from on high." The upshot is that while Wisdom is praised as the source of visible creation's form and beauty, she herself remains invisible. Where and as God wills, her work in creation may be discerned, but she may not be identified with any creature and remains at a certain remove from creaturely experience: capable of being heard, perhaps, in the voice of the prophets, but certainly not seen with the eyes or touched with the hands. We are thus left with something of a paradox: Wisdom is truly the image of Israel's God, through whom God wills to be known, and yet for all the writer's celebration of Wisdom's all-pervasive radiance, she remains strangely distant and elusive.

It is in this context that early Christian attitudes toward Jesus appear especially significant. Given that Jesus is confessed to be the Wisdom of God (1 Cor. 1:24; compare Luke 7:35; 11:49), it is no surprise that he should also be described as the image of God. Yet the fact that he himself, as a human being, is also a direct descendent of Adam (Luke 3:23-38; compare Rom. 1:3; Gal. 4:4) signals that unlike the disembodied power of the books of Proverbs and Wisdom, he shares the corporeality of the first human pair. This combination of properties is highlighted in Colossians' declaration that in Christ "the whole fullness of deity dwells bodily [*somatikos*]" (Col. 2:9; compare 1:19). The physicality of Jesus is brought into still higher relief in the Johannine tradition. For though preferring to describe Jesus as the "Word" (*Logos*) rather than the image of God, the writer of 1 John refers not only to "what we have heard," but also to "what we have see with our eyes, what we have looked at and touched with our hands" (1 John 1:1)—a use of language that is possible because this word "became flesh and lived among us" (John 1:14).[21] The point in both cases is clear: in Jesus God has come into the world in such a way that the physical form of a human being provides genuine and, indeed, unsurpassable knowledge of God. Jesus thus seems to function as an image in precisely the sense that the Law and Prophets reject, inasmuch as he is able to say of himself, "Whoever has seen me has seen the Father" (John 14:9).

In this way, a counter is offered to the theological concerns underlying the Old Testament's suspicion of a material image of God. Far from leading the worshiper away from God, Jesus in his very corporeality provides the definitive mediation between Creator and creation. God remains transcendent and unknowable by any human power; but by confessing the human being Jesus as God's image, Christians find themselves able to affirm that the unknowable God has come among us in knowable form.[22] In Jesus the world is thus confronted with the claim to have been provided with an objective referent, visible and tangible, against which all claims about God may and must be tested. If we want to know about God, we have to look at this image; and if we will not look at him, our knowledge of God will be flawed.

Suspicion and Affirmation in Conflict: The Iconoclastic Controversy

Though the central position of Jesus within Christian worship and theology was firmly established by the time that the earliest books of the New Testament were written, nothing could be more mistaken than to suppose that this led to a softening of views on the use of manufactured images in worship. On the contrary, early Christians not only took up Jewish ridicule of pagan religious images, but, convinced that they alone had kept faith with God's covenant, even turned the charge of idolatry against the Jews themselves.[23] In a statement for which parallels could be found in virtually any Christian writer of the first four centuries, Origen of Alexandria insists that Christians not only avoid the worship of images, "but when necessary . . . readily come to the point of death in order to avoid defiling their conception of the God of the universe by any act of this kind contrary to his law."[24] The fact that the person of Jesus was worshiped was not in any way taken to imply that any other creaturely form (including even a material depiction of Jesus himself) was a fitting object of liturgical attention.

Notwithstanding this background, however, by the sixth century icons—pictures of Christ, Mary, the apostles, and other saints produced for liturgical use—were an integral part of worship in the Byzantine church. While the sequence of events that led to this incorporation of images into Christian worship is far from clear, the increasingly visible, public character of the church in the aftermath of the conversion of Constantine was in all probability a precipitating factor, and the process was certainly well under way by the fifth century.[25] Nor was it hard to provide a basic justification for this development. After all, though Jesus was understood to provide an objective and unsurpassable referent for our knowledge of God, he had ascended to heaven and thus was no longer physically present on earth. How then was he to be known in the present? Obviously, it was necessary to have some enduring record of Jesus' life:

> [For] since all these things actually took place and were seen by men, they were written for the remembrance and instruction of us who were not alive at the time in order that though we saw not, we may still, hearing and believing, obtain the blessing of the Lord. But seeing that not every one has a knowledge of letters nor time for reading, the Fathers gave their sanction to depicting these events on images . . . in order that they should form a concise memorial of them.[26]

The liturgical use of images was thus justified in the first instance on pedagogical grounds.[27] Nor was it simply a matter of making use of pictures where recourse to the biblical text was impossible or impractical. Even for those with the time and ability to read, icons were valuable in their own right as an augmentation of the biblical narrative:

> The representations of scenes in colours follows the narrative of the gospel; and the narrative of the gospel follows the narrative of the paintings. Both are good and honourable. . . . [For] when we see the same thing [described in Scripture] on an icon we perceive the event with greater emphasis.[28]

Far from leading people away from the true God, icons brought them nearer the divine. In contemplating these images, they are "lifted up to remember and have earnest desire for their prototypes."[29]

While the history of iconoclasm is as difficult to trace as that of the iconophilia it opposes, it is clear that iconodule arguments were not persuasive to many Christians. Iconoclasts were quick to cite against defenders of images not only the Second Commandment, but also the fact that the written testimony of "the Fathers" (that is, orthodox theologians writing prior to the fifth century) was overwhelmingly hostile to liturgical use of images, which was identified with idolatry and paganism. While the iconodules invoked in their defense Basil of Caesarea's claim that "the honour of the icon is conveyed to the prototype,"[30] the fact that Basil was referring to the intratrinitarian relationship between the Son and the Father—and not to that between icons and the person of Christ—made the significance of his claim doubtful at best when it came to assessing the propriety of icons.[31] From the iconoclasts' perspective the issue was not whether the honor paid to an image redounded to the one portrayed, but whether any image crafted by human beings could genuinely portray the divine: the affinity between divine prototype and iconic representation that the iconodules affirmed was rejected in principle by iconoclasts as simply inconsistent with Christian belief in divine transcendence.[32]

In this context, however, it is important to remember that the iconoclasts were as fervent as their opponents in confessing that Jesus was the image of God. Moreover, they demonstrated a genuine appreciation for the need for some enduring witness to Jesus' materiality in their affirmation that the Eucharist was the one genuine icon of Christ.[33] Where they refused to concede any ground was in their insistence that no icon could be countenanced other than one (like the Eucharist) directly formed by God. In order to understand the force both of this argument and of the iconodule response, it is necessary to look briefly at some of the salient features of the doctrine of the incarnation with which both parties were working and which proved decisive in the orthodox vindication of icons at the Second Council of Nicea in 787.

Two features of incarnational theology upon which both iconoclasts and iconodules were agreed was that the divine essence was uncircumscribable (and thus incapable of depiction) and that the human being Jesus was fully divine. In one way or another all of the six ecumenical councils preceding the Second Council of Nicea were concerned with working out the implications of these two points, but the crucial principles upon which the resolution of the iconoclastic controversy turned were defined at the fourth, the Council of Chalcedon, which took place in 451. At issue was the relationship between Creator and creature in the person of Jesus. Was the divine Word to be distinguished from the human Jesus (as seemed to be necessary if the separate integrity of the divine and human natures was to be preserved)? Or were divine and human in him blended in such a way as to constitute a new and distinctive form of being (as seemed to be required if Jesus was to be confessed as just one person)? As it happens, both alternatives were rejected in favor of a definition according to which Jesus was confessed "in two natures, without confusion or change, without division or separation . . . together in one person and one hypostasis."[34] In the course of subsequent efforts to defend this formula of "one person in two natures," the orthodox position came to affirm that Christ's human nature had no existence independent of the Word.[35] The union of divine and human in Christ was therefore not to be understood as the joining of two discreet, preexistent entities (whether on the model of two boards glued together or of divine "software" programmed into human "hardware"), but rather of the Word identifying Jesus' fully human life as the Word's own.[36]

Both sides in the iconoclastic controversy were zealous proponents of this Chalcedonian Christology, but the fact that each drew somewhat different implications from the Council's definition led each to accuse the other of violating its basic principles. The iconoclasts argued that since in Christ the divine and human natures were neither confused nor divided, any icon of Christ would have to depict both natures in their proper distinction and yet without separation. Yet, they noted, everyone agreed that divinity was by nature uncircumscribable, and thus incapable of being given physical form on an icon. It seemed to follow that the iconodules were caught on the horns of a dilemma, since any putative depiction of Christ presupposed either that the divinity could be depicted in the humanity (which would mean a confusion of Christ's two natures), or that the humanity alone was being depicted without the divinity (which would imply their separation).[37] On these grounds the iconoclast Emperor Constantine V felt quite justified in concluding that "anyone who makes an icon of Christ has failed to penetrate to the depths of the dogma of the inseparable union of the two natures of Christ."[38]

The iconodules, however, countered that it was their opponents who had failed to take the measure of Chalcedon. They granted that the divine nature could not be circumscribed, and that it was therefore the (circumscribable) human nature that was the basis for iconographic representation; but they insisted that the unity of the person of Christ made it absurd for the iconoclasts to charge them with idolatry, since the human nature of Christ was *precisely in its humanity* inseparable from the divine. John of Damascus put it as follows:

> I boldly draw an image of the invisible God, not as invisible, but as having become visible for our sakes by partaking of flesh and blood. I do not draw an image of the immortal Godhead, but I paint the Son of God who became visible in the flesh. . . . The flesh assumed by Him is made divine and endures after its assumption . . . [so that] flesh became the Word, yet remained flesh, being united to the person of the Word.[39]

From this perspective, it was the iconoclasts who were dividing the person of Christ by suggesting either that the depiction of his human form somehow failed to include his divinity, or worse, that the incarnation somehow altered Christ's human nature in such a way as to render it incapable of representation. For the iconodules, the point was not that the icon portrayed Christ's divinity (for it is indeed unportrayable), but that in portraying his humanity it genuinely portrays Christ and thus points the beholder to contemplate both the fact and the character of his divinity.[40]

It was this argument that proved decisive for the dogmatic vindication of icons at the Second Council of Nicea in 787.[41] To be sure, strictly speaking it applied only to the depiction of Christ, but it was clear to those on both sides of the dispute that once this case had been made, there could be no serious objection to icons of Mary and the saints.[42] The central issue in the iconoclastic controversy was whether or not it was as the incarnate, corporeal Jesus of Nazareth—and thus as a being capable of material depiction—that the divine Son was "the image of the invisible God" (Col. 1:15).[43] To the extent that an affirmative answer to this question is judged to be orthodox, it follows that the material is able to mediate genuine knowledge of God to the extent that it conforms to the one true image of God that is Christ. Here the fact that human beings were created in that image was decisive, since it implied that to portray Christ accurately required depiction of those who were being conformed to his image (Rom. 8:29; 1 Cor. 15:49) and were thereby becoming participants in his divine nature (1 Peter 1:4).[44] In pointing us to Christ, images of the saints also serve the iconic function of pointing us to God.

Summary and Assessment

In the course of the iconoclastic controversy, the tension between the suspicion and affirmation of images found in Scripture was resolved christologically. The Decalogue's prohibition of images was not simply dismissed, but it was reinterpreted in light of the wider history of salvation. Thus, while the Second Commandment had enduring value insofar as it taught the impossibility of physically depicting the divine nature, its prohibition against bowing before images (the LXX uses the verbal form of *proskynesis*) was not meant to be a permanent bar to religious iconography and was intended only to restrain the Israelites' tendency to idolatry.[45] The coming of Jesus marks an end to this blanket prohibition by making it clear that the point of the Second Commandment was not to denigrate the representational power of the material, but to leave open a space for its appropriation by God:

> In former times God, who is without form or body, could never be depicted. But now when God is seen in the flesh conversing with men, I make an image of the God whom I see. I do not worship matter; I worship the Creator of matter who became matter for my sake, who willed to take His abode in matter; who worked out my salvation through matter. Never will I cease honoring the matter which wrought my salvation![46]

Because the Son was coeternal with the Father, the triune God had never been without an image; but in the Old Testament period the image remained as invisible as the prototype and was known only through types and shadows. With the incarnation, however, it assumed a visible form that can be honored in its visibility only by being depicted iconographically.[47]

Thus, while both iconoclasts and iconodules confessed Jesus as the image of God, for the latter the significance of the incarnation radiated beyond the flesh and blood of Jesus to render *all* matter potentially revealing of the divine. Because Christ, as the true image of God, is the ground of all creaturely existence (Col. 1:16; John 1:3), human beings are authorized, according to John of Damascus, to "make images of every form we see" so that in Christ we may "combine our experience with reason, and thus come to knowledge."[48] Thus, while the saints and martyrs are worthy of special reverence by virtue of their conformity to Christ, all human beings are for Christians fit objects of veneration insofar as they have been created in God's image.[49] Even angels, though naturally without bodies and thus invisible, participate in this new economy of the material, because God has "clothed in forms and shapes things which are bodiless and without form . . . lest we should be totally ignorant of . . . bodiless creatures."[50]

Although there is much to admire in the iconodule reflection on the wider significance of the incarnation for theological attitudes toward the material, there remain significant difficulties with the epistemological significance attached to icons in the Orthodox tradition. The reservations expressed by Hans Urs von Balthasar are significant:

> We cannot say that the theological arguments proposed in favor of icons always sound very convincing. . . . [They] scarcely measure up to the Old Testament's ban on images, a ban which was never expressly revoked in the New Testament, or to the marked restraint and dearth of images of the early Christian period. By contrast, we are given much food for thought by the argument of the iconoclast Constantine V, which says that a merely human representation of Christ—unavoidable, since the divine side of his being remains irrepresentable—constitutes an assault upon Christology and must eventually lead to Nestorianism. Constantine's argument is valid at least by

> way of a permanent warning against allowing the Image of himself that God made to appear in the world . . . to be extended without any critical distance whatever into other images.[51]

To be sure, von Balthasar is quite clear that he intends here only a call for vigilance ("critical distance") rather than a thoroughgoing iconoclasm, but his remarks do highlight the potential problems associated with an uncritical enthusiasm for icons as a medium of human knowledge of God.

One forceful critique of Orthodox iconography comes from Alain Besançon, who notes that notwithstanding the iconodule emphasis on the positive significance of the incarnation for the Christian understanding of matter, icons themselves suggest very little enthusiasm for the everyday world of the material. Instead, the icon is "an instrument of contemplation through which the soul breaks free of the sensible world and enters the world of divine illumination" and, as such, "remains steeped in the Platonic spirit."[52] This judgment is substantiated by the highly stylized depiction of the figures on icons, as well as by the symbolic weight attached to the colors and poses used. It is also reflected in a general trend in the history of Orthodox iconography toward the depiction of dogmas rather than events. Noting that the more earthy stories from Jesus' ministry (especially those associated with eating) have never figured prominently in iconic representation,[53] Besançon points out that throughout the medieval period the subject matter of iconic depiction tended more and more toward the abstract and conceptual rather than the narrative and physical.[54] The cumulative effect of these features leads him to suggest that the icon is less a full-throated celebration of the incarnation than the expression of "a compromise between the full vision of Christ's humanity and the symbolic abstractions tolerated by iconoclasm."[55]

Perhaps the most evident piece of iconic stylization, the pervasive use of gold, provides a partial response to this critique. The gold of the icons is the divine light that emanates outward from the image depicted and thus is a reminder that the matter affirmed in the icon is matter that has been transformed in the same way that Christ was on the Mount of the Transfiguration. From this perspective, there is no reason why one should expect icons to look "realistic" according to earthly standards, because they depict matter that has become transparent to the uncreated light of Christ. In this respect, they are designed to lead the beholder beyond the everyday world, but they are not for that reason hostile to the world; rather, they depict the glorified destiny of the material order under the triumphant lordship of Christ.

At this point, however, it is necessary to ask how the iconographer knows that the image he fashions is accurate. Given the prospective character of icons as intimations of glorified existence, the problem here is less the lack of a clear historical basis for the iconographic conventions regarding the form of Jesus, Mary, or the apostles than whether human beings who are still in history can have a sure enough sense of history's consummation to justify turning away from the dynamic and evolving fullness of creation to a palette limited to a relatively small number of conventional forms. Here von Balthasar's worry about the uncritical identification of image with reality returns, with iconic art running the risk of being hostage to an over-realized eschatology so confident of its vision of the future as to have nothing to learn from the present.

It was a genuine achievement of iconodule theology to recognize that the incarnation implied a wholesale reevaluation of the significance of matter as a medium of knowledge of God. Insofar as the eternal image of God has taken flesh, the material cannot be regarded as an insurmountable barrier to knowledge of God. Nor can such knowledge be limited (as the iconoclasts thought) to the dimensions of Jesus' physical body. Because God has in Christ taken on the material conditions of creaturely existence ("born of a woman, born under the law"), knowledge of God must include all those other material factors—the people, the places, the events—that condition Jesus' creaturely existence. In their insistence on the value of depicting scenes from the Gospels, as well as Jesus' later followers, the iconodules understood this point. Nevertheless, they arguably set their sights too narrowly. As a result, the canons governing the production of icons, though designed with the admirable aim of checking the introduction of purely subjective elements on the part of the artist, may all too easily translate into an unwillingness to see the light of Christ shine through any but a limited number of established forms.[56] Consequently, though it may be true (as Orthodox theologians in particular are keen to stress)[57] that as material beings we cannot get along without material images, the risk that we will conform those images to our own sensibilities raises the question of how our imaging of Christ is to be kept from the ever-present temptation to idolatry. An adequate response to this question will require a more detailed exploration of how our knowing of Christ (and thus of God in Christ) is related to our knowing of other objects in the world around us. To this possibility we turn in the next chapter.

chapter 3 The Image of God in Christ

The Problem of Knowing an Unknowable God

The previous chapter explored a fundamental tension at the heart of theological reflection on the image of God. All parties can agree on the basic principle that an image is a source of knowledge, and that an image of God therefore opens the door to genuine knowledge of God. To the extent that all Christians follow Col. 1:15 in confessing Jesus of Nazareth as the "image of the invisible God," they would appear to be committed to the principle that there is genuine knowledge of God in Christ. Moreover, the iconodule argument that the incarnation creates a situation in which the whole material realm to be pressed into the service of imaging God would appear to suggest that genuine knowledge of God is now a universal human possibility. In this respect it is undoubtedly true, as Dumitru Staniloae has argued, that the images, as media for human knowledge of God, "are not merely the products of the incommensurability between God and man, but also of the likeness between man, as spirit, and God."[1] We in time can know God in images because God has an image eternally in God's own trinitarian life.

At the same time, however, there are other dimensions of Christian reflection that belie this optimistic assessment. Two issues are of particular importance here. First, though Christians confess that Jesus is risen and thus alive in his humanity, they also confess that the body perceived by the disciples during the forty days after Easter is now physically absent from the world and will remain so until Christ's return in glory at the end of time (Acts 1:9-11). This point highlights the temporal and spatial limits to our perception in a way that raises genuine questions regarding the accuracy of any images that we might construct. Thus, while it may be possible to grant the iconodules the principle that in light of the incarnation the fabrication of an accurate image of God is possible, it remains open to question whether or not any given image fits the bill.[2]

Even apart from this, however, stands the more basic concern that the divine nature is infinite and therefore incapable of being comprehended (and thus fully known) by finite human minds. As even the most fervent of iconodules acknowledged, the incarnation changes nothing in this respect.[3] The divine nature remains fundamentally uncircumscribable and thus incapable of physical representation. Since what cannot be represented remains hidden to our minds, it follows that God remains for us essentially unknowable. God may have an image internal to the divine life; but given the infinite nature of the one whose image it is, this fact in itself would not appear to resolve fully the question of human knowledge of God.

This tension between the confession that God is genuinely known in Christ and that even in Christ the divine nature remains fundamentally beyond all creaturely comprehension defines a basic problem for Christian theology: the need for clarification regarding what Christians mean when they say that human beings either can or cannot know God. Writing more than a century before the iconoclastic controversy, Maximus the Confessor offers one of the most succinct answers to this difficult question in the tradition: "Divinity and divine things are in some respects knowable and in some respects unknowable. They are knowable in the contemplation of what pertains to divinity and unknowable as regards divinity in itself."[4]

The distinction Maximus draws here is the basis for the traditional distinction between cataphatic (or positive) theology on the one hand, and apophatic (or negative) theology on the other. In one respect, there is genuine knowledge of God that makes meaningful talk about God possible. At the same time, because God is beyond all speech as God is beyond all knowledge, we are compelled to deny any exact correspondence between the divine essence and the qualities that we rightly predicate of the created world. The trick lies in honoring both these convictions, as Maximus makes clear in his *Centuries on Love*:

> If you are about to undertake the task of theology, do not seek out God's essence, for neither the human intellect nor that of any other being under God can grasp it; but try to discern, as far as possible, the qualities that pertain to God. These include eternity, infinity, indeterminateness, goodness, wisdom, and the power of creating, preserving and judging creatures, and so on. For he who discovers these qualities, to however small an extent, is a great theologian.[5]

Good theology begins and ends with a recognition of God's unknowability; but Maximus is careful not to equate this unknowability with utter ignorance, because he holds that God *is* known in God's qualities or attributes. The great theologian (literally, one who talks about God) thus emerges as a person who strikes the right balance between saying too much and saying too little.

While the basic distinction between divine knowability and unknowability may appear unobjectionable in itself, the fact that the person of Jesus does not figure in either of the above quotations raises the question of whether Maximus himself succeeds in striking the proper balance between them in his characterization of the theologian's task. After all, though Paul was willing to grant that from the beginning of the world God's "eternal power and divine nature, invisible though they are, have been understood and seen through the things [God] has made" (Rom. 1:19-20), he immediately makes it clear that until the coming of Jesus this knowledge served only as the occasion for blasphemy and idolatry on the part of Gentile and Jew alike (Rom. 1:21; 3:9-11, 21-22). From this perspective it seems necessary, as theologians from Luther to Barth have been keen to stress, to draw a sharp line between genuine knowledge of God in Christ and all forms of "natural theology" that claim to derive knowledge of God from creation in general.[6] Accordingly, Maximus's views on the possibility of knowing God through contemplating God's eternity, infinity, and the like seem a textbook example of what Luther decried as a "theology of glory": instead of focusing on Jesus, it seems, we are directed to "the contemplation of created beings" as the visible signs of God's invisible essence.[7]

Before dismissing Maximus out of hand, however, it is important to recognize that a narrowly christocentric interpretation of Jesus of Nazareth as the one knowable manifestation of an essentially unknowable God also runs into problems with respect to maintaining the proper balance between apophatic and cataphatic theology. Most obviously, it is predisposed to some form of subordinationism. After all, if God is inherently unknowable, and Jesus is knowable, then it seems to follow that in encountering Jesus we encounter something less than God.[8] If, on the other hand, we follow the First Council of Nicea in affirming that the Word made flesh is fully divine, then Jesus must be no less unknowable in essence than the Father to whom he bears witness: even as "no one knows the Father except the Son," so "no one knows the Son except the Father" (Matt. 11:27). These two points make it clear that a theologically adequate account of human knowledge of God cannot rest on a contrast between the transcendence of the Father and the immanence of the Son. Moreover, since Maximus is as well (if not better) known for his insistence on Christ's historical particularity as for his commitment to apophaticism, it is worth exploring in greater depth his views on how Jesus figures in his understanding of what we can and cannot say about God.

The Logic of Knowing and Unknowing in Maximus

Any evaluation of the tension between God's unknowability and God's knowability in Maximus's thought requires some preliminary investigation into his views on what "knowing" means. Given that none of Maximus's writings takes the form of a systematic exposition of doctrine, generalizations are risky. All the same, the basic structure of Maximus's epistemology seems straightforward enough. He describes knowing as a process of abstracting conceptual images from created beings.[9] Knowing thus involves an ascent from the particular data of sensory experience to the noetic realm of concepts. Because God's absolute simplicity precludes the process of categorization and abstraction that underlies the formation of concepts, however, God cannot be an object of knowledge in the strict sense of the term.[10]

The problem lies in working out how this fundamental principle of divine unknowability fits with the idea that God *is* knowable in God's attributes. In light of Maximus's insistence that God cannot be enclosed in a concept, it would seem doubtful that such knowledge qualifies as knowledge of *God* at all, since the divine attributes (eternity, infinity, wisdom, goodness, and the like) look to be nothing more than a series of conceptual abstractions. Maximus's epistemology would thus appear to render the idea of human knowledge of God vacuous by leaving no middle ground between a divine essence that is beyond every concept and a list of knowable qualities that are nothing more than concepts.

Maximus is able to offer a third option between these two seemingly exclusive alternatives by virtue of the fact that he refuses to equate the divine attributes either with God's essence or with concepts abstracted by the creaturely intellect. Since knowing relates to concepts, this third option means that the human intellect's apprehension of the divine attributes is not "knowledge" in the strict sense of the term. Maximus instead describes it as participation (*methexis*).[11] At the same time, he insists that this participation remains intellective in character, since human beings are by nature intellectual creatures, and grace always honors the integrity of created natures.[12] The ineradicably intellectual character of human being thus makes it possible to continue to speak of human knowledge of God, even though God's absolute transcendence of conceptual categories dictates that this "knowledge" has a decidedly unintellectual form that can be described with equal accuracy as "hyperknowing" or "unknowing."[13] Instead of grasping God through the abstract medium of the concept, the participatory knowledge of which Maximus speaks involves the intellect's being grasped by God in a way that transcends its whole conceptual apparatus.[14]

Participation in God thus refers to a state of contemplation in which concepts are left behind. On one level this is hardly surprising. After all, to the extent that concepts are abstracted from particulars, they are effectively detached from them and thus cannot be a mode of genuine participation in them.[15] So Maximus teaches that participation in God comes through a divine penetration of the intellect that overcomes the opposition between subject and object characteristic of conceptual knowledge.[16] Developing this line of thought, Maximus distinguishes the divine attributes both from the (unparticipable) divine essence and (merely knowable) concepts abstracted from created reality by classing them as objective dimensions of divine being that are open to participation by creatures.[17] Consistent with their being open to creaturely participation, these attributes are effectively understood by Maximus to be the immediate source of creation's structure and stability. Because they are genuinely of God (Maximus says that they pertain to God *ousiodos*, or essentially), they do not have any temporal beginning and thus are not themselves creatures. Nevertheless, creatures can participate in them because they belong to the category of God's works (that is, how God is) and are therefore distinct from the unknowable divine essence (what God is).[18]

We thus come to "know" God when and as the uncreated divine works that structure and sustain creation supervene on (and thereby illuminate) the concepts that our intellects abstract from creation. In this process the divine attributes that underpin creation as a whole become manifest to us in what Maximus calls the *logoi* of individual creatures.[19] Perhaps best defined as the "intrinsic meaning" each creature has been given by God, a creature's *logos* is both its own ontological ground and an ineradicable sign of God's providential care for and presence in all things.[20] That we generally fail to see these signs is a consequence of our sinful predilection to see creatures as nothing more than a means to our own selfish ends; but we become able to perceive them as we acquire the capacity to deploy our intellects dispassionately. As Maximus himself puts it, "The intellect functions in accordance with nature when it keeps the passions under control, contemplates the *logoi* of created beings, and abides with God."[21]

Yet as crucial as the *logoi* are to Maximus's understanding of creaturely knowledge of God, they are by themselves incapable of granting more than a "mediate and partial apprehension" of God.[22] They are the medium of human knowledge of God, but the intellect cannot attain participation in God solely on the basis of its contemplation of the *logoi*. Even when the intellect has stilled its passions sufficiently to be able to focus on creaturely *logoi* without distraction, knowledge of God remains beyond its natural capacity.[23] Although Maximus allows that the intellect naturally seeks out the transcendent cause of created beings, he nowhere suggests that it is capable of discovering this cause on its own.[24] As contemplated by the natural power of the intellect alone, the *logoi* of creatures are words out of context whose wider significance cannot be understood until God takes the initiative and shows us their meaning.[25]

In describing how God leads the intellect beyond this contemplative dead end, Maximus speaks of a sudden illumination comparable to the granting of sight to the blind. However dedicated the intellect may be in pursuit of the ultimate, the intellect operating on its own can never ascend beyond the realm of opinion. Genuine knowledge of the *logoi* as concrete manifestations of God's presence and power is possible only when God's own Logos reveals their place within the wider context of divine providence.[26] In other words, the many *logoi* of creation can only be read and understood in their relation to the divine Logos that is their source.[27] This shift in the intellect's perspective produced by the revelation of the Logos is so radical as to prompt Maximus to compare it with the resurrection from the dead:

> All visible realities need the cross, that is, the state in which they are cut off from things acting on them through the senses. All intelligible realities need burial, that is, the total quiescence of the things which act upon them through the intellect. When all relationship with such things is severed, and their natural activity is cut off, then the Logos, who exists alone in Himself, appears as if risen from the dead. He encompasses all that comes from Him, but nothing enjoys kinship with Him by virtue of natural relationship. For the salvation of the saved is by grace and not by nature.[28]

Apart from the Logos, our knowledge of creatures lies idle; but the intellect illumined by the Logos "will perceive pre-existing in God all the *logoi* of created things."[29]

It would therefore be mistaken to interpret Maximus's vision of the Christian pilgrimage as a steady ascent from the material world to God, in which grace is needed only for the final step from nature to supernature. The revelation of the Logos is not simply the final rung on the contemplative ladder, but the source of orientation without which it is impossible even to begin the climb. This is certainly not to minimize the importance of spiritual discipline: Maximus notes repeatedly that it is impossible to recognize the Logos when the intellect is consumed by passion. But the point remains that no amount of spiritual dedication could break through to the Logos if the Logos had not already broken through to us. Thus, while there is a correspondence between the Logos and created nature (since "He encompasses all that comes from Him"), there is no "natural" pathway from creation to the Logos (since "nothing enjoys kinship with Him by virtue of natural relationship").

Maximus's Christological Particularism

The impossibility of deriving the Logos from experience is reflected in Maximus's refusal to separate the Logos from the particularity of Christ. As the one through whom the Logos "reveals both Himself and the *logoi* of all that has been and will be brought into existence by Him," the person of Christ stands at the core of Maximus's understanding of human knowledge of God.[30] In contrast to any suggestion that salvation might be conceived in Neoplatonic fashion as a more or less natural progression up the great chain of being, Maximus's soteriology is resolutely personal.[31] Thus,

> the saints are said to receive Christ's intellect. But this does not come to us through the loss of our own intellectual power; nor does it come to us as a supplementary part added to our intellect; nor does it pass essentially and hypostatically into our intellect. Rather, it illumines the power of our intellect with its own quality and conforms the activity of our intellect to its own. In my opinion the person who has Christ's intellect is he whose intellection accords with that of Christ and who apprehends Christ through all things.[32]

Once again, the key category is participation. But now it is clear that to participate in God is not to be elevated to some abstractly considered sphere of "divinity" but to be incorporated into the particularity of Christ's story, which encompasses the whole of creation.[33] The Christian perceives the same world that every other person does, and she perceives it as a human being; but what she once perceived through the uncertain medium of her own concepts and opinions she now beholds in the clear light of Christ.[34]

So long as we live on earth, the revelation of the divine Logos does not affect so much *what* we see (that is, Christ instead of creatures) but *how* we see (that is, creatures in their relationship to Christ), as grace enables the mind "to see with knowledge what is [already] in front of it"[35] This emphasis on the epistemic centrality of Christ precludes the kind of theology of glory to which Luther objected; and by integrating knowledge of Christ with knowledge of the creation as a whole, Maximus also rules out a Marcionite rejection of material creation as a means by which God may be known. Seen in relation to the divine Logos who is their source and center, the many creaturely *logoi* "draw to [God] all those who use well and naturally the powers given to them for this purpose."[36] Through grace these creaturely *logoi* come into focus as the component parts of the extended story of how God governs the world. In this way they are enabled to function as genuine sources of knowledge of God.[37]

The christological focus of Maximus's thinking comes to the fore in his interpretation of the transfiguration. In line with the principle that grace functions to change how we see rather than what we see, Maximus does not understand the disciples' experience on Tabor as the result of any objective change in Jesus' appearance. Instead, the disciples are enabled to see what was there all along by virtue of "a change in the powers of sense that the Spirit worked in the[m], lifting the veils of the passions from the intellectual activity that was in them."[38] This change allowed them to see the Logos in his glory and *on that basis* also to see clearly the divine glory in the *logoi* of created beings.[39] The disciples' knowledge of these lesser *logoi* is symbolized by Jesus' shining garments, which in Maximus's view can with equal justice be interpreted as symbolizing "the words of Holy Scripture" or "creation itself." Neither, he argues, is comprehensible in itself; each can be read only in the light of Christ. Because he is their common origin of Scripture and nature alike, however, in him it also becomes apparent that both "are of equal honour and teach the same things; neither is greater or less than the other."[40]

For Maximus both the revealed law of the Old Testament and natural order can be interpreted rightly only in the light of Christ, who is the sole touchstone of their meaning and truth. This christological focus undercuts any attempt to interpret Maximus as laying the groundwork for a natural theology based on contemplation of the physical world alongside biblical revelation as separate-but-equal paths to God. Whether dealing with the written *logoi* of Scripture or the unwritten *logoi* of creation as a whole, right interpretation depends on discerning the overarching context of God's will as disclosed in God's own incarnate Logos.[41] Consequently, our interpretation of nature and Scripture alike must at every point be subordinated to the Jesus of the Gospels.

It follows that no Christian theology worthy of the name can ever allow the many *logoi* to supplant the one Logos. The latter is the ontological ground of the former, and the transfiguration symbolizes how this order of being is preserved in the order of knowing, inasmuch as Jesus is evidently the source of light that illuminates his garments and not the other way round. Indeed, the vision of the transfigured Christ functions as a parable for the way in which God is genuinely known in Christ while remaining essentially unknowable, since the shining forth of divine glory from Jesus' face shows that his human nature is exceeded by the Logos even as it is also the Logos's own genuinely perceivable form. That the light streaming out from this incarnational center proceeds to illumine—and exceed—the rest of creation as well, confirms Jesus as the necessary reference point for all human knowledge of God.[42]

In light of this analysis of the transfiguration, it should be clear that Maximus's claim that God is known through God's attributes involves no sidestepping of Jesus as the one root of all human knowledge of God. On the contrary, it must be seen as the attempt to do justice both to God's knowability and God's unknowability in a specifically christological context. If God is unknowable in essence, then taking flesh cannot change this fact. To the extent that Jesus is confessed to be truly divine, his essence must be every bit as far beyond creaturely comprehension as that of the God he calls Father. In the flesh no less than out of it, God can only be known through the divine attributes. But all this does not mean that God is knowable in creation in a general sense, apart from Christ. On the contrary, Maximus insists that it is only through the incarnation that it proves possible for God's attributes genuinely to be known, since only the fact of God's taking flesh allows us to ascribe those attributes to their proper subject and thereby avoid idolatry. For while God's attributes have permeated creation from the beginning, it is only in the light of Christ that they become visible to fallen humankind in their proper relation to the will and work of God.

Apophasis and Cataphasis

It is from within this christological context that Maximus's understanding of the relationship between apophatic and cataphatic theology is most profitably interpreted. Here, too, certain texts appear at first blush to suggest that theology entails a progressive abstraction from the particularity of Jesus to some purely spiritual reality:

> If you theologize in an affirmative or cataphatic manner, starting from positive statements about God, you make the Logos flesh, for you have no other means of knowing God as cause except from what is visible and tangible. If you theologize in a negative or apophatic manner, you make the Logos spirit or God as He was in His principal state with God: starting from absolutely none of the things that can be known, you come in an admirable way to know Him who transcends unknowing.[43]

There is a sense in which for Maximus the Pauline "Christ crucified" is preliminary, since the goal of the incarnation is that we know and experience Christ's glory as one of the Trinity and not to limit our horizon to the details of his life "according to the flesh."[44] Though we can come to know Jesus only by attending to the limitations of his historical existence, for Maximus piety demands that we recognize that the point of his coming was to lead us beyond those limitations.[45]

Yet while Maximus does see a process of growth as integral to the human encounter with the Logos, this process never involves abstracting the Logos from Jesus. After all, since the Logos is *homoousios* with the ineffable and unknowable God, perception of the naked Logos is impossible by definition. It follows that Maximus's vision of spiritual growth has nothing to do with an ascent from *Logos ensarkos* to *Logos asarkos*. There is no getting beyond or behind Christ's flesh.[46] Spiritual maturity has to do instead with what is seen *in* this flesh. Where the beginner sees only the flesh of the crucified, who "had no form or majesty" (Isa. 53:2), the mature Christian sees the glory of the one who is "most handsome of men" (Ps. 45:2).[47] For while the human being Jesus is the Logos from the moment of his conception, he cannot be seen as such apart from that enhancement of the senses that comes through grace. The goal of contemplation is therefore not the impossible one of leaving Christ's historical particularity behind, but rather of seeing God's glory in that particularity, as happened on Mount Tabor.

Even if Maximus can in this way be cleared of more blatant "theology of glory," it might appear that the spiritual ascent he describes still has the effect of turning attention away from the details of Jesus' ministry in first-century Palestine to his exaltation beyond time and space as ascended Lord. If the goal of the believer is to advance in spiritual maturity so as to share the disciples' vision of Jesus' ineffable glory, it would seem to follow that the momentum of theology pushes inexorably away from affirmative (or cataphatic) speech about Jesus "according to the flesh" to a resolutely apophatic stance. The story of the transfiguration, in which the disciples' ascent of Mount Tabor is associated with their seeing Jesus transformed beyond earthly categories, would seem to exemplify such a progression. In his most extensive discussion of this episode, however, Maximus interprets it in such a way as to suggest that the experience of apophasis is the basis for cataphasis rather than the other way around:

> For I think that the divinely fitting events that took place on the mount of the Transfiguration secretly indicate the two universal modes of theology: that is, that which is pre-eminent and simple and uncaused, and through sole and complete denial truly affirms the divine, and fittingly and solemnly exalts its transcendence through speechlessness, *and then* that which follows this and is composite, and from what has been caused magnificently sketches out [the divine] through affirmation.[48]

This ordering of theological methods follows the logic of the narrative. On the mountain the disciples do indeed perceive a "light from the face of the Lord," which represents "a hidden apophatic theology" and thus bears witness that God "is by essence beyond ineffability and unknowability";[49] but this experience is the *starting point* of the story, not its climax. The practical significance of this (apophatic) light is that it makes cataphatic theology possible by disclosing God's activity as creator, governor, and judge of the world (as symbolized, respectively, by Jesus' garments, Moses, and Elijah). God in God's self remains beyond the grasp of the human mind: what the disciples come to know in the light of the transfiguration are the positive attributes that identify this unknowable God as redeemer of the world.[50]

We thus return to the point with which the chapter began: an insistence that God is ever unknowable in the divine essence, but knowable in the attributes that pertain to that essence. Maximus's excursus on the transfiguration makes it clear that these attributes are not to be conceived as a set of *properties* to be contemplated in isolation either from one another or from the particularity of the biblical narrative, but as a series of interconnected *events* linked by their common relation to the Logos who is their source and end. It follows that Maximus's focus on the attributes in no way leads to the marginalization of Jesus, since it is only in the light of the one Logos that we are able to see the many created *logoi* as manifestations of God's power and presence.

The relationship between apophasis and cataphasis that emerges from this perspective cannot be described in terms of a fixed sequence. To be sure, because God's essence is unknowable, all theologizing must ultimately end in silence. Yet Maximus's reflections on the transfiguration make it clear that he also sees apophasis as the starting point of theology, since it is the experience of the ineffable glory of the incarnate Logos that makes it possible for us to speak intelligibly about those features of God's will and work in the world that can be described. Thus, at the same time that Maximus stresses the importance of not being distracted by created *logoi* in the contemplation of the Logos, he is equally clear that we only know the Logos (and through the Logos the triune God) only in the "intimations" shown us "in the manifest divine works performed in the flesh."[51]

If the perspective on Maximus presented here is accurate, his conception of theology is grounded in a constant turning to the incarnate Logos that both prompts and is enhanced by a further turning to the details of God's work in the *logoi* of creation. The epistemological priority of the divine Logos is crucial: we cannot regard the many creaturely *logoi* as a basis from which to ascend gradually to the one Logos of God. Instead, we must have first encountered the Logos for us to see the *logoi* in their relation to God. But neither does the revelation of the Logos mean that we can simply leave the many *logoi* behind.[52] On the contrary, the experience of Christ as creator points us to particular creatures as those objects of God's providential care without which our understanding of the divine identity is impoverished.[53] Moreover, insofar as this christologically informed contemplation of creation invariably refers us back to the transcendent Creator who is its source, apophasis and cataphasis stand in a relationship of mutual complementarity centered on the figure of Jesus as the one in whom Creator and creature are one.

Jesus' status as the source of the unapproachable light that illuminates creation implies that for Maximus the incarnation, far from constituting an exception to or mitigation of God's transcendence, is the definitive witness to it. In the enfleshed Logos God is revealed as the one who is utterly unknowable but who is nevertheless known as the source and end of all that is knowable.[54] Moreover, because what we know of God derives from the study of God's attributes as these are perceptible in creation, our quest for knowledge of God drives us to the comprehensive study of creation as a whole, since it is precisely by contemplating what is knowable—the *logoi* implanted in all creatures that structure their existence in time and space—that we testify to God's unknowability as Creator, Redeemer, and Judge of the world.[55]

Apophatic Christocentrism

At first blush it would appear that the effect of apophatic theology is invariably to draw one away from the concrete and particular. This is certainly the view of one of the foremost interpreters of Orthodox theology, who sees in apophasis "a tendency toward ever-greater plenitude, in which knowledge is transformed into ignorance, the theology of concepts into contemplation, dogmas into the experience of ineffable mysteries."[56] There is certainly more than a hint of this in Maximus, who speaks repeatedly in his works of the need to transcend the physical, the temporal, and the historical in order to contemplate the spiritual, the eternal, and the heavenly. At the same time, however, analysis of Maximus's position is rendered more complex by the fact that his apophaticism is deeply intertwined with Christology. Thus, while he follows earlier theologians like Dionysius the Areopagite in affirming that God is not reducible to any conceptual category, he also goes beyond his predecessors in deriving the recognition of this irreducibility specifically from the believer's encounter with the person of Jesus. God's transcendence of our conceptual categories is fundamental to Maximus's thought, and it is crucial to his vision of the Christian life that we seek to attune ourselves to this transcendent reality by training our minds to ascend above the flesh to the spirit; but he is also clear that this ascent has its end no less than its beginning in our encounter with the Word made flesh.

Andrew Louth has described the way in which Maximus roots human understanding of God's unknowability in the vision of the transfigured Jesus as constituting a "Christological turn" in apophatic theology.[57] Whereas Dionysius treats the need to alternate between apophaticism and cataphaticism as a purely logical function of theological predication, Maximus ties it specifically to the logic of the incarnation, "as a movement between God's own hidden life and his engagement with creation."[58] In other words, it is understood not primarily as a reflection of the inherent limits on the creaturely cognition (though it is also that), but as a function of God's mode of being toward (and for) the creature. God's ineffability is therefore not a principle derived from contemplation of divinity in the abstract, but is rather a truth that is revealed to us as God comes to us in Jesus Christ and which, as such, becomes the ground of all that we can know and say of God.

In his meditations on the transfiguration in particular, Maximus shows that when we know all created entities in Christ (and for Maximus to know them otherwise is not really to know them at all), we are brought face-to-face with the unknowable God. But the God who in this way encounters us as unknowable is for that very reason not simply unknown. Once again, God's unknowability is not a general metaphysical principle. It is a function of God's identity as the world's creator, ruler, and judge; and for Maximus this identity is uniquely revealed in the life of the incarnate Logos. This close correlation between apophasis and Christology has important implications for the practice of theology.

Abstracted from this christological framework, a purely apophatic theology would be a theology of an unknown God, such that (as noted in the last chapter) we would finally be driven to silence as we came to realize that all our theological language invariably fell short of its intended object. As the resources of language exhausted themselves, a "negative way" of speaking would invariably issue in the negation of speaking altogether. The logic of unknowability is different. Here, too, theological language has a profoundly apophatic function: it is justified only as it honors (and thus bears witness to) God's transcendence of every conceptual category. Yet because the God here is not simply unknown, this apophatic function does not result in the simple exhaustion of cataphatic forms of speech. Because we know God as unknowable through Jesus Christ, the apophatic aim of theology is necessarily and irrevocably anchored in this bit of historical particularity.

The problem is that cataphatic approaches to Jesus and his ministry can easily lose sight of this apophatic end. As we have had occasion to note at several points already, there is nothing about any manufactured image of

Jesus that guarantees its deployment will succeed in bearing witness to God's transcendence. The iconoclast concern that too facile a faith in images can lead to Nestorianism is presaged in Maximus's warning that it is all too easy to conceive even the divine Logos "according to the flesh," thereby reducing God to the realm of the knowable—and thus of the controllable.[59] We therefore need to take care to represent Jesus in such a way that the Logos who comes *in* the flesh is not reduced *to* the flesh.

How is this done? It is a commonplace of preachers and theologians alike that telling Jesus' story rightly is an ongoing challenge, but one thing that should be clear from the foregoing analysis of Maximus's thinking is that we do not honor Jesus' centrality by only talking about Jesus. That would amount to trying to secure a place in the kingdom through those cries of "Lord, Lord" that Jesus himself expressly repudiates (Matt. 7:21). The reason such a strategy cannot succeed is that it abstracts Jesus from the wider context of creation within which the incarnation is located, as though it were possible to cut the Logos free of the myriad earthly attachments that accompany the act of taking on creaturely existence. If the incarnation means nothing else, it means that the Logos cannot be seen or talked about in isolation, but only in relation to concrete details of character and circumstance (details like "Nazareth," "friend of tax collectors," and "crucified under Pontius Pilate") that constitute the particular identity of the Word made flesh.

Nor can this process of contextualization be restricted to the immediate circumstances of Jesus' earthly ministry. Because the incarnate Logos is the source and measure of all creaturely being, a full account of Jesus' identity includes the whole of creation no less than the particular features of the biblical narrative. God's relationship to the creation is defined by Jesus, but it is by no means limited to him; rather, in and through him it goes all the way down. It is on this basis that Maximus can affirm that "the natural and the written law . . . teach the same things."[60] As already noted, in saying this Maximus is not setting the natural world alongside the story of Israel as alternative paths to God. On the contrary, he is arguing that in the same way that neither "law" is legible apart from Christ, so attention to both is integral to grasping (and being grasped by) the fullness of Christ's identity as the divine Logos.[61]

The good theologian is the one who is able so to speak of these two laws as to make it clear that both of them derive from and point to Christ. This double movement is reflected in the transfiguration itself, inasmuch as the brightness of the light on Tabor forces the eyes to look away from Christ to the spiritual landscape he illumines, even as it inevitably draws them back to him as the source of that illumination. Because God's essence is beyond the grasp of creaturely knowledge, there can be no creaturely knowledge of God in God's self. We know God only as God comes into creation and, as the brilliance of the transfigured Christ makes clear, even then the divine essence remains beyond our grasp. What we see and know is the creaturely form that this essence sustains and illumines, and because this creaturely form is bound to (and thus illumines) every other, our knowledge of it cannot rest content with (even if it must take its start from) the brief span of his life in first-century Palestine. Instead, it calls for a deliberate and ongoing engagement with the whole of creation as that which "pertains" to the Logos. And that means that Christians face the ongoing task of discerning how the whole of creation actually does pertain to the Logos as its source and end.

As wide-ranging as this exploration may be, however, the impulse behind it remains apophatic. The goal is not to assemble an encyclopedic knowledge of things in themselves, but to know things in Christ and thus to be able better to identify Christ as that one through whom the unknowable God encounters us. In this process (and contrary to the apparent sense of the quotation from the *Centuries on Love* at the beginning of this chapter [p. 34]), this disciplining of language and concept in the service of theology does not proceed by means of a progressive abstraction from the concrete and particular, but through sustained and deliberate attention to the particular as it exists in and is illumined by Christ.[62]

This manner of relating the apophatic and cataphatic moments of theology to the person of Jesus has important implications for the way in which the invisible God finds a visible image. Maximus's reflections are fully consistent with the idea that Jesus, as the incarnate Logos, is the one genuine image of God. In the words of Hans Urs von Balthasar,

> whoever strives to go beyond this, whoever deems that the Father is still not visible enough in the Son, has not given sufficient thought to the fact that the Father has revealed himself in the Son, the "radiance of his glory and the expressive image of his being," the "total heir" not only of his historical revelation, but of his entire "universe" (Heb. 1:3). Nor has he sufficiently pondered the fact that, after this Word, who is the Alpha and Omega, the Father has nothing further to communicate to the world, neither in the present aeon nor in the aeon to come. He has not considered that, as Irenaeus often repeats, the Son is *the* visibleness of *the* Invisible One, and that this paradox, with the simultaneity it expresses, remains the *non plus ultra* of revelation.[63]

What Maximus brings out, however, is something more of the way in which the knowledge of God we receive through Jesus is problematic in its own way. As von Balthasar's words make clear, it is not problematic because it is incomplete or deficient, as though the being of the Father were not fully visible in the Son. Rather, it is problematic because the divinity made visible in Jesus—precisely because it is fully divine—is finally as incomprehensible to the created intellect as that which remains invisible. As Maximus puts it quite unambiguously in a later work: "The more he becomes comprehensible through [the incarnation], so much the more through it is he known to be incomprehensible."[64] In short, the knowledge of God we encounter in Jesus remains problematic because visibility does not mean control. The fact of the incarnation does not mean that divinity is now circumscribed by a creaturely form in such a way as to be summoned at will by means of adherence to an established set of dogmatic or iconographic formulas. In this sense, the dictum that the finite is incapable of containing the infinite (*finitum non capax infiniti*) is fully justified.[65]

And yet the fact remains that in Jesus what was invisible is made visible. In him God is truly and unsurpassably known. If God is not contained in Jesus, it remains the case that in Jesus we encounter nothing less than God. The point (as Maximus brings out with exceptional force) is that the infinite exceeds or overflows the finite in the same way that the light of the transfiguration exceeds the limits of Jesus' physical form. The problem, then, is not that the infinite God remains unknown in Jesus in the same way that God remains unknown in any finite form, because Jesus is genuinely the image of God and thus the one such form in whom God may be known. The problem is that to know God we must know Jesus, and Jesus' identity exceeds the bounds of his physical form as surely as did the light of the transfiguration. As the one Logos of God, Jesus is the maker of all the lesser *logoi* that constitute the creation as a whole (John 1:3; Col. 1:16), so that his story is inseparable from theirs: if we can only determine the meaning of the many *logoi* by reference to the one Logos who shapes and sustains them, it is also true that our knowledge of the Logos unfolds by reference to the many *logoi*. It makes a difference for our knowledge of Jesus—and thus for our knowledge of God—to know that he called Matthew the tax collector, Paul the Pharisee, and the perhaps equally disagreeable person in the next pew. Likewise, it makes a difference to know that the human form Jesus assumed emerged only through billions of years of biological evolution, and that the star that sustained the network of life he shared will eventually grow cold.

Two conclusions may thus be gleaned from this chapter's investigation of Maximus the Confessor: (1) theology has the apophatic goal of reminding the church of God's radical transcendence of every conceptual category; and (2) this goal is fulfilled by focusing cataphatically on the particularity of Jesus of Nazareth. Crucially, however, this focus on Jesus as the Logos of God is not honored by a "Jesusolatry" that sees in him the cancellation rather than the revelation of divine unknowability. To follow that route would be to undermine the apophatic character of Christian theology from the start. Rather, to see Jesus in his particularity is to see him as Maximus argues the disciples did on Tabor: in relation to the totality of the world of which he is the source and end. Christ is thus honored as the manifestation of what cannot be seen by attending patiently and deliberately to the whole of what can be. It is in this way, as the one in whom "all things hold together," that he is "the image of the invisible God" (Col. 1:17, 15).

With respect to the larger project of investigating the epistemological implications of Jesus' status as the divine image, Maximus's analysis reinforces the concerns expressed at the end of the last chapter over the kind of restrictions on the range of subjects permitted within Orthodox iconography. Inasmuch as the whole of created reality is illumined by Jesus and thereby bears witness to him as Lord for those with eyes to see, there is little basis for regarding only certain episodes of his life as fit subject matter for iconic depiction, and still less for a preference for abstract subject matter. In the same vein, von Balthasar's judgment that "after this Word . . . the Father has nothing further to communicate to the world" also requires some correction. For while it is true that all God has to communicate to human beings is contained in Jesus, Jesus does not come upon us in isolation, but only in relation to the whole of the history he has come to redeem.[66] And this means, in turn, that if the Father has nothing more to communicate apart from Christ, the content of what has in fact been communicated in Christ is very much still in the process of being worked out, even if the church may (on the basis of its belief in divine immutability) stand firm in the conviction that nothing of what it has yet to perceive of Christ will prove inconsistent with what it has already seen.[67]

In this way, analysis of Maximus's views on human knowledge of God highlight the difficulties surrounding the appropriation of the biblical confession of Jesus as the image of God. Specifically, it points to the fact that as much as Jesus represents the ultimate source and norm of all Christian claims to know God, discerning his image is far more problematic than might first appear to be the case. The problem is not simply that any amount of information available about the historical Jesus is subject to (possibly well-intentioned) selection and distortion by human beings trying to make sense of it, but that Jesus' life exceeds the parameters of his historical existence in first-century Palestine, however exhaustive an account of the latter may be available. A comprehensive answer to the question of who Jesus (and, therefore, of who God) is cannot be secured by any amount of historical investigation into the figure of Jesus of Nazareth—precisely because (as the disciples discovered on Tabor) the one who encounters him is ineluctably pointed beyond him to the whole reality of which he is the origin and ending. The next chapter will begin the task of working out the implications of this fact for the practices of the church as its members seek to know the God who has taken on flesh in Christ.

chapter 4 The Image of God in Human Beings

Developing Protocols of Discernment

The Divine Image in Christ and in Us

The previous two chapters have aimed to establish two basic points. First, the biblical claim that God has an image grounds the Christian conviction that God can be known. In Christian thinking, however, the idea of a divine image is not understood to imply any weakening of belief in God's transcendence of the world in general or of our conceptual categories in particular. The divine image does not render God either circumscribed or circumscribable; on the contrary, in the very process of making God known, it confirms God's transcendence of human knowing.

The second point—that the image of God is none other than Jesus of Nazareth—gives these rather abstract claims more definite shape. The story of Jesus not only respects the Old Testament principle that the divine image is not of human making, but also confirms that it exceeds every created form, including Jesus' own humanity. At the same time, because Jesus is the image of God in his flesh-and-blood existence, his particularity cannot be interpreted as a fortuitous (and potentially dispensable) pointer to a God whose transcendence allows no image. In the words of Hans Urs von Balthasar,

> it is impossible to dissect the objective Christ into a form, whose sole property it is to "appear" externally, and a formless light which is what remains for the religious interiority. The whole mystery of Christianity, that which distinguishes it radically from every other religious project, is that the form does not stand in opposition to infinite light, for the reason that God has himself instituted and confirmed such a form.[1]

In short, the fact that God has an image means that God can be known, and the confession that Jesus is that image means that God is known in him. It follows that the story of Jesus is the unique and unsubstitutable touchstone against which all talk about the nature and character of God (that is, all claims to know God) must be tested.

This summary of a specifically Christian theological epistemology is complicated by two factors. First, the fact that Jesus is no longer physically present on earth (a point acknowledged by Christians and non-Christians alike) would appear to vitiate his significance as the one genuine source for human knowledge of God. To be sure, the manufacture of icons is a means of addressing this concern (and it is worth noting in this context that the defining features of icons of Christ were believed to be based on images dating from his lifetime), but I have already had occasion to note the difficulties of supposing that the selective and highly idealized depictions of Jesus in the tradition of Orthodox iconography constitute an adequate representation of Jesus of Nazareth. Not even the written Gospels can be thought to compensate entirely for Jesus' absence, for though their collective rendering of Jesus' career remains for Christians the touchstone for all subsequent claims regarding his character, no such narrative may be confused with Jesus himself.[2] This is not because of some deficiency in the Gospels as historical sources (as though they provided an insufficient quantity of information about the "historical Jesus"), but simply a reflection of the Christian conviction that their status as Word of God is derived from—and thus in principle always answerable to—the concrete reality of the Word made flesh.[3]

Second, even if Jesus were still among us in the flesh, an exclusive identification of the image of God with his historical persona would stand in tension with the equally biblical claim that humankind as a whole was created in God's image and its apparent implication that God may be known in all human beings without distinction. The last chapter's review of Maximus the Confessor's theology might seem to go some way to addressing this issue, insofar as it showed the importance of distinguishing the claim that Jesus of Nazareth, as the divine image, is the touchstone for all our knowledge of God from the very different idea that he is the only source of such knowledge. As the Orthodox tradition in particular emphasizes, the glory that overflows the limits of Jesus' body on Tabor can be read as a parable of the impossibility of his life being seen and known for what it is in isolation. Like every human story, Jesus' can be told and understood only in relation to other human stories and, ultimately, in relation to the story of the whole of cosmos from creation to consummation.[4] In this respect, the claim that humankind was created in God's image does nothing to undermine or qualify the unique character and significance of Jesus' status as the image of God par excellence. On the contrary, the stories of other human beings have value precisely because they enhance our understanding of Jesus' story.

Yet merely stressing human beings' role in shaping our understanding of Jesus fails to distinguish them adequately from other creatures. Since the context of Jesus' birth, ministry, and death ultimately encompasses the whole creation, there is no part of it that does not contribute to our understanding of his story. According to Genesis, however, human beings alone in all creation were made "in the image of God," and this would seem to imply that their relationship to Jesus is qualitatively different from that of all other creatures. It follows that something more needs to be said about human beings than that they contribute to our knowledge of God by helping to contextualize Jesus' story. If all creation bears testimony to God's glory (and thereby aids in the discernment of the divine image), Scripture declares that human beings participate in that image in a more direct way: they do not simply shape its context, but are part of its content.

The most obvious way of accounting for this distinction between humankind and all other creatures is to connect human beings' status as creatures made in God's image with the fact that Jesus, the one true image of God, was himself a human being. As noted in chapter 1, some version of this idea has been a feature of Christian theological reflection for a long time, and it appears to have solid biblical roots in Paul's teaching that human beings are destined to be conformed to the image of Christ (Rom. 8:29) through a process of transformation that is already under way (2 Cor. 3:18).[5] Yet Paul's language suggests that humanity's bearing Christ's image is more a matter of destiny than of origin (see 1 Cor. 15:49), and this same eschatological tone is shared by the most significant non-Pauline parallel to this idea in the New Testament: "what we will be has not yet been revealed. What we do know is this: when he is revealed, we will be like him, for we will see him as he is" (1 John 3:2). If, as these passages suggest, the manner in which human beings share Jesus' image remains hidden, it is hard to see how experience of other human beings can be integral to our discerning God in the here and now.

The recognition that there is no immediate identity between our experience of human beings, whether considered individually or collectively, and the divine image is important as a means of honoring the soteriological point that the believer's life is "hidden with Christ in God" (Col. 3:3); but it should not be viewed as the last word on the question. The relationship between Christ and the rest of humanity is grounded in the fact that the Word, in taking flesh, has joined the divine destiny to that of human beings in a way that has no parallel with any other creature. This is not to imply that human beings are necessarily destined for a greater degree of blessedness than all other creatures, inasmuch as Paul (in Rom. 8:21) and the writer of Revelation (Rev. 21:5) see God's plans as encompassing the redemption and renewal of creation as a whole. But it does mean that human beings have a unique role to play in that renewal process by virtue of the character of their relationship to Jesus (see especially Rom. 8:15-17, 19; compare James 1:18). In the varied metaphors found in the New Testament, Jesus does not simply relate to us as original to copies, but as vine to branches (John 15:5), cornerstone to building stones (1 Peter 2:4-6), husband to wife (Eph. 5:31-32), and head to members (Col. 2:19).

While each of these metaphors implies that human beings are joined to Jesus' life in a way that other creatures are not, the last of them is particularly significant owing to the fact that its use within the New Testament places it beyond the realm of mere metaphor. For while the identification of a particular social group as a "body" of which constituent individuals are "members" was a commonplace of ancient Mediterranean political rhetoric, in the hands of Paul the image functions quite realistically.[6] In writing to Christians in Rome and Corinth, he does not tell them that they are "a" body in the general and more or less ill-defined way that any social group might be so conceived, but rather that they are *the* body of *Christ* (1 Cor. 12:27; compare Rom. 12:4-5). This assertion entails two closely related claims: first, that Christians derive their identity from this particular human life; second (and no less important), that the full shape of this life is inseparable from the total number of those who, having been baptized "into" him (Rom. 6:3; Gal. 3:27; compare Acts 8:16; 19:5), are now part of his story.[7] This solidarity is affirmed most forcefully in Paul's vision on the Damascus road, when the risen Lord identifies himself as "Jesus, whom you are persecuting" (Acts 9:5); but it is also implicit in the earthly Jesus' declaration that the account he will give of himself before the Father includes an account of his followers (Matt. 10:32; Luke 12:8). And it clearly underlies Paul's conviction that those who have been baptized into Christ's death will share in the life of his resurrection (Rom. 6:5-8; compare 1 Cor. 15:12-18).

The church's status as the body of *Christ* means, in the first instance, that the identity of this corporate whole is defined by the particularity of Jesus' career as the crucified and risen one. In line with this principle, Paul can speak of believers "always carrying in the body the death of Jesus, so that the life of Jesus may also be made visible in our bodies" (2 Cor. 4:10). The principle that Jesus is the source of the ecclesial body's identity is reflected in the subsequent development of the corporate metaphor in Colossians and Ephesians, where Christ is spoken of more specifically as the "head" of the body that is the church (Eph. 1:22-23; 5:23; Col. 1:18). This development of the metaphor means that the identity of the body cannot be understood as a composite of the various individual identities of the church's members and, correspondingly, rules out the reduction of Jesus' identity to that of the community.[8] Because he is the head, Jesus stands over against the community as the one "from whom the whole body, nourished and held together by its ligaments and sinews, grows with a growth that is from God" (Col. 2:19; compare Eph. 4:16). There is thus no possibility that the engrafting of new members will change the body's identity; it is rather the members whose identities are transformed by being "nourished" and "held together" under the head. At the same time, however, the claim that Christ's body is corporate and, as such, does experience growth in its members means that even Jesus is not called the "image of God" because he exhausts that image, but because he is the source of its identity and unity.

In this way, the New Testament characterization of Christ's risen life as a corporate reality provides a specifically Christian basis for making sense of the claim that all human beings participate in the divine image. Interpreting the divine image in terms of the body of Christ rules out the reduction of the *imago dei* to any attribute or property possessed by individual human beings in isolation from their relationship to Christ, since the only common factor that unites the various members (who, according to Rom. 12:4 and 1 Cor. 12:14-18, are otherwise characterized by irreducible diversity) is their incorporation under a single head. Instead, Paul's use of somatic language allows human beings' status as creatures made "in" God's image to be understood as referring to their having been called to be members of—and therefore quite literally "in"—the body that defines that image.[9]

Through the process of being grafted into the body of Christ, human beings are conformed to his image (Rom. 8:29; 2 Cor. 3:18). Because this transformation is a matter of taking up a particular function within the body, however, it would be a mistake to understand it as a matter of being molded into so many carbon copies of Jesus. Paul's language suggests rather that our being conformed to Christ's image is better interpreted in a more open-ended way, as a matter of taking on the particular form—quite distinct in both beauty and function from that of Jesus the head—to which we have been called as members within the body.[10] Such an interpretation has the advantage of bringing into relief the basic point that while Christ is the head of the body—so that it is properly called *his* body—he is not himself the *whole* body: while Jesus' particularity defines the church's identity, the body is not reducible to the head. At the same time, however, the distinction between head and members rules out any divinization of the church, which is not the continuation of the incarnation, but a body whose life is at every moment dependent on the gift of Christ's Spirit.[11] Indeed, the refusal to collapse Jesus into the ecclesial body is crucial for appreciating the way in which the diversity of the body's members, in their distinction from the head, can help guide the church to an appreciation of Jesus' transcendence of every human reality, ecclesial or otherwise.

To understand the church's simultaneous identity with and distinction from Jesus, consider that there are two ways in which I may be encountered by another: in the second person, through my efforts at communication in word and deed (for instance, speaking, offering a gift); and in the third person, through the mere fact of my physical presence (for instance, being present to view, blocking the aisle on the bus). These two modes of encounter stand in an asymmetrical relationship to one another. On the one hand, I cannot encounter someone in the second person unless I also encounter her in the third: if I am to offer her a gift, I need to obtrude physically on her space. Even if this obtrusion is mediated by some sort of messenger or go-between, it is only possible to speak of *my* encountering her if it is clear that the third party is acting in my name. On the other, I can certainly encounter someone in the third person without encountering him in the second, as when I cross someone's path without addressing her.[12]

In both cases it will be true that the person has encountered me, yet the character of the encounter will be quite different depending on whether or not it includes second-person address.[13] Where the latter is absent, the other must determine what she can about my identity on her own, making what inferences she can on the basis of whatever aspects of me she perceives. By contrast, when I encounter someone in the second person, I disclose myself in such a way as to attempt to shape her apprehension of who I am. She is, of course, free to make her own judgment regarding the accuracy or significance of my self-disclosure; but to the extent that she recognizes my address as an attempt at self-disclosure at all, she is not simply thrown back on her own resources.[14] Moreover, having once encountered me in the second person, any future interpretation of my being based on third-person encounters will be conditioned by this knowledge. Indeed, it seems fair to say that the context provided by second-person encounters allows third-person encounters to become epistemically productive in a way that they could not be apart from them: one can interpret another's physiognomy better after having come to know her in the second person. And, of course, as acquaintance deepens, second- and third-person factors will intertwine to provide a cumulative picture of the individual, with information acquired in each mode correcting one's judgments of the individual's character in such a way (it is to be hoped) as to provide an ever more accurate understanding of the identity of the one encountered.

Translated to the figure of the church as the body of Christ, the distinction between second- and third-person encounter makes it possible to hold that the church marks the locus of Christ's objective presence in the world without suggesting that Christ's objectivity is either exhausted by or in every respect identical with that of the earthly, historical community. Insofar as the church is specifically Christ's body, he is the source of its identity. Yet this identity is not some kind of ghostly presence suffusing the body as a whole. It is, rather, a function of Christ's status as the head: a distinct member of the body with its own risen and ascended objectivity that remains distinct from that of the other members.[15] The whole body is and remains his as an object of third-person encounter, but the head alone determines where and how the body will be a means of second-person encounter. It is only as the head makes use of the words and actions of its members on earth to address particular people that the church becomes—quite independently of its own capacity or control as a creature—the place where Christ himself can be said to speak and act.

It is in this way that Jesus' status as the image of God is inseparable from his status as head of the body that includes an indeterminate (to us) number of other human members.[16] In this context, Jesus' assertion that "as you did it to one of the least of these . . . you did it to me" (Matt. 25:40) should be understood quite literally as a function of his identity as the Christ and not simply as a metaphorical expression of his personal commitment to the vulnerable. For while it is true that the Word is the divine image from all eternity and quite independent of the presence or absence of a created order, with the incarnation Jesus has irrevocably bound his identity to those he has come to save, such that henceforth the divine image can only be discerned in its fullness through a comprehensive act of perception that includes both head and members. It follows that if we want to see the image of God, we need to look at other human beings, not as the source or norm of this image, but as those whose life under the head renders them the ongoing locus of its manifestation.

The Difficulty of Isolating the Divine Image

Human beings reflect the divine image only indirectly, insofar as their lives are understood to be constituted and sustained by relation to the head.[17] Nevertheless, if only Jesus alone, as the incarnate Word, is the image of God in the strict sense, the logic of the incarnation forces the conclusion that this image can be discerned in its fullness only within the corporate body of Christ (the *totus Christus*). Yet even this guarded formulation of the relationship between image of God and the body of Christ may seem to claim too much. After all, isn't the plain meaning of passages like 2 Cor. 4:4 and Col. 1:15 that Jesus is the image of God in himself, without reference to other human beings? The problem with this objection is that it presupposes the possibility of speaking of Jesus "in himself," as if there were any point in his life that he was not already the head of his body and could therefore be identified without reference to it. Biblically, the election of Christ is inseparable from the election of human beings in Christ. Jesus is logically prior as the immediate object of God's eternal election;[18] but the concrete content of that election is nothing other than God's choosing of humankind.[19] Thus, while Christ and the church can and must be distinguished as head and members, they cannot be separated without denying their unity as one body, established for all time by God's primordial act of election "before the foundation of the world" (Eph. 1:4).

The language of headship needs to be stressed to make clear that the task of discerning the divine image in the many members of the Christ's body does not undermine the central significance of Jesus. Other human beings are not the image of God in the way that Jesus is. They do not provide knowledge of God considered by themselves—a point reflected in the fact that the theme of humanity's creation in God's image is mentioned at the outset in the Old Testament only to be ignored until Jesus' coming in the New. To draw again on the language of Paul, it is only once human beings have moved from being "in" Adam to being "in" Christ that their creation in the image of God becomes theologically significant: they image God only insofar as they are seen in Christ, who in this as in every other dimension of human existence is the only "point of contact" between humanity and God. In the epistemological sphere no less than elsewhere, Jesus' words hold true: "apart from me you can do nothing" (John 15:5). In this way, the correlation of the image of God with the body of Christ confirms that the *imago dei* is, in its essence, a divine reality into which human beings are engrafted only by virtue of—and in strict dependence on—the Word's having assumed flesh. Human existence in God's image is at no point a matter of human beings possessing divine attributes, but exclusively and irreversibly of God having taken on human ones. We become "participants of the divine nature" (2 Peter 1:4) only because God has in Christ participated in human nature, and thus only by the fact that we—apart from any merit or capacity on our side—share the humanity God has assumed.

And yet, having been joined into this body, which is nourished and sustained by Christ alone, other human beings do disclose the divine image. In their lives God is glorified (John 15:8) and therefore known. Again, this glorification of God is concretely nothing other than the glorification of Jesus. Its source is the Spirit (John 16:14); and it takes place specifically through Jesus' body, which, having been raised from the dead by the Spirit's power (Rom. 1:4; 1 Tim. 3:16), is now built up by the same Spirit through the addition of new members in baptism (1 Cor. 12:13), so that "through the church the wisdom of God in its rich variety might now be made known to the rulers and authorities in the heavenly places" (Eph. 3:10). In short, while it is the Spirit who establishes Jesus' identity as the divine image, the Spirit does not do so apart from constituting and revealing that image in its full corporate identity as the body of Christ. As Jesus himself makes clear, the Spirit's witness to him is bound up with that of the disciples (John 15:27; Acts 1:8), who, as the medium of Jesus' glorification (John 17:10) are the ones in whom Jesus' life is made visible (2 Cor. 4:11). They are an ineradicable component of his identity (John 17:21-23), so that ultimately Jesus' story cannot be told without telling their story as well (Matt. 10:32-33).[20]

Nor can this relationship be conceived as limited to the visible church. For though it is only in baptism that a person takes up her place in the body of Christ as a member under the head, Christ has been made "head over all things" (Eph. 1:22) quite independently of human affiliation with the church. Indeed, because Christ's headship is in this way the cause rather than the consequence of human salvation, even non-Christians must be regarded as members of his body.[21] Thus, while it is in the church that the members live explicitly as Christ's body, the work of the Spirit in building up the body is evidently not confined to the church. Indeed, although the augmentation of the visible church must be regarded as the goal of the Spirit's work, its ground is the fact that the pouring out of the Spirit at Pentecost has *already* established (in the words of the Orthodox theologian Nikos Nissiotis) "a personal connection between [Jesus] and all human beings" that is the condition for all further growth of the church as a body through time.[22] After all, human beings can become members of the church only because they have been created by God to be members of Christ's body even prior to their baptism.

Once again, the fact that Jesus' story is inseparable from that of the members of his body does not mean that his story is reducible to that of humanity in general, or even to that of the church in particular. Jesus does not live a generalized human existence, but his own, quite specific life, marked by particular events like "born of the Virgin Mary," "suffered under Pontius Pilate," "was crucified, died, and was buried." Now it is a widely recognized fact that the pictures of Jesus' particularity that emerge in both scholarly and popular accounts of his life generally bear an uncomfortable similarity to the particularity of their authors. Liberals produce a liberal Jesus, feminists a feminist Jesus, political radicals a revolutionary Jesus, social conservatives a Jesus who champions "family values." Without suggesting that all such reconstructions are equally wide of the mark, this tendency to cast Jesus in one's own image highlights a difficulty that lies with any proposal suggesting that our knowledge of Jesus (and, by extension, about God) is tied to our knowledge of other human beings. Even if the logic of the preceding paragraphs is accepted, one might well ask how it is possible to honor its conclusions without thereby giving license to human projects of self-deification.

In order to address this very legitimate concern, it is important to stress once again that the image of God does not refer to a property possessed by human beings intrinsically. Because the primary referent for the *imago dei* is the life of Jesus in its entirety, the Bible provides no basis for raising up any particular human attribute as a "point of contact" with divinity. As already discussed in chapter 1, attempts to isolate some such quality (whether it be rationality, freedom, self-consciousness, relationality, or anything else) fail on a number of counts. On the one hand, they undermine divine transcendence by implying that certain aspects of created existence are somehow ontologically more proximate to God than others; on the other, they invariably turn attention away from the concrete reality of Jesus as the true *imago dei* by focusing on some conceptual abstraction that can be subject to theological analysis without any necessary reference to the particular features of Jesus' life as it was lived "under Pontius Pilate."

Insisting that the image of God refers specifically to Jesus rules out the possibility of directly identifying any aspect of oneself with the divine, as though the *imago dei* were a possession that human beings could hold over against God. Likewise, it rules out focusing on some aspect of Jesus' existence—an aspect ("kenosis of patriarchy," "suffering love") that, of course, other human beings might also embody in their own contexts—as decisive for understanding what it means to say that he is God's image. Against all such tendencies to abstraction it is necessary to insist that there is no basis for interpreting the divine image in terms of a concept that, however characteristic it may otherwise be of Jesus' own life, can be made a subject of reflection independently of him. Once again, the *imago dei* is not a property or characteristic of Jesus' existence as a human being; it *is* that existence in its entirety. This point underlies the fundamentally *epistemological* significance of the divine image, for it is a basic feature of trinitarian theology that the underlying *ontological* relationship between the first and second persons of the Trinity that grounds Jesus' status as the image of God is ineffable. All we are given is the assurance that God is truly encountered in this life, such that no account of who God is can be considered accurate that is not centered on it.

As it happens, the particular form of this one human life implicates the totality of other human lives. Because the image of God takes specifically human shape as a life with and for other human beings, its contours are fully resolved only in the destiny of humankind as a whole. It follows, paradoxically, that the historical person of Jesus does not exhaust the divine image, *precisely insofar as he defines it*. As members of (*mele*, 1 Cor. 12:27) or participants in (*metochoi,* Heb. 3:14) Christ, we are the means of his glorification (John 17:10) even as he is the source of ours (John 17:22).[23] Jesus' priority as source and center of this glory dictates that ontologically this relationship is one of absolute dependence of humankind on Christ;

epistemologically, however, it is one of mutual definition, though even here Jesus' role as the source of human glory dictates that this interdependence is decidedly asymmetric. Rowan Williams has characterized this asymmetry in the following terms:

> The creative act of God in all this can only be articulated in terms of two quite irreducible moments: the establishing in the life of Jesus of a unifying point of reference, and the necessarily unfinished ensemble of human stories drawn together and given shape in relation to Jesus. . . . Thus, in theological terms, human history is the story of the discovery or realization of Jesus Christ in the faces of all women and men. The fullness of Christ is always *to be* discovered, never there already in a conceptual pattern that explains and predicts everything; it is the fullness of *Christ* that is to be discovered, a unity that holds together around this one story.[24]

These twin ideas—that it is the face of Christ that is to be discovered in the faces of others, and that it is *only* in this way that the face of Jesus can be discovered—means that the process is not simply a matter of trying to discern a reality one already knows in an unfamiliar context (like trying to see a mother's features in the face of her son). What one sees in the face of the neighbor must be consistent with what one already knows of Christ (otherwise it would be meaningless to identify the reality found there as Christ's), but the principle that the fullness of the image is not restricted to Jesus means that what one sees will also be something genuinely new. The aim, in other words, is not to shoehorn our experience of other people into a preexisting vision of Christ, but rather to allow that vision to be reshaped by those with whom the image of God in Christ is irrevocably bound.

Hans Urs von Balthasar once wrote, "The authentic saint is always the one who confuses himself the least with Christ and who, therefore, can most convincingly be transparent to Christ."[25] The preceding paragraphs should make clear the truth of this statement. As von Balthasar rightly notes, transparency to Christ does not mean that the individual loses her own identity; on the contrary, her ability to show forth Christ effectively depends precisely on her maintaining a clear sense of her own being as someone utterly different from Christ. But this point suggests a further truth that von Balthasar leaves undeveloped in this passage; namely, that this kind of transparency is also a feature of Jesus' identity as image of God, insofar as genuine encounter with him (like that experienced by the disciples on Mount Tabor) is one in which the glory of God's image overflows his person to include the particularity of other human beings.

The ontological priority of Jesus as the source and measure for talk about the divine image means that this mutual transparency is asymmetric; but it is nonetheless real, and it is reflected in the biblical idea of the church as the body of Christ. The body is one; but if we want to know it in its fullness, we cannot look only at its head but need also to pay attention to the other human beings who are its members. This point helps us to make sense of the way in which the phrase "image of God" can be applied both to Jesus in particular and to humankind in general. The problem is how we can honor this principle without so confusing Christ and the neighbor that we either limit our vision of Jesus to what we see (or think we see) in other human beings or, alternatively, refuse to acknowledge as "made in the image of God" any aspect of our neighbor that does not conform to our existing vision of Christ. In either case, we run the risk of seeing of Christ only what we want to see, thereby failing to discern precisely that aspect of the divine image that may be most crucial to our acquiring accurate knowledge of God.

Protocols for Discerning the Body

The importance of identifying those through whom the body of Christ—and thus the image of God in that body—is to be discerned cannot be underestimated. As Bruce Marshall (building on earlier insights of George Lindbeck) has argued convincingly, the meaning of Christians' utterances about God are fixed by the practices in which they engage.[26] Clearly, then, the insistence that the meaning of the phrase "image of God" is christologically determined will not prevent it carrying radically different meanings, depending on which human lives Christians perceive and receive as disclosing Christ in the present. Attention to the ways in which the church struggles to identify particular individuals as worthy of attention in this regard will therefore be crucial for an adequate theology of the *imago dei*. To the extent that such means of discernment are the subject of communal reflection and cultivation, they will bear a strong resemblance to what Daniel Bell calls a "technology of desire," understood as a collection of concrete practices deployed to steer human desire toward God as the only end offering true repose.[27]

Bell's language of "technology" has been criticized on the grounds that it ultimately reduces to "technique": an impersonal, quasi-automatic process that comes perilously close to a kind of ecclesial justification by works.[28] Whatever the merits of this critique as applied to Bell,[29] I agree that the mechanistic connotations of the term *technology* render it infelicitous in an ecclesial context. In an effort to preserve what I take to be Bell's desire to highlight the difficulty of shaping human perceptions in the face of social and cultural pressures that steer human desires away from the love of God in Christ and, correspondingly, the extent to which the discernment of God's image requires the deliberate cultivation of particular sensibilities within the church, I will instead employ the term *protocol*. There is nothing especially theological about this word. It is rooted in the language of international relations and can refer either to the etiquette of formal diplomatic exchange or to those draft agreements that provide the basis for the preparation of more formal documents. As such, however, "protocol" has the merit of connoting, on the one hand, a relatively formal, mutually agreed set of conventions directed toward a particular end without, on the other, suggesting either inflexible procedure or guaranteed results. In this way, talk of "protocols of discernment" is consistent with the belief that the possibility of seeing the image of God in others is ultimately a matter of grace. At the same time, it reflects the conviction that such discernment will not flourish in an environment where basic Christian practices like the reading of Scripture, prayer, and common worship are neglected. From this perspective, the goal of outlining protocols of discernment with respect to the *imago dei* may be compared to the deployment of various philological, grammatical, archeological, historical, literary, and pastoral "protocols" in the service of biblical interpretation.

Granted that the term *protocol* offers an attractive combination of regularity and flexibility, however, it remains necessary to say something more about how protocols relate to the discernment of the divine image. Perhaps the most important thing to be said here is that *protocols* of discernment should not be equated with *criteria* of discernment. In other words, protocols are not meant to provide a standard over against which a particular claim regarding the content of the divine image is to be evaluated, but rather are to be understood as means of focusing perception in such a way that such criteria might be applied more productively. In this way, protocols of discernment can be conceived as defining the parameters of ecclesial behavior within which it makes sense to enquire about the content of the divine image. In much the same way, the protocols governing the conduct for judge, jury, attorneys, witnesses, and others in a law court establish the framework within which it is appropriate to make judgments regarding a person's guilt or innocence—without themselves providing the criteriology for the verdict. Similarly, the criterion against which Christian vision of the divine image is to be measured is the person of Jesus himself as depicted in Scripture and not any set of ecclesial practices. But given the fact that even the Jesus of Scripture is all too easily fashioned into an idol after the reader's image, there is every reason for the church to commit itself to disciplined reflection on the kinds of practices in which it should be engaged in order to help counter its tendency toward idolatry that contents itself with some image other than that of God.

In a culture where the fundamental equality and inherent dignity of all human beings are regarded as self-evident, the claim that subscription to specific protocols is necessary if God's image is to be discerned in the neighbor may sound strange. Yet while there can be no denying the very practical gains the idea of human equality has meant for many marginalized groups, it would be a mistake to assimilate the liberal principle that "all men are created equal" to the Christian conviction that "all of you are one in Christ Jesus" (Gal. 3:28). The modern, political notion of equality defended by thinkers like John Rawls is predicated on the idea that all persons share a fundamental identity that implies their basic interchangeability. This runs counter to the vision of Christian unity described by Paul, who devotes considerable energy to highlighting the difference (and thus the fundamental noninterchangeability) among the members of Christ's body (Rom. 12:4-8; 1 Cor. 12:4-31; compare 7:7). In line with this contrast, the Rawlsian model of an "original position," in which people are considered without regard to the particularities that differentiate them one from another, is radically opposed to a vision in which discernment of the image of God depends precisely on attending to the unique and unsubstitutable identities of individual human beings.[30]

The Pauline vision of the many diverse members of Christ's body thereby undercuts traditional interpretations of the *imago Dei* as referring to some common quality shared (albeit possibly in different degrees) by all human beings. At the same time, however, to speak of knowledge of the image of God requiring attention to the whole of the human family might also seem to imply that the differences between people are finally of no great matter. After all, if every human being contributes equally to our perception of God's image in Christ, it becomes a matter of indifference at whom we look in any particular instance. For while all people command our attention in principle, and each may be expected to contribute something different to our knowledge of God, there is no reason to direct our gaze in one direction rather than another. Under such circumstances it might be thought both natural and legitimate to begin with those who are most familiar to us; but a problem with this strategy is that it seems calculated to reinforce our already existing perceptions of the divine image in Christ and therefore to be especially open to the risk of idolatry. On the other hand, a purely reactive focus on the unfamiliar is not much better, since our judgments of what is unfamiliar are themselves simply a reflex of what we know best and thus no less arbitrary or potentially misleading.

It is in response to this double-edged challenge that serious thought about the shape of "protocols of discernment" is important. The Christian tradition offers many guides for helping the church in the ongoing task of framing an accurate picture of the image of God in Christ, but two are particularly helpful in providing an initial orientation to the process of developing protocols that are both appropriate and effective. The first and most well-established is the canonization (and subsequent veneration) of certain exemplary believers as saints. The second takes the form of the "preferential option for the poor" advocated by liberation theologians. While these two practices are by no means mutually exclusive, the particular activities that they entail differ sufficiently in their orientation and organization to constitute distinct (though, as I will argue, closely related) protocols. As such, they merit separate examination.

The Veneration of the Saints

While the formal process of canonization is limited to the Roman Catholic and Orthodox churches, the practice of highlighting the sanctity of particular individuals (for instance, Thomas Cranmer, Dietrich Bonhoeffer, Martin Luther King Jr.) is by no means uncharacteristic of Protestants.[31] Whatever form it takes, this practice reflects a deep-seated Christian conviction that though all the faithful have been elected to be saints (Rom. 1:7; 1 Cor. 1:2), certain believers are especially worthy of the title because their lives reveal the image of God with particular clarity.[32] At the same time, the fundamental Christian conviction that Jesus alone is the image of God dictates that the example of those with this capacity to reveal the divine image is kept subordinate to the christological prototype. Consequently, in those churches where saints play a formal role in the liturgical life of the community, there is a clear distinction, identical to that which we have already seen in relation to icons, made between the reverence (*dulia*) paid to saints and the worship (*latria*) of which God only is worthy.[33]

In earliest Christian thought, the capacity to disclose the divine image was associated preeminently with the martyrs, who, as the etymology of their title suggests, were seen as the supreme examples of witness to Christ.[34] By persevering in their faith to the point of death, they had lived out fully Christ's command that his followers "take up their cross and follow me" (Matt. 16:24). The martyrs' conformation to the pattern set down by Christ meant that their sacrifice was understood in the churches as more than the comparatively abstract and impersonal act of dying for a cause. It was, rather, an iconic representation of Christ rooted in personal communion with Jesus.[35] Thus, Luke depicts the proto-martyr Stephen praying, "Lord Jesus, receive my spirit" (Acts 7:59), in echo of Jesus' "Father, into your hands

I commend my spirit" (Luke 23:46).[36] The same basic pattern is found in *The Martyrdom of Polycarp*, the oldest piece of hagiographic literature outside of the New Testament, dating from the mid-second century. Not only is Polycarp praised for "a martyrdom conformable to the gospel,"[37] but the parallels between his death and Christ's are highlighted through numerous details in the narrative, including his prediction of the mode of his execution, the date and manner of his arrest, and his being encouraged by a heavenly voice. Nevertheless, the difference between Christ and the martyr remains clear: "For we worship this One as Son of God, but we love the martyrs as disciples and imitators of the Lord."[38]

However sharp the distinction between the martyr and her christological prototype, however, the very fact that Polycarp's end (along with those of many others in the church's first century) was thought worthy of being recorded indicates that martyrs were accorded a definite, if theologically subordinate, place in the memory of the church. It thus comes as little surprise to find that the narrative describes the annual celebration of the martyr's death "as a birthday, in memory of those athletes who have gone before, and to train and make ready those who are to come after."[39] If all Christians had been grafted into Christ's body, martyrs like Polycarp quickly came to be seen as "the *membra Christi* par excellence," to the extent that their physical remains became the preferred sites of eucharistic worship, with local communities raising churches over their graves.[40] With the eventual political triumph of Christianity as the official religion of the Roman Empire, the effect of believer's devotion to the memory of the martyrs extended to the physical reordering of civic space, as cemeteries that were traditionally located outside the city walls became the site of new church construction and the focus of popular worship.[41]

The martyrs' reflection of Christ's death makes it natural that they should function as foci for ongoing Christian reflection on the image of God, but this particularity raises the question of whether their life is the only sort that is capable of revealing the contours of Christ's body in the present. Ultimately, the church judged that it was not. A groundbreaking figure in suggesting a broader understanding of the saint was the Egyptian monk Antony, who became the subject of a new form of hagiographic literature at the hands of Athanasius of Alexandria. The parallels between Christ and the saint characteristic of earlier martyrologies are preserved, to the extent that a military commander is reported to have said of him, "Truly this man is a slave of God!" in clear imitation of the Gospel accounts of the centurion's reaction to the crucified Jesus (Matt. 27:54; Mark 15:39).[42] Yet Antony's imitation of Christ did not extend to the point of suffering a martyr's death. According to Athanasius, he had hoped for such an end and had even "seemed to grieve that he had not been martyred" during the Great Persecution of the early fourth century, but a central thesis of Athanasius's biography is that Antony's survival is no obstacle to his acquiring exemplary status for other believers, Indeed, Athanasius argues that "the Lord was preserving him for our benefit and that of others, so that he might become a teacher to many in the discipline he had learned from the Scriptures."[43]

Athanasius was quite aware that his eulogy of Antony represented a bid to broaden the category of believers worthy of veneration. In this respect, Athanasius's *Life of St. Antony* functions as a significant step in the process by which saints' lives were transformed from a fixed pattern designed "to reflect the original, normative example of Christ's own life" to a much more variegated type of literature focused on the challenge of "how one form of particularity (the life of Jesus) can be mediated into a very different context with its own equally specific demands and challenges."[44] Whereas saints like Polycarp had been martyrs in their body, Antony represented a new breed as "a martyr to his conscience."[45] At the close of the *Life*, Athanasius highlights this distinction:

> Our Lord and Savior Jesus Christ glorifies those who glorify him. He not only leads into the kingdom of heaven those who serve him to the end [namely, the martyrs], but even in this place, those who hide themselves and are eager to withdraw he makes famous and proclaimed everywhere because of their virtue and for the benefit of others.[46]

Yet exactly what were the conditions of being counted as one of this expanded class of martyrs? As the above passage suggests, Athanasius clearly saw submission to monastic discipline as a sign of exemplary piety, but the fact that the many nameless monks that appear in the narrative are evidently not seen as being in Antony's class suggests that the life of the hermit did not provide the same kind of automatic guarantee of sanctity as meeting a martyr's death. And while Athanasius highlights Antony's acts of healing, exorcism, and prognostication, as well as his continued physical vigor in old age,[47] there is no indication that he has a specific criteriology of sainthood in mind. Indeed, he makes it quite clear that Antony's reputation was already firmly established at the time of his death, so that his job as biographer was not to demonstrate what was already well known, but only to exploit it for the edification of others.[48]

All this suggests a process of identifying saints that, while not exactly democratic, at least has a markedly populist character. The ground for the judgment that a particular person is specially transparent to Christ is in the first instance that she is perceived and celebrated as such at the local level.[49]

Even where more formal procedures for vetting candidates for sainthood have been introduced, this populist element remains at the root of the process, since the responsibility for presenting individuals for consideration as worthy of veneration continues to rest ultimately with local constituencies. Thus, while among Catholics in particular the process of canonization is both rigorous (involving no less than three distinct stages of review by the magisterium) and highly centralized, the criteria remain relatively general and open ended.[50] Successful candidates (with the exception of martyrs, who remain a separate class) must be vindicated with respect to doctrinal purity, heroic virtue, and miraculous intercession after death, but these criteria are primarily negative and fall far short of defining a positive picture of what qualifies as saintly behavior.[51] That judgment depends in the first instance on local communities' impressions of individuals in a way that (as the cases of Francis of Assisi and Catherine of Siena show) provides an opening for models of sanctity that may run against the established social and religious conventions.[52]

The evidence, however, suggests that this opening is not particularly wide. Statistical analysis of Catholic saints who died between the eleventh and the seventeenth centuries shows that nearly 40 percent were of royal or noble birth, and if urban patricians and others of "good family" are included, the number climbs to over 60 percent. By contrast, the number of saints from poor backgrounds stands at around 16 percent over the same period.[53] The fact that these percentages remain relatively stable over a span of seven centuries suggests a permanent bias in favor of the upper classes that is all the more striking when it is remembered that the well-to-do made up only a tiny fraction of the overall population.[54] To be sure, saints of wealthy background often became famous precisely for their devotion to the poor (again, Francis of Assisi is an obvious example). Moreover, once an individual of whatever rank achieved recognition for sanctity, his or her exalted status with respect to all members of the community alike did function to suppress class differences.[55] Nevertheless, the dominance of persons from the upper classes as objects of cultic veneration is indicative of the degree to which popular visions of the divine image were far more inclined to reflect established social norms than challenge them.

One crucial reason for this disparity in the representation of rich and poor is undoubtedly that the options available to people of different classes affected their likelihood of achieving special status. Like Francis, Thomas Aquinas had to overcome family objections in order to pursue his vocation (his mother thought the Dominican order beneath him), but the renunciation of privilege that did and does make such stories compelling is inseparably bound up with the principals' affluent backgrounds. The same options for displaying heroic virtue simply were not available to the poor, who had nothing comparable to renounce. It is thus no surprise that the most prominent characteristic of saints drawn from the poorer classes is a capacity for wonder working, which was one of the few ways in which those denied access to political power, wealth, and education could display their holiness.[56] In much the same way, both the overall number of women saints and the types of careers associated with them turn out to be very limited when compared to men.[57] In this context, it comes as little surprise that in the current Roman liturgical calendar male saints outnumber female by three to one, and married women are hardly represented at all.[58]

Whatever the combination of reasons that may have contributed to the class and gender imbalance among those Christians venerated for their perceived holiness, the mere fact of its existence creates serious problems for any broadly inclusive idea of the divine image. Moreover, the fact that those venerated by the community tend to have benefited from the profoundly unequal distribution of social goods within western Europe contrasts with Jesus' own explicit reversal of accepted social values in the Gospel narratives (see, for example, Mark 10:13-31; Luke 6:20-26; 16:19-31). This is not to deny that those individuals who have been judged worthy of veneration are transparent to Christ for the reasons celebrated with the community of faith. Still less is it to minimize the significance of those occasions when an individual achieved renown in spite of flagrant disregard of popular conventions regarding suitable behavior.[59] But it is to observe that the image of God that emerges from the cult of the saints is a highly selective one that tends to focus on a limited number of stereotypical character traits (for instance, virginity, obedience, patient endurance of physical pain, not to mention an often powerful streak of anti-Semitism) and results in a correspondingly straitened vision of the will and work of God in the world.[60] In this respect, the process of canonization suffers from some of the same limitations already noted in relation to the production of icons.

A different (though closely related) risk in seeking to identify the image of God in Christ by reference to certain exemplary persons of faith is the potential that these individuals will displace Jesus as the focus of Christian devotion. As has already been noted, such developments run counter to both official church teaching, with its formal distinction between the veneration of saints and the worship of the Trinity, and the conventions of hagiographic literature itself, in which pains are generally taken to emphasize the saint's disclaiming of divine prerogatives. Here again, Athanasius's biography of Antony is typical: "It was not by giving commands that Antony healed, but by praying and saying the name of Christ, so that it was clear to everyone that it was not Antony who was doing this, but the Lord, who was, through Antony, expressing his love for humanity and healing those who suffered."[61]

Despite such attempts at clarification, by the sixth century saints had shifted in both popular understanding and officially sanctioned practice "from being primarily witnesses in a partnership of hope to being primarily intercessors in a structure of power and neediness" modeled on secular relationships of patronage.[62] As the Protestant Reformers would later point out, the momentum of devotional practice tended to overwhelm technical distinctions between *dulia* and *latria*, with saints effectively interposing themselves between the worshiper and Christ as the immediate object of faith and hope.[63] The fact that officially recognized saints tended to exemplify a fairly narrow selection of evangelical qualities only compounded the difficulty by eclipsing those aspects of Jesus' identity that run counter to prevailing social and anthropological prejudice. In light of these points, it is hard to avoid the conclusion that the veneration of saints is at best a very incomplete solution to the problem of discerning the body of Christ in the world.

The Preferential Option for the Poor

A rather different approach to the politics of discernment also finds its most thorough development in Catholic thought, though it has also been the object of considerable (and to a certain degree independent) reflection in Protestant circles. The idea that society's poor are crucial to genuine discernment of God's presence in history is a hallmark of the many theologies of liberation that have emerged throughout the Christian world over the last forty years.[64] Moreover, insofar as the poor are identified specifically with those "of little or no importance, and without the opportunity to give expression themselves to their sufferings, their comraderies, their plans, their hopes,"[65] they represent precisely that majority segment of the population largely marginalized by the traditional practices of canonization. The significance of the poor in the thinking of liberation theologians is not the mere fact of their presence (which is clearly not new), but their increasing refusal to be regarded as people "of little or no importance" denied "the opportunity to give expression themselves to their sufferings."

Liberation theology thus begins not merely with registering the fact of poverty, but with declaring the objective injustice of this fact as revealed in the protests of the poor themselves.[66] In this way, its proponents implicitly question whether the best (or at least the only) way for the church to identify persons to serve as guideposts for Christian faith and practice is the formal process of canonization. The liberationists' preferential option for the poor is emphatically not based on claims regarding either the heroic virtue of the poor, or any other characteristic that might be supposed to make them stand out from the norm as especially important. On the contrary, the reason that the poor are the focus for liberation theology is precisely that they *are* the norm: by definition "of little or no importance" and therefore anonymous. The goal of the preferential option is precisely to challenge this condition by "giv[ing] people a name and a face."[67] The root of this perspective is Jesus' own ministry, recorded in the Gospels as one of proclaiming good news specifically to the poor (Luke 4:18; cf. Isa. 61:1). The challenge to which liberation theologians call the church is precisely to place itself in such a way as to attend to the lives of the poor as those to whom God, who has identified with them in the ministry of Jesus, would have us attend.

Because the poor are by definition invisible for those in power, to attend to them as persons means viewing the poor on the poor's terms, in solidarity with them and under the same threats that they face. Any other strategy merely reinforces the anonymity of poverty, however much it may be motivated by genuine feelings of sympathy toward poverty's victims.[68] This commitment to lived solidarity with the poor, in turn, demands an active participation in their political liberation here and now as the concrete realization of their release from enforced anonymity.[69] This prioritization of active commitment means that formal theological reflection emerges only subsequently (though necessarily), as a "second step" of critical reflection on Christian praxis.[70] This in no way entails the sidelining of theological reflection. The Bible in particular retains a definite theological priority as the ideological framework for Christian faith and practice, but, liberationists argue, it can only be good news for the poor to the extent that it is read by the poor.[71] In this context, liberation theologians point out that there is no neutral perspective available from which to appropriate the truth of Scripture or the theological tradition. All theology is done relative to a particular interpretive framework that establishes the criteria against which it is to be evaluated, and liberation theologians frame their interpretation of Scripture and tradition in terms of their accountability to the poor.[72]

Importantly, this hermeneutical decision is itself justified by reference to God's prior decision, definitively realized in the incarnation (though already anticipated in Old Testament passages like Isa. 1:11-17 and Amos 5:21-24), to encounter humanity as a whole in and through the poor. Though Jesus remains a particular human individual, the shape of his individual life is one of absolute commitment to others, such that commitment to (and thus knowledge of) him is inseparable from a parallel commitment to them. The conclusion follows that religious awakening will take the form of a "conversion to the neighbor":[73] "The modes of God's presence determine the forms of our encounter with God. If humanity, each person, is the living temple of God, we meet God in our encounter with others; we encounter God in the commitment to the historical process of humankind."[74]

Needless to say (and in line with the principle that Jesus is the head of all people irrespective of their having been baptized), whether or not the neighbor in question is herself a Christian is irrelevant to this perspective.[75] Once again, the theologically central status of the poor (as the neighbor whose situation calls most immediately for our commitment) does not depend on their confessional stance any more than it does on their moral virtue. The implication for the church is that its discernment of Christ in the present is as much, if not more, a function of its encounter with those who may well be outside the church as it is a matter of reflection on the lives of those—apostles, saints, and theologians included—who definitely stand within it.[76]

If the narrowness with which its boundaries are drawn in practice creates problems for the model of discernment based on veneration of the saints, however, the sheer breadth of experience that liberation theology opens up for the discernment of Christ constitutes its chief weakness. This comes out especially clearly in the way in which liberation theologians Leonardo Boff and Jon Sobrino have attempted to broaden precisely the category of the martyr to include anyone who dies in the cause of justice."[77] As William Cavanaugh points out, the effects of this move are theologically questionable:

> Boff and Sobrino seem to assume that the content of Christ's life, death, and resurrection can be isolated apart from their form. Thus, Sobrino's "central criterion for martyrdom," that it be "unjustly inflicted death for love's sake," leaves him no choice but to recognize even those who resort to armed violence as potential "martyrs by analogy." . . . One difficulty with this account is that it ends up straining analogy to the breaking point. The ancient martyrs are *defined* by their nonviolence. . . . The martyrs choose death rather than apostasy or violent resistance precisely because their deaths mirror that of Jesus on the cross.[78]

In short, in attempting to expand the field in which Christ may be discerned, the liberationist perspective ends up diminishing its capacity to provide any firm criteria against which to judge whether or not what is discerned is in fact the body of Christ. Consequently, while Christian understanding of the body of Christ becomes much more inclusive, it risks becoming correspondingly less distinctive. The truth of the insistence that "encounter with the Lord occurs in our encounter with others," especially the poor, becomes transformed into the claim that the poor rather than Jesus are "the bearers of the meaning of history," in a way that threatens to eclipse the theological significance of Jesus as the unique source of salvation.[79]

Cavanaugh sees the problem here as a reduction of the Christian life to acting out an abstract (and correspondingly vague) principle like "love" or "justice" rather than seeing it as "a highly skilled performance learned in a disciplined community of virtue by careful attention to the contours of the Christian life and death as borne out by Jesus and the saints."[80] The same sort of critique has been developed by Daniel Bell, who is concerned that liberationist ecclesiology results in a church "that traffics in abstract values and apolitical options" in a way that ultimately undermines the very sort of resistance to oppressive social forces that the "preferential option for the poor" was intended to foster.[81] Importantly, the problem for Bell and Cavanaugh is not that liberation theology is too political, still less that liberation theologians merely cast God in their own image, or put themselves in God's place.[82] The problem is, rather, that liberation theology's living out of the preferential option for the poor fails to be political enough. As Bell puts it,

> At best the [liberationist] Church inspires or motivates Christians under the force of the value of love or the preferential option for the poor to move into the real world of social conflict. In the era of savage capitalism, this will not suffice. Such a vision does not nourish resistance; it only leads to the sense of crisis that currently afflicts the liberationists. This is because in the era of savage capitalism, resistance . . . hinges not on getting one's signs and values and religious options right, but on authorities, practices, apparatuses, on techniques of desire.[83]

Liberationists operate from a profound awareness of the fact that every telling of the Christian story is constituted by those it excludes (as well as by the often unrecognized "master narratives" that define the social order within which it is told). The difficulty is that this very sensitivity, especially when combined with an ecclesiology that views the church in primarily moral rather than institutional terms, tends to undermine the normativity of any such story in a way that risks obscuring the political distinctiveness of Christianity as a particular way of life. In light of this difficulty, the question is whether the preferential option for the poor can maintain the critical edge that liberationists rightly seek to bring to bear on theological anthropology without dissolving the particularity of the body of Christ into the vagaries of general ideological precepts. To the extent that the criticisms of Bell and Cavanaugh are on target, the possibility of answering this question in the affirmative will depend on reshaping the preferential option as a more explicitly ecclesial protocol of discernment lived out in specific practices rather than as an open-ended commitment to comparatively abstract principles.

Conclusion

It is tempting to view the protocols of discernment represented by the cult of the saints on the one hand and the liberationist preferential option for the poor on the other as instantiating elitist and populist perspectives, respectively. Even cursory examination of the two perspectives, however, renders such a categorization problematic: the process of canonization has significant populist elements from beginning to end, and liberation theologians are by no means insensitive to the importance of an ecclesiastical center standing over against the margins.[84] The difference between the two approaches to discernment is probably better described in terms of contrasting tendencies within the two processes, each of which implicitly takes the interplay of center and margins for granted. Thus, the cult of the saints reveals a fundamentally centripetal tendency to give greater precision to the outline of the image of God, while the preferential option for the poor exhibits a centrifugal problematizing of the established boundaries of Christ's body.

This fundamental difference shapes the strengths and weaknesses of the two approaches. In highlighting the exemplary lives (and deaths) of the saints and martyrs, the church succeeds in providing models of christoform existence that extend beyond the physical and temporal parameters of Jesus' life in a way that hones the community's understanding of its own beliefs and practices, including especially what it means by the word *God*.[85] This is not to deny the fact that the meaning of the Christian story in any given instance is also constituted by cultural vectors that are not explicitly included in that story, but it is to affirm the role of communal practice in determining communal meaning:

> Since in the nature of the case the sentences which express this community's most central beliefs are held true chiefly, and perhaps only, by members of this community, it is mainly this community's own practices which fix the meaning of its utterances and the contents of its beliefs. Not only corporate practices, but those of individual members can have this role. This holds

> particularly for the actions of those individuals—the saints—whose practical mastery of the complex connections among the community's central beliefs and of what it is right to say in ever-changing situations best embodies the community's grasp of the meaning of its own claims.[86]

In the saints, in other words, the church recognizes those who from whatever background have provided the appropriate lived context within which to interpret its claims about reality in general and God in particular. The determination that such judgments are best made retrospectively (normally, only after a saint has died) can be seen as an implicit acknowledgment of the incompleteness of the divine image revealed in Christ and the church's consequent inability to predict in advance what that image will look like when lived out in bodies constituted differently biologically, socially, and historically.[87]

Unfortunately, however compelling this process may appear in theory, and however inspiring the examples of individual saints may prove in practice, a purely statistical analysis of canonization suggests that the impact of unspoken, cultural narratives on the church's construal of its own identity is profound. Even though a recognition that the shape of a sanctified life is not limited to a rigid repetition of Jesus' career is implicit in the expansion of the category of saints beyond the class of martyrs, there exists an enduring tendency to make saints' lives conform to well-established (and officially sanctioned) models.[88] Furthermore, the fact that those approved for cultic veneration as saints in the West are overwhelmingly both male and upper class show the degree to which patterns of canonization reflect wider cultural assessments of value and power. This judgment is confirmed by a closer examination of the relatively small number of medieval and early modern saints who were women or from the poorer classes. By and large, saints who were women or poor tend to fall within a limited range of types conforming to the wider society's views of acceptable behavior for members of these groups (so that, for example, the women tend to exemplify the virtues of humility and obedience rather than military or intellectual prowess). As a result, the extent to which the process of canonization succeeds in aiding the discernment of the divine image in history appears to be seriously compromised by its tendency to reinscribe the (largely unspoken) narratives that perpetuate the existing social order. In this way, the cult of the saints runs the risk of obscuring the central reality of Christ (albeit in a way rather different than traditional Protestant polemic might suggest) by undermining Jesus' own identification with "the least" (Matt. 25:40, 45; compare Mark 9:36-37) and his insistence that "what is prized by human beings is an abomination in the sight of God" (Luke 16:15).

The obscuring of Jesus is also a problem for a politics of discernment that proceeds on the basis of a preferential option for the poor. In this case, however, the problem is not that of the interposition of a culturally conditioned substitute for Jesus, but the dissolution of Jesus as a figure with a clearly defined (if incomplete) narrative identity. Precisely out of a concern to avoid the idolatrous elevation of any individual or group in the place of the divine, the preferential option for the poor demands a perpetual and deliberate destabilization of the Christian story that exposes the exclusions that its telling inevitably entails. The effect of this process is to run the risk that the figure of Jesus will continually recede from view as the focus of the Christian story in favor of abstract concepts like "love," "justice," or "inclusion." In the process, Jesus is reduced to an exemplification of ethical principles rather than their measure and thereby ultimately ceases to be viewed as indispensable.[89]

It must immediately be emphasized that these are tendencies and risks, not inevitabilities. Notwithstanding the relative class and gender bias in the communion of officially canonized saints, the absolute population is large enough to include a significant (if not preponderant) number of figures who actively subvert established social norms in a way that sharpens the church's perception of the body of Christ. Likewise, there is no shortage of liberation theologies with an intensely christological focus.[90] The fact is that the ecclesiological dynamics underlying both the cult of the saints and the preferential option for the poor are equally capable of being fruitful means of discerning the divine image in practice. The significance of figures like Juan Diego, Harriet Tubman, Martin Luther King Jr., and Oscar Romero within liberation theologies indicates that the two approaches are by no means mutually exclusive, even if their respective strengths lie in different directions. A natural question to ask is, thus, how adequate protocols of discernment might deploy their undoubted strengths to overcome both the exclusion of the human other implicit in all theological language and the obscuring of the divine Other that invariably follows.

As Joerg Rieger has argued, a crucial question that must be asked in any attempt to sort out the strengths and weaknesses of different theological positions is, Who benefits materially from a particular approach?[91] This question is all the more urgent when the figure of Jesus or one of the saints is claimed as the property of the church as a whole. Under such circumstances, it is all too easy to conclude that every believer benefits equally from particular liturgical practices. All too easily ignored are the subtle ways in which the experiences of certain groups are privileged in ways that cannot readily be perceived, let alone theologically justified. Recognition of such hidden biases and attention to the mechanisms that perpetuate them hold open the possibility for seeing the divine image as a reality that takes shape "between God and the excluded" in a way which, if taken seriously, undermines illusory claims to objectivity and thereby opens the way for a broader range of experience to be taken seriously as a source of human knowledge of God.[92] The difficulty lies in determining how to counter those practices that prematurely close our notion of the divine image without thereby leaving it so wide open as to undermine its clarity as an image. The next chapter will attempt to move in that direction by suggesting how a christologically focused concept of *dulia* provides a means of bringing the politics of discernment embodied in the cult of the saints on the one hand and the preferential option for the poor on the other into a mutually corrective relationship that guards against either too close a correlation or too sharp a distinction between our knowledge of the divine and the human other.

chapter 5 Discernment as Communal Discipline

The Protocols of Service

Discernment and Dependence

The previous chapter argued that although Jesus alone can lay claim to the distinction of being the image of God, the fact that Jesus has this status as a human being implicates the whole of humanity in the discernment of that image. In support of this position, it is important to stress that Jesus is not "Savior" in the abstract, but specifically the Savior of Mary, Peter, John, and so on, down to you and me and those who will come after us. It follows that full knowledge of who he is includes knowledge of those he came to save. After all, one would not imagine one had an adequate knowledge of an individual in the absence of any knowledge of the spouse to whom she had joined her life. How then can it be supposed possible to claim adequate knowledge of Jesus apart from knowledge of those for whom he has joined his life in order to make one body (Eph. 4:4)? Our seeing the divine image—and thus our knowledge of the God whom it images—is therefore dependent on our knowledge of other human beings precisely because it is dependent first and foremost on Jesus himself.

At the same time, because Jesus is a particular individual with a particular history, the image he bears is not related to all human beings in the same way any more than his physical presence is. It follows that the choice of human beings in whom we search for the image is not a matter of indifference. After all, discernment does not describe a generalized looking around, but a deliberate and careful effort to pick out relevant information from a mass of potentially distracting data. It is not a natural capacity, but a skill that requires training and practice in order to counter the inherent limitations and biases of one's own historically and socially conditioned perspective. In the last chapter we examined two approaches to the task of discernment in the church and noted that while each helps to guide perception of the divine image, each also is marked by tendencies that work to block discernment by obscuring its christological ground. In the case of the cult of the saints, the risk is that the pressures of the social order may cause a particular version of the divine image to intervene between the individual believer and Christ in a way that short-circuits the ongoing process of discernment by prematurely closing off other voices. By contrast, the preferential option for the poor can have the opposite effect of allowing the image discerned to grow too diffuse to maintain definite contact both with the particularity of Jesus and with the life of the church. In the one case the divine image is rendered prematurely concrete; in the other it risks becoming permanently abstract.

There is a way in which these contrary tendencies can be viewed as the product of the different positions of the persons in question with respect to Jesus' saving work. The fact that normally no one can be canonized until after he or she has died (and, indeed, until after the church has had a sufficient amount of time—fifty years in modern Catholic canons—to reflect on them as dead individuals) highlights the extent to which the saints are those who have experienced the full effects of Jesus' saving work. They have been visibly called out of darkness into his marvelous light (1 Peter 2:9) in a way that is manifest to the church at large. By contrast, the poor are those who are an object of God's concern insofar as they remain anonymous and thus persons in whom the power of God has not been made visible to the church. The church looks to them because it *expects* God's saving power to be revealed among them, while it looks to the saints as people in whom God's saving power *has been* revealed. In looking to the saints, the church bears witness to what it has been given to know of God as the contours of the divine image have been filled in historically; in looking to the poor, by contrast, the church testifies to its continuing ignorance of that image as it continues to be manifested in the power of the Spirit that blows where it wills, begetting new saints "not of blood or of the will of the flesh or of the will of man, but of God" (John 1:13). In short, the saints exhibit God's work in retrospect, the poor in prospect.

As sharp as this contrast between the canonized and the anonymous poor may appear, it nevertheless serves to highlight what, from a strictly theological perspective, the members of the two groups have in common: namely, that they depend entirely on Christ for their identity. As noted in the previous chapter, the saints are those believers who, by confusing themselves the least with Christ, have become most convincingly transparent to Christ.[1] Likewise, the poor are defined in the Bible precisely by the fact that they have no refuge but God (Ps. 14:6; compare 12:5; 70:5; Isa. 25:4; 41:17; Jer. 22:16), who is their only hope (Job 5:15-16; compare 1 Sam. 2:8; Ps. 9:18; 72:2-3; 109:31). The rest of the human family stands in a problematic relationship to Christ precisely to the extent that they have some other guarantor of their identity apart from him, whether it be their race, nationality, gender, class, family, profession, or religion. In so doing, they have constructed idols for themselves by supposing that their status as persons can be secured by reference to some reality other than God. To that extent, they fail to be transparent to Christ, because they have interposed some factor between themselves and him as a source of value and thus have not regarded knowledge of Christ as that supreme value in comparison to which any other gain can only be counted as loss. This stands in contrast to the saints and the poor alike, inasmuch as the former refuse to claim anything for themselves and the latter have effectively been rendered incapable of so doing.

In different ways the saints and the poor both show that dependence—indeed, absolute dependence on God—lies at the root of human identity. Yet (*contra* Schleiermacher) this relationship of dependence is not a generalized ontological fact that can be known by anyone through a bit of disciplined introspection. Rather, its meaning can be discovered only by looking outward at those whose lives exemplify it in particular ways.[2] The form of a person's dependence is a function of her calling in Christ. Thus, while every saint may be able to repeat Paul's claim that "it is no longer I who live, but it is Christ who lives in me" (Gal. 2:20; compare 1 Cor. 15:10), the effect of Christ living in Mary Magdalene is very different from his life in Thomas Aquinas. Correspondingly, to take a saint as a model of Christian behavior (see 1 Cor. 11:1; Phil. 3:17) is not to engage in slavish repetition of someone else's calling, but to strive to copy another's fidelity to Christ in one's own calling.[3] Here again, one potential benefit of attention to particular saints in the life of the church is precisely to remind individuals of the *plurality* of callings in Christ, each of which contributes in its own, unsubstitutable fashion to our understanding of who Christ is, and thus of who God is.

Needless to say, the dependence on Christ that characterizes the lives of the poor is different. It is certainly not something to be desired or imitated. When Jesus tells the rich young man to sell all his goods (Matt. 19:21 and parallels), it is not so that he may become poor, but so that he may give the proceeds to the poor and thus alleviate their poverty (compare 2 Cor. 8:9). In this context, it is important to emphasize once again that liberation theologians see their work not as a benevolent attempt to help the poor (in which case it would not differ from traditional practices of Christian charity), but rather as a reaction to what Gustavo Gutiérrez calls the irruption of the poor, in which those who have long been ignored refuse to be ignored any longer.[4] As such, it is not a celebration of poverty, but rather a mode of reflection occasioned by the recognition that the refusal of the poor to accept their poverty is itself a fact of theological significance from which the church at large both can and must learn.[5] The same point animates Ada María Isazi-Díaz's insistence that encounter with the poor is not simply a matter of listening to them describe their experiences, but also of allowing them "to interpret . . . what happened to them."[6]

The complementarity of the cult of the saints and the preferential option for the poor thus lies in the degree to which both processes constitute "protocols of discernment" that in different though related ways help the church to recognize the divine image. The saints show the church how God's will for human beings has already been revealed in the past; the poor are decisive for the church's quest to identify the divine image in the present. The basic complementarity of these two aspects of discernment lies in the fact that the saints provide a living, ever expanding, and concrete embodiment of the divine image in its essentially christoform character (one that, significantly, is often marked by just the kind of turning to the poor advocated by liberation theology). At the same time, the preferential option for the poor provides a deliberate counter to the tendency (evident in the actual practice of canonization in the churches) for the church to ignore the poor in favor of more respectable folk in its quest for examples of Christ's Spirit at work in the present day. Yet given that the saints are not always poor and that the poor are not always saints, the question naturally arises of whether these two protocols are finally essential to the church or simply practical and in theory dispensable expedients for reining in extremes. Doubtless the saints and the poor alike will always be with the church, but does the church really need to attend to them as a matter of ecclesiastical protocol in order to fulfill its calling as church?

This question can be asked in another way. Granted that the saints and the poor are both characterized by a relationship of utter dependence on God that makes them uniquely transparent to Christ, in what sense, if any, is the church dependent on them? After all, notwithstanding a residual respect for martyrs and other heroes of the faith, Protestant Christianity has by and large repudiated the notion that commerce with the saints plays any necessary role either in the church's public liturgy or in the private piety of its members.[7] And notwithstanding the ecumenical influence of liberation theologies, the idea of a preferential option for the poor is arguably even more contentious as a proposed mark of the true church.[8] Given this evident lack of consensus, any claim that either protocol is integral to the life of the church requires further justification.

Dependence and *Doulia*

In the context of reviewing both the veneration of icons and the cult of the saints, I mentioned the term *dulia* as the technical designation for the honor paid to the saints, as distinguished from the worship (*latria*) due to God alone. More recently (and in a thoroughly nontheological context), the American philosopher Eva Feder Kittay has deployed the term *doulia* as a means of describing relationships that address certain forms of dependence characteristic of human society in general.[9] Her way of using the word provides a basis for developing the theological concept of *dulia* in a way broad enough to cover both the cult of the saints and the preferential option for the poor as variations of an interrelated set of protocols geared toward refining the discernment of the believing community.

Kittay is not a theologian, and she introduces the concept of *doulia* as part of a philosophical analysis of human equality that she develops with the aim of promoting a more robust system of social welfare. It is her contention that the individualist accounts of equality associated with modern liberal political theory are inadequate because they operate with an unrealistically narrow understanding of the person and, consequently, fail to attend to relationships of dependence that prevent all citizens enjoying equal access to and enjoyment of social goods. Specifically, she notes that the liberal image of the free and responsible citizen as the basic political unit lacks the depth needed to take account of the ways in which actual societies are constituted by persons who are not autonomous, but whose special needs render them dependent on the care of others:

> Whether we say that we are fully cooperating members of society throughout our lives, or over the course of our lives, the idealization is questionable at best, or pernicious at worst. It springs from the Kantian position that autonomy is that feature of human existence that gives us our dignity. But it fosters a fiction that the incapacity to function as a fully cooperating societal member is an exception in human life, not a normal variation; that the dependency is normally too brief and episodic to concern political life, rather than constituted by periodic, often prolonged phases of our lives whose costs and burdens ought to be justly shared.[10]

In place of the classic liberal vision of the autonomous individual, Kittay takes the pervasive fact of dependency in human existence as a sign that what gives an individual value is not any intrinsic capacity, but rather the extrinsic fact of her having been the object of someone else's care.[11]

As important as the fact of dependence is for those in need of care, however, Kittay's aim in critiquing liberal theory is the fate of those who provide care as much as the situation of those who receive it. She contends that care of dependent persons transgresses the liberal model of "justice as fairness" insofar as the relationships established between the dependent and the caregiver have a status of being at once uncoerced and yet not voluntarily chosen—a logical possibility that is simply not recognized in liberal theory's implicit identification of absence of coercion with active choice.[12] In contrast to the functionally specific, interventionist style of care characteristic of the professional doctor, lawyer, or therapist (all of whom have considerable latitude in defining the parameters of their interactions with clients), the dependency worker's obligations exceed any formal set of voluntarily assumed contractual obligations (so that, for instance, a private nurse to a severely disabled individual is not morally free to leave when his shift is over if his replacement has not arrived).[13] These constraints condition the freedom of such workers as social actors in such a way as to put them at a relative disadvantage when it comes to claiming the goods necessary for social thriving.[14]

This line of analysis leads Kittay to define dependency work as a relationship of care in which the focus of the individual's activity is the thriving of the other rather than the self.[15] Moreover, it is Kittay's contention that because such relationships are necessary to the broader health of society, they cannot be treated as matters of private choice that can be ignored when it comes to negotiating the distribution of social goods. It is at this point that she introduces the concept of *doulia* (which she derives from *doula*, a term for a postpartum caregiver who supports the mother so that the latter can care for her baby) to describe a political framework that takes seriously the social implications of dependence. The essence of Kittay's position is simply stated:

> *Just as we have required care to survive and thrive, so we need to provide conditions that allow others—including those who do the work of caring—to receive the care they need to survive and thrive. . . .* For just as the caregiver has a responsibility to care for the dependent, the larger society has an obligation to attend to the well-being of the caregiver.[16]

As Kittay defines it, the concept of *doulia* is thus multifaceted. It refers generally to the ethic of care required in a social environment marked by dependence, but its focus is not exclusively the dependence of those who themselves need the care of others. Indeed, the fundamental concern that drives Kittay's argument is not the adequacy of the care received by people who are radically dependent on others for their well-being (though she is by no means insensitive to this issue), but rather the lack of care provided to caregivers, whose dedication to those who are radically dependent undermines their ability to flourish in a society that views such dedication as a private option rather than a public necessity.

Kittay's analysis complicates the phenomenon of dependence by refusing to see it as a marginal phenomenon in political discourse. Her related observations that we are all at some time radically dependent on others and that care for dependent persons is necessary for the continuation of society as a whole means that the service provided by caregivers cannot be viewed as limited to those individuals under their charge. Even fully functional members of society are dependent on the work of caregivers, insofar as they could not function as they do if someone were not tending the young, the ill, and the enfeebled. In this context, the central thrust of *doulia* (as Kittay's derivation of the term from the work of the postpartum caregiver indicates) is *caring for the caregiver*: guaranteeing that the necessary conditions are met in order to ensure that the effect of caring for dependent individuals is not the social marginalization of the caregiver. In this respect, her analysis highlights the dependence of the dependency worker: while not intrinsically vulnerable in the way that their charges are, dependency workers' dedication to those who are unable to care for themselves renders them vulnerable in a manner that requires the compensating service of *doulia* in order for them to enjoy their fair share of social goods.

In short, *doulia* names the appropriate response to the fact that in caring for the vulnerable, caregivers have assumed a position of vulnerability that benefits society as a whole. To practice *doulia* is to ensure that those who have assumed this position of vulnerability are not disproportionately disadvantaged thereby. In this context, Kittay argues, the exercise of *doulia* cannot be treated as an act of private charity or of contractual arrangement between individuals. It must rather be seen as a social practice that requires the formulation of specific policies aimed at pinpointing the identities and needs of those who have become vulnerable through their care of others. As such, it requires that the wider community reframe its self-perception so as to recognize the ways in which its own identity is bound up with its attitude both to those on its margins, and to those whose care for the marginalized risks their own marginalization.

The relevance of Kittay's model of *doulia* for the discernment of the divine image in human beings lies here. In answer to the questions of John the Baptist, Jesus defines his own identity in terms of his relationship to the marginalized (Matt. 11:2-6 and parallels; compare Luke 4:16-21). That the message he proclaims is truly gospel is in this way validated by the fact that it is received as such by the poor, so that in Jesus the divine image appears precisely as a person whose own humanity was given over to the care of others (Matt. 20:28 and parallels) and who for that reason was "highly exalted" (Phil. 2:9). Jesus himself makes it clear that this practice is to be a model for those who follow him (Matt. 20:26-27 and parallels). At the same time, the biblical writers recognize that this kind of work requires external support: Jesus himself was served by women "who provided for him out of their resources" (Luke 8:2-3 9 [NRSV alternative reading]; compare Matt. 26:6-13 and parallels), while Paul refers to the support he and others have received from congregations (Gal. 4:15) as well as from select individuals (Rom. 16:13; Phil. 2:25; Philemon 11, 13).[17]

If this is the case with the figures who define the divine image for Christians (see 1 Cor. 11:1), it would seem to follow that discerning the divine image is a process more complicated than identifying certain predetermined qualities in individuals. Certain individuals exemplify the divine image by being peculiarly transparent to Christ; but the judgment that any individual has this status would seem to be bound up with the degree to which his or her ministry is experienced as gospel by those on the church's margins. In this way, oddly enough, the discernment of the divine image in the saint is inextricable from the process of taking seriously its presence in those whose marginalized status may place them outside the church altogether. As argued in the previous chapter, both the formal process of canonization and the purely economic fact of poverty have serious shortcomings as a means of discerning individuals in a way that honors simultaneously both the breadth of the divine image and its ineradicably christoform character. When seen as two complementary protocols within a larger process of communal discernment, however, both can be given their due.

Though developed as a means of furthering discourse on political equality in a liberal society, Kittay's concept of *doulia* helps to address the problem of discernment in the church by drawing attention to the ways in which communities are constituted by lines of mutual dependence. This perspective provides a framework within which to see saints as individuals who in their service to the community of faith acquire a vulnerability that calls for their being served in turn by that community. At the same time, Kittay's analysis militates against conceiving the individual believer in general and the saint in particular in terms of an ideal type by highlighting the degree to which dependence, vulnerability, and the patterns of marginalization that both entail are constitutive features of human social organization under the conditions of history. All this is not to compromise the christological criterion against which all talk of the image of God is to be measured. On the contrary, it reaffirms the Pauline insight that the unity of the body under Christ does not preclude but rather presupposes a multiplicity of genuinely different, non-interchangeable, and mutually dependent members. This recognition, in turn, suggests that the process of discerning the image of God in the world is a complex progress that properly combines fidelity to existing models of human life (in the veneration of the saints) with a challenging of those very models (in the preferential option for the poor). As a practice that seeks to render the relationships of dependency within the community transparent and to affirm in concrete, political terms their value for the community as a whole, Kittay's category of *doulia* is worthy of serious theological reflection. I will therefore use the rest of this chapter to explore how it might inform the discernment of the divine image in the specifically ecclesial processes of canonization and the preferential option for the poor.

The *Dulia* of the Saints

It is striking that Kittay describes the network of practices needed to sustain a community in the face of human dependence with the same term used within Catholic theology to describe the veneration of the saints. Needless to say, the mere fact of terminological convergence says nothing about the degree to which the two concepts are genuinely parallel; moreover, the idea that the saints in glory stand in any need of "care" on the part of the church militant would seem doubtful at best.[18] Nevertheless, the fact that the language of service or care figures in both discussions does at least suggest a direction of inquiry. To what extent is the *doulia* Kittay envisages consistent with the Catholic understanding of the *dulia* the faithful render to the saints?

Western theology owes the distinction between *dulia* and *latria* to Augustine.[19] As with so many other classic theologoumena, however, it is necessary to look to Thomas Aquinas for systematic analysis of *dulia*. Significantly, this analysis comes in the second part of the *Summa Theologiae*, in the context of Thomas's reflections on the exercise of justice in human communities. Also worthy of note is the fact that in Thomas's sequential treatment of the virtues that contribute to justice, *dulia* is coupled with obedience as one of two constitutive forms of respect (*observantia*). It follows that in order to understand *dulia*, it is first necessary to have some familiarity with what Thomas means by respect.

Thomas understands respect as a generalized form of piety, which is, in turn, derived from religion. As religion instantiates human veneration of God as the source of existence, piety in Thomas's thinking takes the form of veneration of parents and country (including all fellow citizens) as the immediate source of our life under God.[20] Within this more general context of social relations, respect is the veneration of that more restricted group of human others who in some way stand *in loco dei* insofar as they contribute to the perfecting of human life.[21] As the subsequent articles make clear,

Thomas principally has those who exercise direct authority in particular spheres of life (for instance, political and military leaders, as well as teachers). Such people help to perfect lives by guiding them to a particular goal in the same way that a sailor pilots a ship.[22] The two chief tokens of respect are honor, which is the acknowledgment of preeminence, and homage (*cultus*), which consists in the practical subordination of one's will to the one to whom respect is due.[23] By way of qualification, however, Thomas also notes that when service to those in authority is rendered with the aim of serving the public good rather than in recognition of the particular dignity of an individual, the operative virtue is better described as piety rather than respect.[24]

In Thomas's view piety explicitly entails the material support of those to whom it is owed as well as honorific recognition.[25] The same point is carried forth in his discussion of *dulia*, where he affirms that this virtue entails external, physical actions and not merely a set of mental attitudes.[26] And while it is clear that Thomas has in mind here primarily honorific actions (that is, physical postures struck or words spoken), the biblical text he uses to support his position is 1 Tim. 5:17, which speaks of a "double honor," and which Thomas (following Jerome) interprets in financial terms.[27] Importantly, Thomas goes on to affirm that while the exercise of *dulia* entails that some superiority be acknowledged in the one to whom *dulia* is shown, this does not necessarily refer to a blanket judgment about the comparative merits of this other with respect to oneself. He puts it this way:

> Now someone's good qualities can be counted outstanding not only in comparison to the one doing honour—as though the one honoured must always excel the one doing honour—but also in their own right or by comparison to others. From this point of view excellence or superiority in any line gives a person a claim to honour. There is nothing to say that the one honoured must be better than the one doing him honour; it is enough that he be superior either to others or to the one doing him honour in some respect, even if not altogether (*simpliciter*).[28]

Following from this pattern of differential ability (and, correspondingly, differential obligation), Thomas argues that everyone is due some honor in principle.[29] Indeed, it is precisely the relative character of the honor associated with *dulia* that distinguishes it from *latria* in Thomas's analysis, since the unique character of the honor owed God derives from the fact God is the only other to whom every human being is subject in every respect.[30] In this way, the logic of *dulia* is quite different from that of *latria*. The latter glorifies (and thus testifies to) God's independence with respect to the creaturely realm, while the former, understood specifically as a form of public testimony given before other people,[31] highlights the mutual dependence of human beings: the honoring of a person's special worth is part of the economy by which that worth becomes socially productive.[32]

This having been said, the tone of Thomas's reflections on *dulia* may still appear in spirit rather far removed from Kittay's idea of support for caregivers. For example, he states that *dulia* in its strict sense refers to the reverence a slave owes a master,[33] and thus seems far more interested in maintaining existing positions of power and privilege than in redressing imbalances in the way that Kittay envisions. At the same time, however, it is important to remember that Thomas, too, sees *dulia* ultimately as a matter of justice. The fact that he defines justice as "the lasting and constant will of rendering each his due" would appear to substantiate his essentially conservative outlook.[34] And yet this appearance is belied by the distinction Thomas draws between general justice, which is directed to the common good, and particular justice, which is directed to the private good of the individual.[35] *Dulia* falls under the rubric of particular justice, but it is for this very reason subordinated to requirements of general justice, since for Thomas distributive questions of what is due any given individual as an individual cannot be separated from the larger question of the common good, because human beings are inherently social.[36] In this context, the *dulia* rendered to others has as its ultimate rationale the good of society as a whole.

Of course, it is very easy for those in power to appeal to the good of the wider society as a means of securing their own privileged position against any possible criticism. Liberalism emerged at least in part as a reaction against just this tendency, insisting (albeit not always consistently) on a basic equality of all persons as a means of guarding against the attempt to lock any particular class of people into a position of permanent marginalization on the basis of an appeal to the health of the collective. Unfortunately, this way of tackling the problem of inequality tends invariably to set the individual over against society in a zero-sum framework in which individual freedom stands in an inverse relationship to social cohesion. Such a vision bears little relation to Aquinas's christologically informed view of human destiny, in which the individual is simply incapable of flourishing as an autonomous monad. Insofar as Kittay is eager to challenge the liberal tendency to view relationships of dependence as exceptions within the larger social order, she can arguably be seen to have a certain level of common cause with Thomas. Even though her conceptual framework remains heavily indebted to liberal notions of equality (for example, she articulates her position in distributive terms, as a matter of providing a level playing field for those subject to relative disadvantage by virtue of their roles as caregivers), her proposals also seem open to interpretation in the direction of Thomas's understanding of general justice, according to which a given class of individuals is due particular honor by virtue of their social role.

At the same time, the fact that Kittay associates such honor precisely with individuals whose vocation leads them to take on a position of social vulnerability provides a basis for reshaping Thomas's categories in a way that challenges a practice of *dulia* that simply serves further to entrench existing power relations. Furthermore, though Kittay herself does not write from a theological perspective, her focus on those who assume positions of vulnerability in service to others meshes well with specifically theological concerns. According to Thomas, *dulia* is owed to human beings insofar as they share a limited portion of God's supreme authority (*participat quamdam similitudinem divini dominii*).[37] As shown preeminently in the ministry of Jesus, however, the way in which God exercises that authority is by rendering the divine self supremely vulnerable: taking the form of a servant and undergoing the most brutal of criminal executions (Phil. 2:7-8). If humans are owed *dulia* to the extent that they share in divine authority, it would seem to follow that vulnerability would be an appropriate touchstone for identifying suitable candidates—and one that would almost by definition challenge existing social perceptions of human worth.

The danger with this model is that it might tend to reinscribe traditional practices of charity, in which the poor are viewed as largely passive objects of largesse rather than as active historical agents. Such practice has been subject to sustained critique by liberation theologians in particular as captive to an individualistic view of the person that is incapable of either recognizing or challenging socially embedded structures of immiserization.[38] Perhaps still worse, it tends to operate from the presupposition that the well-off know what the poor need, so that the gift of charity need entail no commitment to listen to the poor, let alone to allow one's understanding of what constitutes genuine assistance to be changed by them. In order to avoid this kind of captivity to regnant social norms and provide a basis for discerning new and surprising dimensions of the divine image, it is necessary to develop an account of *dulia* that attends to the agency of those on the receiving end of care no less than that of the ones providing it. To this end, it is necessary to reexamine the liberationist idea of a preferential option for the poor.

The *Dulia* of the Poor

The vulnerability of the poor is hardly a matter of controversy. Deprived both of basic resources and access to the engines of power that distribute them, the poor are defined as such by their special vulnerability to hunger, homelessness, disease, and death. As argued in the previous chapter, however, a straightforward application of the preferential option for the poor is of questionable value for the theological task of discerning the body of Christ—and thereby the image of God—in the world. The problem is quite simply that focus on the poor as such ultimately renders the christological referent at the heart of Christian talk of the image of God superfluous. Rather than the source and norm of Christian reflection on human being, Jesus risks being reduced to the status of a paradigmatic instantiation of an abstract principle—with the inevitable weakening of his unsubstitutable significance for Christian faith and practice. No less problematically, a focus on the poor as the bearers of history's meaning can suggest a theological valuation of poverty that sits somewhat uneasily with the liberationist insistence that poverty is an evil to be resisted.

Certainly Jesus' own ministry is one that both promises and pursues the elimination of poverty, not its spread. If the poor are the object of Jesus' blessing, this is not grounded in any sort of positive estimation of poverty as such, but because of the conviction that God will intervene to bring it to an end (Luke 6:20; compare 16:19-26). It is precisely this hope for an ultimate end to poverty that governs Jesus' insistence that his followers give to the poor (Matt. 19:21 and parallels; Luke 14:13; compare 19:8). The result of this activity may be that one becomes poor, but that is not its goal. It should therefore come as no surprise that a crucial element in Paul's ministry is precisely to relieve the poverty of those Christians in Jerusalem whose dedication to the needs of others (as recorded in Acts 2:45) put them in need (Rom. 15:26-27; 1 Cor. 16:1-4; 2 Cor. 8:1-7; Gal. 2:10; compare Acts 11:29). In short, poverty is of concern to the New Testament writers as something that is to be overcome, not as a state that is of value in its own right.[39]

At this point, it is important to reclaim Gutiérrez's emphasis on the irruption of the poor (as opposed to the mere fact of poverty) as the starting point for a theology of liberation. To focus on the irruption of the poor is not to attribute value to poverty as such, since such irruption is nothing other than the act by which the poor register their refusal to accept poverty as God's will. As the legacy of the struggle of the poor against poverty shows, however, this refusal to be poor does not amount to a rejection of vulnerability. On the contrary, resisting the structures that create and maintain people in poverty exposes one to increased risk at the hands of the principalities and powers that have an interest in maintaining the status quo. The character of this pattern of vulnerability is suggested by the following biblical passage:[40]

> There was a certain man of Ramathaim, a Zuphite from the hill country of Ephraim, whose name was Elkanah son of Jerosham. . . . He had two wives; the name of one was Hannah, and the name of the other Peninnah. Peninnah had children, but Hannah had no children.
>
> Now this man used to go up year by year from his town to worship and to sacrifice to the LORD of hosts at Shiloh. . . . On the day when Elkanah sacrificed, he would give portions to his wife Peninnah and to all her sons and daughters; but to Hannah he gave one portion, because, though he loved her, the LORD had closed her womb. Her rival used to provoke her severely, to irritate her, because the Lord had closed her womb. So it went on year after year; as often as she went up to the house of the LORD, she used to provoke her. Therefore Hannah wept and would not eat. Her husband Elkanah said to her, "Hannah, why do you weep? Why do you not eat? Why is your heart sad? Am I not more to you than ten sons?"
>
> After they had eaten and drunk at Shiloh, Hannah rose and presented herself before the LORD. (1 Sam. 1:1-9a, translation altered)[41]

Hannah's story illustrates what liberationists mean by the irruption of the poor. Because she is barren in a society where women are valued for their ability to produce progeny, she is objectively without status and thus subject to ridicule by her fertile rival, Peninnah. Evidently, she endures what becomes an annual rite of public humiliation for years, and although her husband, Elkanah, protests his love for her, there is no evidence that he makes any effort to protect her from Peninnah's taunts.[42]

One day, however, she simply refuses to take it anymore. Rather than withstand to yet another round of torment, "Hannah rose." There is no hint given as to what prompted this sudden departure from years of quiet submission. Perhaps Elkanah's words in v. 8 made it clear to her at last that she could expect no relief from within her present situation, but there is certainly no suggestion that she was motivated by explicitly theological concerns, let alone by direct divine inspiration. Nor is the reader given any reason to believe that she had thought through the consequences of her actions for her family or herself. The story simply records that, having endured an intolerable situation for years on end, she suddenly determined not to endure it anymore. She just got up.

At the same time, her story soon acquires a specifically theological focus. We are told that after she got up, she "presented herself before the LORD" and prayed to God to relieve the conditions of her suffering. With no earthly power willing to act on her behalf, she turned to God. As the narrator makes clear, however, this act carried its own set of risks:

> Now Eli the priest was sitting on the seat beside the doorpost of the temple of the LORD. [Hannah] was deeply distressed and prayed to the LORD and wept bitterly. . . .
>
> As she continued praying before the LORD, Eli observed her mouth. Hannah was praying silently; only her lips moved, but her voice was not heard; therefore Eli thought she was drunk. So Eli said to he, "How long will you make a spectacle of yourself? Put away your wine." But Hannah answered, "No, my lord, I am a woman deeply troubled; I have drunk neither wine nor strong drink, but I have been pouring out my soul before the LORD. Do not regard your servant as a worthless woman, for I have been speaking out of my great anxiety and vexation all this time." Then Eli answered, "Go in peace; the God of Israel grant the petition you have made to him." (1 Sam. 1:9b, 12-17)

Hannah's extreme distress is apparent in the fact that her address to God was incoherent: she was not praying in a conventional matter, with the result that her activity was not recognized as prayer at all, but interpreted by the local religious authority as drunkenness. When faced with this kind of verbal assault, however, Hannah protests against Eli's interpretation of her situation and thereby catches him up short. Faced with a woman who affirms that she has been speaking out of her "great anxiety and vexation," Eli changes his judgment from one of blame to blessing. Significantly, Eli accepts Hannah's account of her situation at face value. He does not pry further into the cause of her distress, nor does he attempt to assess the propriety of her petition. Evidently, the testimony of the person before him that she is "a woman deeply troubled" constitutes sufficient grounds for him to bless her action.

This should not be taken to imply that any action by anyone who claims to be "deeply troubled" receives God's blessing. Presumably Eli would have reacted differently if he had seen Hannah going at Peninnah with an ax. Nothing in this story or elsewhere in the Bible suggests that social marginalization secures automatic divine approbation for one's deeds, even if those deeds are aimed at alleviating their suffering. The fact remains, however, that the theologically significant actor in this narrative—the one whose deeds are the immediate occasion for the fulfillment of God's saving purposes—is neither Elkanah (the patriarch) nor Peninnah (the productive citizen in good standing), but the person at the bottom of the small slice of Israelite society depicted in the narrative. Even Eli, the otherwise respectable religious authority, can do no more than give approbation to an event that takes place quite apart from his own initiative.

Nor is this pattern limited to a single story in the Old Testament. As Ronald Thiemann has pointed out, it permeates the narrative structure of the Gospels, where God's purposes seem most clearly revealed not in the disciples, but through a series of obscure and often nameless figures who come to the fore of the narrative only to disappear again once their moment has passed.[43] Often enough, these figures are the ones who take the initiative in approaching Jesus, who assumes a role similar to Eli in saying to those he heals, "Your faith has made you well" (see Matt. 9:22 and parallels; Mark 10:52 and parallels; Luke 7:50; 17:19). These words clearly do not diminish Jesus' significance as the agent of healing, but they do highlight the fact that it is the "irruption" of those in need that provides the occasion for Jesus' power to be displayed. As seen particularly in the story of the Canaanite woman (Matt. 15:21-28), whose request for help Jesus at first rejects, the content of Jesus' gospel is often seen most clearly where persons expose themselves to risk by refusing to accept social marginalization as God's will for them.

In this context, it is crucial to recognize that Jesus' actions in these stories cannot be assimilated to more traditional models of charity. Partly this derives from the fact that Jesus' own actions (for instance, touching the leper or the woman with the hemorrhage) often challenge the uses of power that structure the wider society. This fact cautions against interpreting these actions narrowly as a purely personal matter of charity. Just as significantly, however, Jesus' behavior is significant for the degree to which it seems open to allowing the marginalized to articulate for themselves what constitutes "good news" for them. If this commitment does not always take the precise form of the request, "What do you want me to do for you?" (Matt. 20:32 and parallels), and certainly does not preclude Jesus' taking the initiative, it nevertheless stands as a sign that the content of what is genuinely good for the marginalized cannot be determined without immediate reference to their own perception of what is wrong with their situation.

If Jesus subjects himself to this sort of practice, then it cannot be anything less than obligatory for those who would follow him. In marked contrast to the *dulia* of the saints, this attention to the self-assessment of the marginalized involves a disciplined search for the divine image among those who emphatically do not look like Jesus. The goal of this search is not to model one's own life after that of the marginalized. On the contrary, to the extent that the church's task is that of proclaiming the good news, it is ultimately a summons to the marginalized to conform their lives to Jesus' own in a way that includes a word of judgment lying in, with, and under the good news of grace. But the point remains that in so doing the church does not presume to state in advance precisely what such conformity would entail and recognizes that its own ministry must include an honoring of the marginalized that waits on the activity of the Spirit to define the precise shape of their calling.

The practice of honoring the marginalized constitutes a protocol of discernment that complements the *dulia* of the saints and has resonances with the *doulia* described by Kittay. Its aim is to allow someone to recognize and claim her personhood in an encounter defined by the attempt to communicate to that someone the good news of Jesus Christ. This will undoubtedly entail challenging the marginalized person's sense of herself—no encounter with the gospel can be genuine that does otherwise—but it will also require the discernment of the marginalized person's selfhood by the evangelist.[44] Nor is this latter step merely a tactical matter of finding the most effective existential "hook" for the gospel message in a particular person's life; it is rather integral to the speaker discerning what the gospel message actually is in any given situation. It is in this regard that the *dulia* of the poor is no less crucial to the life of the community as a whole than the *dulia* of the saints, inasmuch as both are necessary to a comprehensive discernment of the boundaries of Christ's body as the locus of the image of God. If we are to honor the saints as those who have instantiated the divine image in the past, we must also honor those on the margins of the community of faith as those who hold the secret to the ways in which that image will take concrete form in the future.

Summary and Conclusions

Interpreted within the framework of care for the vulnerable provided by Eva Feder Kittay's concept of *doulia*, the seemingly very different practices represented by the traditional cult of the saints and the liberationist preferential option for the poor can be interpreted as protocols of discernment that help the church perceive the image of God in history. Since the touchstone of all talk of the divine image is Christ, both protocols are theologically defensible only insofar as they operate in terms of a robustly christological framework. At the same time, however, the deployment of such a framework must take into account the fact that the divine image is not limited to Jesus, but must be understood in terms of the body of Christ considered as a whole, the precise contours of which are still being revealed as new members become engrafted in it. The saints illustrate how Christian callings have been lived out in the past, while the poor point to the inability of the church to foreclose on the shape such callings will take in the future. In this way (and to pick up a theme raised earlier in the chapter), the *dulia* of the poor figures in prospect what the *dulia* of the saints accomplishes in retrospect.

Kittay's reflections are helpful because they provide a basis for addressing the limitations of established practices both of formal canonization and of the liberationist preferential option for the poor. While she uses the term *doulia* to refer to all forms of care given to those who are dependent on the care of others for their survival, her particular interest is that class of people whose need for care is a direct consequence of their own commitment to care for those with exceptional needs. This focus has the effect of problematizing established social practices in ways that can help to highlight the christological criterion against which the church is called to make its judgments regarding the content of the divine image in human beings.

By suggesting that special consideration should be shown to those who have made themselves vulnerable through care for the vulnerable, Kittay offers a corrective to any practice of *dulia* that simply reinscribes established relationships of power and privilege. In this way, her work can be used to reinforce Jesus' insistence that the one who would be great must assume the role of a servant (Matt. 20:26-28; Mark 9:35; John 13:12-15). Likewise, by pointing out that relationships of dependence are an integral feature of life in community, she undermines any ecclesiology that would view the church's relationship to those on its margins as an incidental or exceptional feature of its identity. She thereby helps to remind the church of the degree to which Jesus linked the vindication of his own identity as Christ to his reception by the marginalized of his own day (Matt. 11:2-6 and parallels).

Honoring both these dimensions of discipleship requires that the practice of *dulia* in the church be reconceived as having two foci, reflecting the two categories of people to whom the church has special obligation. First, when the saints' imitation of Christ is viewed quite specifically as a matter of taking on a condition of vulnerability in service to one's vulnerable neighbors, the liturgical practice of *dulia* can be interpreted as a matter of honoring those who by their dedication to the well-being of others have undercut their ability to secure honor by conventional means. To be sure (and in contrast to Kittay's understanding of *doulia*), the church's veneration of the saints is not simply compensatory. Indeed, its significance as a matter of compensation dwindles to nil in a context when veneration is focused on those who, having died, have attained a state of glory in which they are no longer vulnerable. As a result, the benefits of *dulia* accrue not to those who receive it but to those who offer it, inasmuch as believers' acts of veneration help to shape their understanding of the body of Christ in a way that provides an ever-greater diversity of models for faithful discipleship in the present day. Nevertheless, by singling out those whose activities in life cut against such conventional measures of success as independence, security, and control, the two forms of the protocol of *dulia* outlined in this chapter can establish an alternative index of prestige capable of redirecting communal resources in the present toward those engaged in like activities.

As liberation theologians have rightly pointed out, however, the ideal of commitment to the vulnerable is vacuous apart from the practice of taking seriously their identity as agents in their own right, with particular goals, aspirations, and (perhaps most importantly) assessments of their own situation. An engagement with the marginalized that takes these points seriously represents a second focus of *dulia*, the proper conduct of which is integral to making meaningful judgments regarding who is worthy of *dulia* in the first and more traditional sense. At the same time, however, this form of *dulia* should not be conceived as a surrender of christological criteriology in favor of a more generalized commitment to love, liberation, or some other value. The poor as a bloc do not replace the saints as models for Christian behavior, but are rather seen as that group in relation to whom the saints are finally vindicated as saints by following Christ in holding the concrete shape of their own ministries accountable to the poor, even where it may cause offense to the wider community of faith.

This form of accountability does not consist in automatically following wherever the poor lead, any more than authentic *dulia* of the saints involves a wooden repetition of their particular deeds. The aim in both cases is, rather, to discern the image of God through practices that help to identify those persons who challenge our limited and partial perceptions by highlighting the surprising contours of Christ's body. Such persons are by definition exceptional in the sense of standing apart from the norm, but while the exceptional character of the saints lies in their particular visibility within the church, the marginalized are exceptional precisely in their invisibility, which (as Kittay notes) results from the power of normative discourse to shape people's perception of the human. Moreover, the problems associated with bringing the marginalized to light are enormously and unavoidably complicated by the fact that any process by which the church seeks to identify the marginalized reinforces the privileged status of its members in a way that invariably generates new patterns of exclusion to be unearthed.[45]

These two modes of *dulia* go together not only because both have a common end, but because neither is adequate on its own. As noted in the previous chapter, the practices associated with cult of the saints tend to undermine their exceptional qualities by a process of general assimilation to a new (albeit specifically ecclesial) norm. Under the accumulated pressure of this process, the lives of saints continue to be regarded as exceptional, but also (and for that very reason) exhibit progressively less capacity to challenge current practice. Like Jesus himself, they are easily domesticated in terms of established "types" of holiness with which the church becomes all too comfortable.

The *dulia* of the poor serves as an antidote to this tendency by forcing the church to interpret its vision of the gospel in terms that genuinely confront the personhood of those at its margins. This process is not simply a tactical matter of effectively marketing the gospel to a particular population, but precisely of working out what the gospel is in a way that ought to challenge the self-understanding of the proclaimer no less than the one to whom the proclamation is made. In speaking to itself, the church is invariably set on the course of repeating itself in a way that robs the gospel of its quality as news and thereby weakens the hearer's appreciation for its genuine goodness. By contrast, in looking without, the church is immediately faced with the challenge of explaining how what is undoubtedly "news" to the outsider is justifiably claimed as "good." Through this process of confronting the stranger, moreover, Christ and the saints can again become "strange" for the church precisely to the extent that their lives are understood to embody and illuminate the gospel that is proclaimed. And because this renewed sense of strangeness simply reflects the degree to which these lives are exceptional, its impact falls on those outside the church no less than those within in a manner that helps counter any tendency to abstract the content of the gospel from the particularity of Jesus of Nazareth.

This interpretation of *dulia* helps to resolve a problem with which our discussion of discerning the divine image began, namely, how to honor the principle that the image of God is present in all people by virtue of the universality of Christ's claim on humankind, while recognizing that this same christological criterion suggests that the divine image will be most clearly visible in those whose lives deviate from socially normative models of human personhood. By recognizing that a theologically adequate practice of *dulia* will necessarily encompass those on the margins of the church as well as those who have proved model disciples in the past, it is possible to compensate for a one-sided reliance on processes of discernment that are naturally biased in favor of people from more prosperous social classes.

The point is not to question the sanctity of those whose cult has been validated through official procedures, though such questioning may be appropriate in particular cases.[46] It is, rather, to suggest that the picture of Christ's body that results from an exclusive reliance on these procedures risks being not only incomplete (a feature that is unavoidable prior to the eschaton), but also distorted. At its worst, dependence on such procedures narrows the church's capacity for discernment through a feedback loop that reinforces existing prejudices and thus progressively restricts sensitivity to unexpected manifestations of the divine image in the lives of human beings. Given that historical communities can only maintain their identity through time by reference to traditions mediated through a restricted and largely self-regulating class of individuals, it may be assumed that unequal concentrations of power within the church will generate bias with respect to the discernment of saints. The effects of this sociological inertia (which can only dull the church's capacity to discern the divine image in history) can be overcome only by nurturing practices specifically designed to forestall it. A testing of the church's proclamation in light of its reception by those on the church's margins serves just this role.

Properly understood, this form of commitment to those on the church's margins entails no dilution of the claim that all Christian talk of the image of God must be tested against a specifically christological norm. If the church is always called to broaden its appreciation for the diversity of members within the body of Christ, no amount of development on this level can be allowed to undermine the identity of the head. While the "scandal of particularity" can be misused as justification for all manner of ecclesiastical intransigence, it has the virtue of reminding the church that Christian discipleship is not about adherence to principles or ideals (whether a general openness to the world, political liberation, or even care of the vulnerable considered in itself), but to the person of Jesus. It follows that no claim to have discerned the image of God in history can be abstracted from the particularity of Jesus' career. Here, too, the risk is that insufficient care will result in the church simply reinforcing its own prejudices in a way that undermines its capacity to be challenged by Jesus.[47] In short, a fully developed vision of *dulia* will need to be approached in a spirit that compromises neither the particularity of the one whom the gospel encounters nor the Christ whose love is the ultimate ground of that encounter.

Obviously, there is a considerable gap between these more general remarks on the ecclesial discernment of the divine image and the generation of protocols capable of producing the goods in practice. In many respects, however, it is not a matter of generating new protocols at all, since practices aimed at identifying saints and attending to the poor have long been features of the church's life, even if the particular structures associated with both have undergone considerable development and remain quite varied. My aim has simply been to argue that the kind of processes associated with canonization on the one hand, and what liberation theologians describe as the preferential option for the poor on the other, can be viewed as protocols that serve both to foster and to discipline the church's collective will to discern the divine image in history. As such, they have the specifically epistemological function of deepening the church's knowledge of the God who is known to human beings through that image.

Even when such procedures are in place, however, their effectiveness is always limited by the fact that even the most well-intentioned theological judgments are affected by the material and ideological forces shaping the particular social locations from which they are made. Consequently, assessment of criteria like "social vulnerability" and "christological adequacy" will require attention to the particular discursive contexts within which they are deployed. Mary Fulkerson proposes three kinds of questions that need to be asked here:

> (1) how well a theological analytic is able to inspect the effects of the discourse (a Christological grammar, for example); (2) what work is done by the reliance of a preferred meaning upon an "other" (how a fixed Christological norm might continue to produce [excluded] "others" in unacknowledged ways); and (3), given the inevitability of occluded discourses, what they are.[48]

As Fulkerson's own study of different forms of women's theological discourse makes clear, the goal here cannot be the systematic elimination of bias to achieve some imagined purely biblical outlook.[49] The aim instead must be a level of self-critical reflection that is able to identify the visions and blind spots opened by one's own preferred form of discourse as part of making the case that it is theologically appropriate for a given context.

Within this perspective the category of theological appropriateness will have an unavoidably tactical dimension. Again, however, this cannot be reduced to a matter of deciding which of the faith's otherwise timeless truths needs to be affirmed in a given situation. Fulkerson's proposal goes deeper insofar as she argues that theological truths are not timeless, at least not in the sense that their meaning can be detached from their production in, by, and for "a community that is . . . shaped by power, desire, and social location and in which it is [correspondingly] difficult to commit to a particular (disruptive) good."[50] This perspective implies that good theology is not only a matter of discerning what is going on "out there," beyond the bounds of the church, but also of coming to grips with the forces that shape thought *within* the faith community. It is precisely this insight that requires the church's practice of *dulia* to have two foci, one that identifies examples of "good practice" within the community (canonization), and the other dedicated to problematizing the community's notions of good practice in terms of the perception of those at the community's margins (who are likely to have a clearer perception of the community's biases than even the most self-conscious insider).

We seem left with a situation in which the discernment of the divine image that Christians confess to be all around us turns out to be quite challenging. Far from being identified with some more or less easily stable property all people share in common, the *imago dei* turns out to be inseparable from the particularity of individual persons' callings, with all the uncertainty that comes with trying to perceive a calling's eventual outcome and thus the wider context within which it is best interpreted.[51] The problem is compounded by the fact that the focus on the exceptional person that defines the practice of *dulia* appears to render the discernment of the divine image a matter of communal politics that places it far beyond the reach of the ordinary believer. In light of these considerations, it is necessary to ask whether there are other protocols that bring the discernment of the divine image more within the compass of the ordinary, everyday experience of the individual believer. The next chapter will address this question.

Discernment as Personal Discipline

The Protocols of Chastity

Discernment and Distortion

The previous chapter addressed the Christian discernment of the image of God (understood to be the basis for Christian knowledge of God) on a fairly general level. The upshot of this exercise was the claim that the technology of *dulia*, defined as a particular form of engagement focused on exemplary members of the church on the one hand and those at its boundaries on the other, had the capacity both to honor the christological specificity of Christian talk about the image of God and to challenge institutional tendencies to generate an overly narrow and formulaic picture of Christ. As noted toward the end of the chapter, however, whatever value the category of *dulia* may have as a means of highlighting and correcting distortions in Christian practice, it raises its own set of questions. Judgments regarding appropriate forms and objects of *dulia* remain matters of dispute within the church, and decisions taken will invariably produce their own distortions with respect to the form of the divine image in history. These enduring issues highlight the fact that the significance of *dulia* is not that it allows the church to avoid political bias in its communal efforts to discern the body of Christ, but rather that it helps to make the political character of ecclesial judgments more explicit and thus more open to an ongoing process of critical review.[1] *Dulia* amounts to a set of practices that shapes the church as a distinctive community by helping to sustain individuals in particular kinds of countercultural practices—especially practices oriented to promoting the flourishing of those marginalized by the wider society. But the judgments that give particular shape to those practices will depend on always-debatable analysis of the larger context (including those specifically theological and ecclesial as well as more broadly political and cultural dimensions) in which Christian communities find themselves.

The judgments associated with the practice of *dulia* are political in the sense that they are matters of communal deliberation and decision, even though individual believers ultimately carry out particular acts of *dulia*. Moreover, as decisions that are designed to enhance believers' capacities to discern and thereby to participate more fully in Christ's body, they will by their very nature tend to highlight particular, exemplary individuals in a way that might easily be taken to imply that membership in Christ's body is fairly restricted. This phenomenon is familiar enough from the way in which the word *saint* has long since gravitated in popular usage from referring to all the baptized to a much more exclusive club of heroic believers.

At one level this shift can be justified as reflecting the fact (noted by Thomas Aquinas) that only those who live with Christ in glory have been fully incorporated into his body and thus fully reflect his image.[2] The lives of other believers are "hidden with Christ in God" (Col. 3:3), so that however much we are being "transformed into the same image" (2 Cor. 3:18), we do not yet perceive "what we will be" (1 John 3:2). Nevertheless, even Aquinas has no wish simply to limit the possession of the divine image to the saints in heaven. On the contrary, he affirms that such discernment is not limited even to the members of the church militant. Although believers' incorporation into Christ's body is "actualized" in a way that is not the case with those outside the church, the fact that the body—and thus the reality—of Christ exceeds the confessional boundaries of the church demands that Christians attend to the reality of God's image in those who may not look like saints at all.

The vigorous exercise of the preferential option for the poor is one way of ensuring that the process of discernment is not limited to well-established heroes of the faith. Yet while the development of a theologically shaped practice of *dulia* to the marginalized undoubtedly has the potential to serve as a corrective to the distorted views of the divine image that invariably come with the politics of canonization, the process remains a communal one demanding resources of time, energy, and skill that are likely to place it at some remove from the immediate involvement of the average believer. Consequently, whichever aspect of *dulia* is under consideration, it will necessarily entail collective decisions regarding the criteria to be used in the quest to discern more effectively the divine image in history. It is in this context that the identification of protocols of *dulia* helps to suggest how the ensemble of such practices might be deployed in order to maximize the church's openness to forms of the divine image in history by controlling (though certainly not eliminating) the biases that invariably shape this process. Although one could certainly imagine a different set of protocols, any alternative would have the same corporate dimension.

Unfortunately, the quantity of corporate resources that must be deployed to arrive at such decisions ensures that the community will tend to be resistant to any subsequent revisions in its judgments. This inertia is a natural feature of the life of communities, but it also compromises the aim of *dulia*, which is precisely to maximize the church's openness to re-visioning its understanding of the divine image. However much the church seeks to be open to expanding its understanding of God through an ongoing process of self-critical reflection, this very process will inexorably foster the gravitation of the community toward particular images, which, by virtue of their specificity, will tend to work against the church's confession both of God's transcendence of every particular image and of every human being's participation in the divine image. This does not render the process inherently pointless or self-defeating. Social inertia is not an impassible barrier to social change, and overcoming such inertia becomes easier when there are protocols in place that specifically encourage the conscious reshaping of practice (for instance, annual meetings or regularly scheduled changes in leadership). Nevertheless, acknowledgment of *dulia*'s limits does raise the question of whether it might be possible to identify further sets of protocols whose own distinctive characteristics would help the church to discern unexpected dimensions of the body of Christ.

Discernment as Personal Discipline

As should be clear from what has been said above, the quest for further sets of protocols should not be motivated by the idea that the collective processes for discerning Christ's body are in themselves wrong, but rather by the recognition that they can only take the church so far. An obvious alternative to the more collective processes characteristic of *dulia* would be one that centered instead on personal relationships, in which the identity of the others who serve as the focus for discernment is decided by individuals apart from a formal, communally mediated process of selection. Even here, however, it could not be a question of simply abandoning a communal framework for individual preferences. Insofar as any protocols focusing on personal orientation to the other are themselves a dimension of specifically Christian practice, they cannot be equated with the apolitical or the private. On the contrary, they will need to be subject to ecclesial oversight and correction insofar as they, too, will be characterized by the shortcomings, blindspots, and possible distortions of any practice undertaken by fallen human beings. It follows that such protocols will be (relatively) independent of communal scrutiny only with respect to the particular question of which person(s) an individual chooses as the focus for the work of discernment. But the church will be integral in determining the kinds of relationships that are appropriate for such work (for instance, disallowing the relationship of slave and master), as well as how people should behave within them (for instance, excluding physical violence or intimidation).

Acknowledging the role of the community in regulating interpersonal relationships in no way minimizes the contrast between such protocols and the collective procedures that define *dulia*. The shift from the communal to the interpersonal entails the recognition that persons whom it would be quite inappropriate to promote as objects of public veneration or service might nevertheless serve as an appropriate focus for the discernment of the divine image on the part of another individual. Thus, however important veneration of the saints and ministry with the poor may be for the discernment of the divine image in particular individuals (and the consequent expansion of the church's perception of the limits of Christ's body), the fact that they are matters of public witness of the community as a whole mean that they cannot serve as a model for a practice of personal discernment focused on other(s) who are not selected according to publicly mediated criteria of merit or demerit.

While the range of such relationships is potentially very wide, in any individual case the process of selection cannot be arbitrary, since discerning the body of Christ (whether in the context of communal discipline or of personal vocation) is not a matter of looking anywhere, but of looking where Christ appears. In cases like that of the relationships between child and parent, this vocation will be determined largely by biological relationships that the Bible honors (see, for example, Exod. 20:12; Eph. 6:1-4; but compare Matt. 10:37). In others the choice of the other seems more fortuitous, though no less a matter of divine vocation. Consider the biblical account of the first man's response to encountering the first woman:

> "This at last is bone of my bones
> and flesh of my flesh;
> this one shall be called Woman,
> for out of Man this one was taken." (Gen. 2:23)

Though the narrative presupposes sexual complementarity between man and woman, it does not suggest that Adam's exclamation is motivated by his understanding of the woman's reproductive function (which is not mentioned). The stress, rather, is on her particularity (note the triple repetition of the demonstrative "this") as a concrete other recognized by the man as the one with whom his own identity is irrevocably linked. The preceding verse's specification that it was God who brought the woman to the man makes it clear that the man's acclamation is a response to divine initiative. Indeed, it is treated as a calling of such a depth and permanence as to justify disrupting what might otherwise be thought to be the more profound biological bond between parent and child: "Therefore a man leaves his father and his mother and clings to his wife, and they become one flesh" (Gen. 2:24).

Of course, the enthusiasm of the first human pair for life quickly goes sour: celebration turns to accusation (Gen. 3:12) and mutuality to hierarchy (Gen. 3:16). Whatever the weaknesses of patristic interpretations of the fall as a putative historical account of the evolution of human sexuality, they do succeed in communicating the degree to which the current state of affairs falls short of the joyous intimacy suggested by the man's initial response to the woman. Augustine went so far as to identify our incapacity to control feelings of sexual arousal as evidence that something had gone deeply wrong with God's intentions for human beings: in place of free and mutual rejoicing in one another, the experience of lust points to a disordered desire in which the integrity of the other is subordinated to the selfish desire for pleasure.[3]

Though Augustine's views have dominated Western theology, recently Eugene Rogers has suggested a more positive theological interpretation of human beings' inability to master their feelings of desire:

> [Desire] is a way, a particular, embodied way, and hopefully a pleasant, promising way, in which human beings cannot escape from the neighbor, and from the neighbor's claim. The bodies of the desired do not leave even the most devoted misanthrope alone. Rather, inscribed in him or her, inescapably, is the claim of the neighbor, even if wound and cries may have ceased to move compassion. Eros is both inscribed in the image and the last stand of God in human beings, that they might never entirely escape the image of God in their neighbors, however much their powerlessness and vulnerability before that image may distort them into anger, adultery, and murder.[4]

Precisely in its uncontrollability, desire is not subject to the kind of deliberation associated with a measured or calculated choice of the object of one's attention. On the contrary, it can run directly against the conscious wishes of an individual in such a way as to produce the kind of destructive behavior Rogers describes at the end of the passage.[5] Yet, in these cases as well, desire draws one irresistibly toward the other in a manner that reflects, even if only in a broken fashion, the first man's recognition that his life before God is fulfilled only with another. To turn again to the language of Augustine, the experience of desire bears stubborn testimony to the restlessness of the human heart until it finds its proper resting place in God.[6]

The connection Rogers goes on to make between the experience of desire and the divine image is christological. On the grounds that both Christ and human beings in their creation as male and female are the image of God, he argues the sexual desire for union with another reflects God's desire to become one flesh with us in Jesus.[7] Notwithstanding the questionable exegetical grounds for interpreting the divine image in terms of gender difference,[8] the core of Rogers' claim can be substantiated by shifting the focus from discussion of the divine image in Genesis 1 to the language of the two becoming one flesh in Genesis 2. This image of union is taken up again in the New Testament, where the joining of husband and wife is described as "a great mystery" that the writer interprets as foreshadowing that of "Christ and the church" (Eph. 5:32). In other words, the true significance of the union of man and woman described in Genesis is prophetic: it anticipates the union in one eschatological flesh of Christ and the church. That final fulfillment of human being in the one body of Christ thus finds an echo even apart from the church in a relationship, rooted in the power of desire for the other, that reflects the inability to decouple one's own destiny from that of the other.

By interpreting the union of man and woman in terms of the eschatological consummation of Christ and the church, Ephesians 5 relativizes its significance: it can no longer be viewed as the goal of human existence, but only as a symbol of that goal. As already intimated, the Bible certainly does not restrict relationships of great personal intimacy to the relationship of husband and wife. For example, Ruth declares her determination to cling to Naomi in terms no less strong than Adam's celebration of Eve:

> Do not press me to leave you
> or to turn back from following you!
> Where you go, I will go;
> where you lodge, I will lodge;
> your people shall be my people,
> and your God my God.
> Where you die, I will die—
> there I will be buried.
> May the Lord do thus and so to me,

> and more as well,
> if even death parts me from you! (Ruth 1:16-17)

Similarly, David declares that Jonathan's love for him "was wonderful, passing the love of women" (2 Sam. 1:26). And though Jesus does not identify any such single object of devotion for himself, this by no means indicates that he is indifferent to or unaffected by the desire for communion with the neighbor. On the contrary, on the night before his death he confesses such a desire in relationship to a whole community of others (Luke 22:15; John 15:12-13; 17:24).

In line with this variety of biblical passages, the church has experimented with a wide variety of social arrangements for living out this desire for the neighbor, all of which can be understood as establishing specifically interpersonal protocols for the discernment of Christ's body in the other. While heterosexual marriage has tended to be viewed as the preeminent form of such relationship in the modern era, historically it has represented for Christians just one form among many and was by no means generally recognized as the preferred one.[9] Although these alternative vocations have generally taken the form of communal existence defined by an explicit commitment to celibacy, Linda Woodhead rightly notes that "the variety of these communities is often obscured by our blanket use of the term 'monastic' to describe them."[10] And, as already noted, the desire of a parent for her child or of siblings for each other can also serve as powerful examples in still another register of the other in whom Christ confronts us.

As suggested by the fact that even the most diverse forms of monastic practice share the property of being governed according to a rule, this variety does not imply anarchy. The church has generally been happy to honor the relationships among family members on the terms operative in the wider society; but where vocation leads (as foreshadowed in Gen. 2:24) to new arrangements that disrupt these existing relationships, Christians have generally thought it important to define its parameters (by, for instance, specifying the behaviors appropriate to it) and solemnize the process by which individuals enter into it. Again, however, the immediate object of ecclesial concern here is the character of the vocation in question, not the specific qualities of the neighbor(s) with whom one is thereby joined. The church's concern is simply that those taking up a given vocation evince a basic understanding of and suitability for the particular form of life it establishes, and that they undertake it freely. Thus, from the perspective of the church as a whole the protocols of discernment that define these relationships have to do less with the characteristics of the particular person(s) with whom one lives than with one's commitment to relate to them in and through a particular form of life. Moreover, precisely because one's relationship to the neighbor in such relationships is not determined by her possession of a set of predetermined qualities, there is greater freedom to honor her essentially ungraspable character and greater opportunity to wait for the appearance of those unexpected subtleties of personality that may be initially matters of confusion and even pain, but which may on longer acquaintance become occasions of wonder, celebration, and delight.

Chastity as the Virtue of Witness to the Ungraspable Other

Like the collective protocols of *dulia*, the protocols that govern the discernment of Christ through binding personal relationships are a matter of discipline. Picking out those elements of individual character that hold the key to seeing the image of God in the other means allowing time for one's relationship with the other to develop. It is in line with this principle that the church has insisted that the vocations of marriage and monasticism entail a lifelong commitment, in which the mutual fidelity of the participants is crucial.[11] Because human beings enact their relationships bodily, it is entirely appropriate for the Christian tradition to have singled out chastity as the term that best expresses fidelity's meaning in bodily terms. For the status of chastity as a specifically Christian virtue lies not in any demand it makes for the renunciation of the body, but in its stress on the fact that neither the present state nor the ultimate destiny of the self can be abstracted from the body. In this context, chastity should not be understood as the demand to maintain some sort of distance from the other, but as a discipline that establishes the conditions necessary for genuine intimacy within the context of various types of interpersonal relationship. From this perspective, it is imperative from the church's perspective that the love of two sisters for one another, of the monk for his brothers in community, and of spouses all be chaste; but it is no less important to recognize that the form of a chaste relationship will be different in each of these cases.

Karen Labacqz has argued that the lack of shame in the face of total exposure to the other described in Gen. 2:25 ("And the man and his wife were both naked, and were not ashamed") suggests that a crucial feature of human intimacy as intended by God is "appropriate vulnerability."[12] While Labacqz's own reflections focus on sexual relationships, the criterion of appropriate vulnerability can be applied to any of the types of personal relationships described in the previous section, so long as it is understood that what counts as "appropriate" will vary from case to case. Appropriating Labacqz's terminology, chastity may be defined as the discipline of maintaining a state of appropriate vulnerability before the other. Negatively, chastity preserves the integrity of the self by guarding against situations in which one party either controls or is controlled by another, in recognition that such situations are inconsistent with honoring the other as a member of Christ's body. Within the church the protocols of chastity thus refer to those forms of life that shape desire for the neighbor in such a way as to nourish an intimacy based in appropriate vulnerability.

Given that in popular (as well as much specifically Christian) understanding chastity tends to be associated with fear of the body in general and of sexuality in particular, it is important to underscore that its status in the church reflects a high estimation of the body's significance as the fundamental locus for the discernment of the body of Christ and, correspondingly, for human self-expression.[13] Both these points come to the fore in the following passage from Paul:

> The body is meant not for fornication but for the Lord, and the Lord for the body. And God raised the Lord and will also raise us by his power. Do you not know that your bodies are members of Christ: Should I therefore take the members of Christ and make them members of a prostitute? Never! Do you not know that whoever is united to a prostitute becomes one body with her? For it is said, "The two shall be one flesh." But anyone united to the Lord becomes one spirit with him. Shun fornication! Every sin that a person commits is outside the body; but the fornicator sins against the body itself. Or do you not know that your body is a temple of the Holy Spirit among you, which you have from God, and that you are not your own? For you were bought with a price; therefore glorify God in your body. (1 Cor. 6:13-20; translation slightly altered)

Once again, Gen. 2:24 turns out to be a crucial text, but in contrast to Ephesians 5 the reference is very much to the present time rather than to the eschatological union of Christ and the church. Paul begins with the conviction that the bodies of Christians are part of Christ's body and then argues that where intimacy (in this case of an explicitly sexual nature) is entered into inappropriately—that is, where chastity is lacking—the creation of "one flesh" actually undermines the body's integrity rather than (as is the case in the original context of Genesis 2) fulfilling it.[14]

In evaluating the significance of this passage, it is important to note that it does not amount to a blanket demand for sexual abstinence, as though any physical union with another undermined the individual's union with Christ. Though Paul goes on to express definite practical reservations about marriage in the next chapter of the letter (1 Cor. 7:32-35; compare vv. 7-8, 38-40), these do not lead to any blanket condemnation of sexual union. On the contrary, as much as Paul is worried that the desire to please one's spouse may distract the individual from "unhindered devotion to the Lord" (v. 35), he also sees considerable risk posed by unfulfilled sexual desire (v. 9), leading him to advise married persons *against* extended periods of sexual abstinence (vv. 2-5). Moreover, he counsels against divorce, even in those cases where one's partner is not a Christian, on the grounds that both the unbelieving spouse and the children produced by the union are sanctified through the believing partner (vv. 10-16). Obviously, neither of these teachings would make any sense if becoming "one flesh" with another human being in itself constituted a defilement of the believer's union with Christ.

Attention to the details of 1 Cor. 6:12-20 confirms that for Paul believers are not "one flesh" with Christ in a way that would preclude union with any other human being. Instead—and in contrast to the "one body" produced by sexual intercourse (v. 16)—he describes the Christian's relationship with Christ as "one spirit" (v. 17). To be sure, Christians' bodies are members of Christ (a point that Paul will go on to develop in 1 Corinthians 12), but that is precisely the point: Christians are not *joined* with Christ to form one body; rather, they simply *are* members of Christ's one body insofar as they are Christians. Consequently, their becoming "one flesh" with another implicates Christ but in no sense displaces him. Because the believer is here conceived as the mode of Christ's presence in the world rather than as Christ's partner, the opposite of fornication is not abstinence but chastity, understood as a matter of maintaining an appropriate vulnerability that is inconsistent with prostitution, rape, pedophilia, polygamy, and other forms of intimacy in which "the vulnerability is not equal and therefore not appropriate."[15] Only so is it possible to understand how union with a prostitute defiles Christ (1 Cor. 6:15-16) while union with an unbelieving spouse can be a means of the latter's sanctification by Christ (1 Cor. 7:14).

In short, for Paul Christians are not considered over against Christ so much as the means by which Christ is disclosed in and to the world. Paul's insistence that fornication is a sin committed "against" rather than "outside" the body (6:18) is a function of his high estimation of the body's significance as one of Christ's own limbs.[16] The life of Christ with humanity is one of faithfulness, marked by the full giving of himself, and this commitment to the other is glaringly absent in the commercial transaction of prostitution. And yet bodies being what they are, this lack of commitment does not change the character of sexual union: the one who joins with a prostitute genuinely does become "one flesh" with her. As Dale Martin has pointed out, in order to appreciate the force of this argument, it is necessary to recognize that the interpretation of sexual intercourse as union was not especially prominent in Paul's world. Coitus could be described in Greek as *synousia* (literally, "being together with another"), but it was far more common to speak of sex in explicitly hierarchical terms as a matter of penetration and being penetrated (*perainein* and *perainesthai*, respectively).[17] Within this framework there is no question of union of the partners; on the contrary, pleasure was associated exclusively with the activity of penetration (defined as the male role), while the role of being penetrated (socially coded as female) was taken to be a matter of pleasureless submission. It is easy to see how someone operating from within this framework (as some of Paul's Corinthian congregation seem to have been) would not have been inclined to see the frequenting of prostitutes as having particularly serious implications either for their own bodies or for the "body" of the church. Paul strongly disagrees. His ontology of sex on the one hand and of the believer's incorporation into the body of Christ on the other lead him to attribute much greater significance to bodily acts. It is impossible to abstract one's own—or, still more significantly, Christ's—identity from one's body. The fact that God will raise us up again means that the individual's body is integral to the character of the body of Christ both now in history and later in glory.[18]

In short, the believer's and Christ's identity are not finally separable. Paul drives this point home in 6:19-20, when he shifts from a focus on the individual's use of his or her body to the community as a *collective* body: "your [pl.] body is a temple of the Holy Spirit among you . . . therefore glorify God in your [pl.] body."[19] In both verses the visibility of the church is central to the force of Paul's rhetoric. In contrast to the character of traditional Judaism and paganism alike, the central sign of God's presence in the world is not a physical structure, but the believing community (see 1 Cor. 3:16-17; compare 1 Peter 2:4-5). The challenge of glorifying God is therefore not simply a matter either of individual or collective probity (though these are both obviously included), but also the fostering of relations between persons—protocols of chastity—that manifest the church's character as a single body of mutually interdependent members. And insofar as violating such relationships constitutes an act of infidelity to Christ himself, it seems reasonable to infer that honoring them is integral to the process of seeing and knowing the church as Christ's body, the fullness of which is disclosed in the mutual vulnerability of its many members. The next section will attempt to explore the logic of this position further by examining the status of marriage as an appropriate context for the discipline of chastity.

Marriage as a Test Case for the Exercise of Chastity

In a culture where marriage is viewed as the exemplary form of chaste relationship, the idea that it might serve as a "test case" for theological reflection on chastity might seem odd. Yet marriage has not always seemed so self-evidently good for Christians. I have already had occasion to note that Paul expresses important reservations about the practicality of marriage in 1 Corinthians 7, and such reservations are not limited to Paul. For example, Jesus' prohibition of divorce in Matt. 19:3-9 (which by itself might suggest a positive evaluation of wedlock) is followed immediately by the suggestion that he, too, thought that it was "better not to marry" (Matt. 19:10-12). Likewise, Revelation's characterization of the 144,000 who constitute the first fruits of the redeemed as men "who have not defiled themselves with women" (Rev. 14:4) suggests an attitude toward marriage (not to mention women) that borders on the hostile.[20] Nor, if we take seriously the evidence of narratives like the *Acts of Paul and Thecla* and *The Martyrdom of Perpetua and Felicitas*, was this coolness toward marriage among early Christians limited to men. In comparison with texts like these, early Christian endorsement of marriage as found in Heb. 13:4 and (rather more indirectly) in 1 Tim. 3:2, 12; 4:3; 5:14 are notable for their reserve.

Such evidence suggests that, at least among the literate members of the early church, attitudes toward marriage were ambivalent at best and were certainly not marked by a positive appreciation of sexual desire. Though Ignatius of Antioch presupposes that marriage is normative for Christians, he urges couples "to be united with the bishop's approval" so that "their marriage will follow God's will and not the promptings of lust."[21] Writing a generation or so later, Clement of Alexandria set the tone for much subsequent thinking (especially in the West) by emphasizing marriage's procreative function.[22] And while it is certainly worthy of note that as austere a figure as Tertullian can wax lyrical over the blessings of marriage between Christians,[23] the overwhelming consensus of Christian writers was that "virginity is superior to marriage since the latter continually threatens to turn one away from God."[24] Even the so-called Constantinian turn did little to check this basic orientation, with (among others) Jerome in the West and

Gregory of Nyssa in the East affirming the superiority of celibacy in a way that continued to define mainstream Christian thought through the Reformation.[25] Thus, although the overwhelming majority of Christians throughout the patristic and early medieval period continued to be married, the church itself seems to have been only minimally involved in the process.[26]

This lack of ecclesiastical involvement is most obviously explained by the degree to which marriage appeared as a compromise to the life of celibacy that became established early on as the Christian ideal.[27] This enthusiasm for the celibate life set Christianity apart from both Judaism and paganism in a way that marriage did not.[28] Yet by itself this observation begs the question of why marriage tended to be viewed as a vocation that was inferior to (rather than simply different from) celibacy. Paul's reflections in 1 Corinthians 7 provide a clear biblical basis for this perspective (see especially vv. 36-38), but his subsequent reference to the fact that most of the leading figures in the church were married (1 Cor. 9:5)—not to mention the positive view of marriage developed in Ephesians 5—suggests that other perspectives were also current among the first generation of Christians.[29] Moreover, none of these texts suggests that procreation is the purpose of marriage, yet that is the point of view which came to dominate Christian thinking on the subject.[30] It is therefore difficult to make the case that biblical considerations were to the fore here, even if particular passages were open to being exploited to the detriment of marriage.

The link between sexual desire and the fall that was made (albeit in rather different ways) in both the Eastern and Western branches of the church provides a more obvious framework for Christian suspicion of marriage, but these suspicions were present long before the theological elaboration of any such link and thus can hardly have been caused by it. In all likelihood, the roots of Christian ambivalence toward marriage were in the first instance sociological: it just wasn't clear that marriage provided a suitable context for the exercise of chastity in the way that celibate vocations did. Translated into more specifically ecclesiological terms, these doubts focused on whether marriage had the capacity to build up the body of Christ, or whether its role was the purely secular one of providing for the continuation of the species and, still more narrowly, of securing dynastic power and stability.[31] In short, the church's delay in developing a coherent theology of marriage (including liturgical provision for its celebration) can be understood as reflecting uncertainty whether marriage was in fact a forum within which "appropriate vulnerability" was either intended or possible.[32]

Though it may now be difficult to appreciate how marriage could be seen as anything other than the ideal context for the exercise of love, it is important to remember that "it is not simply an error to suppose that in most other societies people married for love; it is a serious misprision to imagine that they would even have *accepted* a correlation between the two."[33] This is certainly not to say that love was unknown in premodern European marriages, only that it was emphatically not seen as matrimony's source or ground.[34] Marriage was a means of transferring property and forging alliances dedicated to the furthering of dynastic, tribal, or national interests through the production of legitimate heirs.[35] In short, it was fundamentally about economics and politics, and most certainly not arranged with a view to meeting the emotional needs or personal fulfillment of the spouses.[36] Seen in this context, the church's insistence on the central role of procreation can be read as an attempt to affirm the goodness of marriage without endorsing the values of economic and political gain that were its primary rationale within the classical world.

Marriage in antiquity was testimony to the fundamental subordination of the individual to the wider society in general and to the needs of the clan in particular. Insofar as Christians did not accept this basic orientation, it is not surprising to find that they viewed marriage with suspicion. In this context, Paul Evdokimov interprets the early church's celebration of celibate vocations as the sign of a fundamental refusal to make the person instrumental to any wider social good and thus as an unconditional affirmation of "the absolute value of the individual above the social."[37] Chastity (*sophrosyne* in Greek) becomes a defining value for this form of life because it was understood as that virtue which secured the integrity of the individual. In a context where sexual intercourse amounted to a *de facto* violation of appropriate vulnerability (as evident in Greco-Roman views on the character and significance of sexual roles), it would be natural to associate genuine chastity with celibacy as the only form of life capable of honoring an individual's capacity to claim and dedicate herself as whole to Christ, with no part held back through the pressure of competing loyalties to spouse, family, or nation.[38] Here marriage would quite naturally have been seen as incapable of supporting a chaste existence.

Such worries clearly lie behind Paul's opinion that it was better for believers to remain single (1 Cor. 7:7). As already noted, however, his reservations are not based on discomfort with sexual intercourse itself (see 1 Cor. 7:3-5). What worries him is the more general point that the married person's inherent obligations toward her spouse will impair her ability to consecrate herself to Christ (1 Cor. 7:32-35). As he puts it, "those who marry will experience distress in this life, and I would spare you that" (v. 28). As a result, marriage seems to be approved only by way of concession, so that though "the one who marries . . . does well . . . the one who refrains from marriage will do better" (v. 38; translation slightly altered).

In line with Paul's suspicions, there remains a persistent tendency in the church to view the preservation of civil society through procreation as marriage's only real justification.[39] Augustine gestures toward something more when he argues that among Christians marriage brings the particular blessing of sanctification in addition to the more general goods of progeny and faithfulness,[40] but he continues to insist that the production of offspring remains "the sole reason why marriage takes place."[41] Thomas Aquinas moves still further in the direction of a genuine appreciation of marriage for its own sake when he argues that the sacramental union of the spouses is the principal good of marriage with respect to dignity (since grace is superior to nature) and essence (since it is a necessary condition of marriage in a way that progeny are not); by contrast, procreation can be considered marriage's principal good only with respect to its intention or end.[42] Yet although the value of marriage is in this way distinguished from the social function of procreation, the continued insistence of the Catholic magisterium that sexual intercourse is consistent with marital chastity only when directed toward procreation suggests a continued tension between the goal of union with Christ and marital union. The reluctance to concede that sexual intercourse has anything other than a "natural" (that is, procreative and thus essentially social) function leads to a situation in which marriage is celebrated in the church as a Christian vocation, but one of its defining features—the one in which each partner is confronted most directly with the concrete, bodily uniqueness of the other—is viewed as lacking any specifically ecclesial value.[43] Within this framework it is hard to avoid the conclusion that marriage is at bottom an impediment to commitment to Christ, at least when compared to the alternative vocation of monastic celibacy.

Given that neither Genesis 2 nor Ephesians 5 connect the "one flesh" union of marriage to the production of offspring, there seem to be good biblical grounds for moving beyond this perspective. Operating from within a tradition that is more open to the idea that sexual intercourse within marriage may be in itself (that is, apart from any consideration of its "natural" functions) a manifestation of chastity, Evdokimov argues that marriage and monasticism represent "two forms of chastity" that are both equally consistent in every respect with a total consecration of the self to Christ.[44] Developing John Chrysostom's claim that the love of Christian spouses "does not have its principle in nature, but in God,"[45] he notes that the married person's relationship to Christ is distinguished from the monk's by being mediated rather than unmediated, but insists that this difference "does not in the least diminish the value of the nuptial union."[46] Marriage is, correspondingly, not viewed as a concession to nature, whether on a social (procreation) or personal (lust) level, but rather as a form of *ascesis*, by which is meant not a denial of the passions but the route to "their healing and transformation."[47] In marriage one dedicates oneself to Christ precisely through an unstinting commitment to the spouse. The specifically ecclesial seriousness of this commitment is reflected in the Orthodox practice of "crowning" the spouses, which symbolizes the character of matrimony as a form of martyrdom, understood in the etymologically original sense of witness to Christ.[48]

Recently, Eugene Rogers has attempted to build on Evdokimov's work in order to stress the fundamentally ecclesial character of marriage over against theologies that would tie marriage too closely to the facts of human biology. To this end, he offers the following definition: "Marriage in Christianity is best understood as an ascetic practice of and for the community by which God takes sexuality up into God's own triune life, graciously transforming it so as to allow the couple partially to model the love between Christ and the church."[49]

Once again, the ascesis of marriage is not a lesser or compromised form of individual commitment when compared with monasticism, but simply one that nurtures the individual's desire for God in a different way. In both cases the believer is called to recognize herself as (wholly and thus physically) desired by God; but in marriage this aim is met through the medium of one's own (equally holistic) desire for an individual human other. In this way, perception of God is bound up with perception of the other: one grows in knowledge of (and thus relationship to) God as one becomes trained to see Christ in the other.[50] Within such a theological vision marriage can be interpreted ecclesiologically as a means of discerning the body of Christ.

The Ecclesiological Dynamics of Marriage

The idea that marriage is a matter of personal discipline in interpersonal relationship is central to the claim that it has a role in upbuilding the church as a whole. Crucial for this way of interpreting marriage is the recognition that the process of discernment toward which it aims takes time. As Rowan Williams puts it:

> I can only fully discover the body's grace in taking time, the time needed for the mutual recognition that my partner and I are not simply passive instruments

> to each other. Such things are learned in the fabric of a whole relation of converse and cooperation. . . . When we bless sexual unions, we give them a life, a reality not dependent on the contingent thoughts and feelings of the people involved; but we do this so that they may have a certain freedom to "take time" to mature and become as profoundly nurturing as they can.[51]

The upshot of this stance is that the wedding ceremony marks the beginning of the couple's relationship rather than some sort of culmination.[52] Needless to say, this is not to say that marriage is something that is entered into casually, but it is to suggest that the kind of reasoning that would tie marriage to some sort of assurance that one has found the "right" person is misguided. As Stanley Hauerwas observes, "we always marry the wrong person."[53] This is neither because we are irremediably stupid when it comes to our understanding of others nor because love is blind, but because people change. Indeed, the act of marriage itself constitutes one of the most crucial such changes, and one whose consequences for our perception of the other we have wed (not to mention for their perception of us) are impossible to anticipate with any degree of certitude. The point of marriage is that it signals a commitment to work through these changes with a particular other in recognition of the genuine uncertainty and risk involved. It is this commitment, understood as an integral part of one's calling to build up the wider body of Christ that is the church, that defines the married vocation as chaste.

In short, over against every understanding of marriage that sees it as a matter of autonomous choice designed to increase personal security (whether through the securing of property, influence, or children), a theology of marriage developed in light of a theology of discerning the image of God will stress that its significance lies in its status as a *calling* that entails *risk*, because at bottom it amounts to joining ourselves to another whom we do not really know.[54] In this respect, the Orthodox practice of placing crowns of martyrdom on the heads of the couple has every reason to be taken seriously as a piece of theologically informed liturgical symbolism. At the same time, however, it must not be interpreted in such a way as to imply that marriage is a life sentence to shared misery. On the contrary, insofar as according to Christian belief martyrs receive their crowns in heaven, the service of crowning bears witness to the joy of those who have already achieved a victory over the partial, broken character of earthly existence. In this way, if the ceremony symbolizes the risk and pain that are unavoidable aspects of marriage, it also celebrates the mutual joy and triumph toward which the union is directed.[55]

With both the dimensions of struggle and joy equally in view, generating a Christian theology of marriage can be seen as an attempt to validate the human experience of being drawn sexually to another person as a matter of specifically ecclesial vocation. As such, marriage stands alongside monasticism as a distinct but in its own way complete manifestation of chastity, interpreted as an ascetic discipline that affirms the integrity of the self in service of the complete consecration of the self to God in Christ.[56] More specifically, this consecration serves the church insofar as it is a project of discerning and rejoicing in the image of God in one's partner. This does *not* mean treating one's partner as some sort of a fleshy filter through which one tries to make out the contours of the historical Jesus. Any such practice would be an abuse rather than a celebration of the other and would fail precisely at the crucial point, which is to see the other as an unsubstitutable member of the same body of Christ of which oneself is also a part and not as a more or less adequate copy of a third person. The point of the encounter with one's spouse (as with the wider church's encounter with the saints and the poor) is not to abstract from her or his particularity to some generalized norm, but precisely to see in this one person who is most emphatically *not* Christ a being who is nevertheless claimed *by* Christ as someone without whom his own story—and therefore everyone else's story as well—would be incomplete.

From this specifically ecclesiological perspective, the protocols of chastity (including marriage and various forms of single living) serve the same end as the protocols of *dulia*. The difference is that in the former the encounter with the neighbor is not mediated through the community in the same way as the latter. To be sure, the *form* of that encounter does continue to be mediated communally through the taking of vows within and before the congregation; but whereas the objects of Christian *dulia* are a matter of communal negotiation in accordance with publicly specified criteria, in marriage one is drawn to another without reference to any clearly defined criteria possessed by that other. In this respect, marriage implies a commitment to what we cannot discern in the other as much as to what we can. Insofar as we are drawn to another by a desire that we do not choose to experience, it is true not only that we invariably marry the wrong person, but also that we do not even control which wrong person we end up marrying!

Needless to say, this should not be taken to imply that the married person will be unable to give reasons why she finds her spouse an appropriate partner, or that the church has no interest in ascertaining the suitability of prospective partners. As traditional practices like the reading of the bans and more contemporary programs of premarital counseling both demonstrate, the personal details of the couple are not by any means irrelevant. Facts do make a difference—but from the perspective of the church as a whole the difference they make is very specific and focused on very particular states of affairs (for instance, the discovery that one party is already married, that the two spouses are within a prohibited degree of consanguinity, or that one partner is being physically abused by the other) that would render a marriage untenable as a source of upbuilding for the body of Christ as a whole. Yet such potential "defeaters" fall far short of a positive criteriology for marriage. However significant it may be on other grounds that two spouses are of more or less the same age or social class, have the same interests, or (most basically) happen to find themselves in close geographic proximity, such facts neither fully explain nor justify their love. After all, if it were to be suggested that another person appeared more suitable when measured against such a list of putative criteria, the lover would not only be unlikely to switch her affections, but also would quite probably be inclined to regard the idea that she should do so as displaying a fundamental misunderstanding of their character.

This misunderstanding would be rooted in the assumption that marriage is at bottom an affirmation of one's knowledge of the other rather than a commitment to the other as one fundamentally unknown who requires the fullness of one's own life to know as a member of Christ's body. Here the contrast with the *dulia* of the saints, which focuses precisely on the life of the neighbor as an already completed whole, is noteworthy. The dynamic in *dulia* is one in which the church acts on behalf of its members by certifying certain lives as particular foci for individual discernment of the body of Christ. Marriage moves in the opposite direction, with individual members doing the work of discernment on behalf of the whole church by virtue of their commitment to celebrate particular others in their unsubstitutability as members of Christ's body.

Nor is this commitment limited to the person of one's spouse. As Linda Woodhead points out, a very practical counter to every attempt to construe marriage as a form of *égoisme à deux* is the undeniable fact that the marriage bond implicates not only the couple, but also a wider circle of family and friends whose relationships both to each other and to the individual spouses are radically altered by the new arrangements.[57] If the dynamics of desire dictate that the married person has only a limited role in "choosing" her spouse, she is even less in control when it comes to selecting her in-laws and offspring.[58] Yet they are all part of the package in a way that can help to bring into relief the ways in which marriage entails discerning the image of

God in the other we don't choose no less (though in an admittedly different way) than protocols of *dulia*.[59]

Whether birthed or adopted, children in particular represent the intrusion (however eagerly welcomed) of a third party into the heart of the marriage, challenging both spouses with respect to their perceptions of each other as well as of the newcomer, whose own calling may lead them down paths their parents neither anticipated nor desired. Here, too, the couple exercise a particular responsibility on behalf of the church as a whole, insofar as they have the primary responsibility for helping the child discern and define her sense of self as a member of Christ's body in the years before (and, in a diminished but nevertheless possibly quite decisive extent, after) attaining maturity. Here, too, the focus of marriage turns on the process of discerning the divine image in another, though now one whose own particular character and, indeed, existence may have been completely unknown prior to marriage.

Conclusion

It has not been the aim of this chapter to present a full-blown theology of marriage. That task would require an entire book of its own. Consequently, many dimensions of married life have not been touched on at all, not the least the church's response to marriages that for whatever reason go badly wrong—an issue on which Christians remain seriously divided. Similarly, a number of equally important (and no less controversial) questions related to the ethics of procreation, including especially the questions of contraception, abortion, and the use of reproductive technologies, have remained unaddressed.[60] Finally, there has been no explicit discussion of the much-debated question of same-sex marriage—though the logic of my argument suggests no intrinsic theological barrier to the ecclesial sanctioning of same-sex unions on the same terms as opposite-sex ones.

Even less has this chapter been an exhaustive account of protocols of chastity. Nothing has been said of the large number of Christians who are not married, except by way of a nod to various forms of celibate life as the principal alternative to marriage as a protocol of chastity in the history of Christianity. Especially in the modern West, however, large numbers of adult Christians are neither married nor under monastic vows. While some will in the course of time move into one or the other of these two states, there is no theological reason for supposing that such a move is in every case either necessary or even desirable. For one thing, the proper fulfillment of either vocation presupposes a willingness to wait on the circumstances of one's own existence that would be belied by any ecclesiastically imposed expectation that every person will invariably decide for one or the other. More substantively, however, such a decision would foreclose the emergence of new protocols of chastity that do not fall within the parameters of either marriage or established communities of celibates.

The aim of this chapter has thus been fairly tightly circumscribed. It has focused on marriage as a particular example of a much wider range of protocols (including, but not limited to, various forms of monastic disciplines) in which the discerning of the body of Christ takes the form of a personal vocation focused on particular others. This process of discernment certainly takes place within and under the care of the wider community of faith, but it is not an affair of the community as a whole in the same way the protocols of *dulia* examined in the previous chapter are. In this context, it is significant that marriage initially struck most Christians as a rather unpromising form of vocation. By virtue of its function as a means of consolidating and extending worldly power among kinship groups, marriage was seemingly predisposed to accentuate the loyalty to mammon that Jesus had declared incompatible with service to God (Matt. 6:24 and parallels). Christian discipleship required total dedication of the individual to Jesus, and it seems to have appeared self-evident to most Christians that marriage by definition was not as compatible with such dedication as other forms of life.

Against this background the church slowly (and not altogether unambiguously) came to acknowledge that marriage could be a vehicle for chaste existence in no sense inferior to unmarried vocations (monastic or otherwise). Specifically, marriage showed itself capable of being reconceived as an ascetic practice in which the spouses express their commitment to the body of Christ through their commitment to take time and space for each other as members of that body.[61] In this way, the appropriate vulnerability between persons that among the earliest Christians was often seen as incompatible with the political and procreative character of marriage slowly came to be seen as capable of being honored in and through sexual encounter. Indeed, far from requiring abstention from the specifically sexual dimension of marriage, it is precisely through the commitment to honor (or, as expressed in the Elizabethan English of the classic Anglican marriage rite, "worship") one's spouse with one's body that the chaste character of marriage is vindicated.

In its various Christian forms, the marriage rite aids this process by providing a hermeneutic for interpreting the union of the couple. By placing what in broader sociohistorical context appears a purely secular matter of biological politics within its liturgical practice, the church provided a "form or rule to the sanctifying possibilities of . . . sex."[62] In so doing, it claimed for marriage the joy suggested by the encounters between lovers depicted in Genesis 2 and the Song of Songs (in both of which, it is important to note, the consideration of offspring is conspicuous by its absence) and thereby points forward to marriage's eschatological significance as a symbolic anticipation of the union of Christ and the church (Eph. 5:31-32). This symbolic interpretation of the married state highlights its role as a discipline of discernment: as Christ and the church form one body, so marriage commits the spouses to see themselves as forming "one flesh" in Christ.

In line with these biblical roots, the church honors marriage as a discipline that both challenges and empowers individuals to pursue the image of God in one neighbor through a lifelong commitment. In its sanctioning of what is effectively an individualized affective drive as the ground for the pursuit of the divine image in history, Christian marriage appears in certain respects as the converse of the politics of *dulia*, in which the effort is made to subsume individual preferences to communally established norms. To be sure, the church also regulates the parameters of marriage, and personal inclination plays a role in individual believers' decisions regarding which saints are to be the object of their personal devotion. Nevertheless, the forms that discernment of Christ's body takes in each of the two cases remain distinct. Where *dulia* is a discipline of the community, marriage is a discipline of individual persons that the church honors as irreducible to any communal project or practice, however much it may define the parameters of its exercise.[63]

At the same time, it would be wrong to overplay the contrast between *dulia* and chastity, as though the drive in the former to see the divine image in the unfamiliar (and uncomfortable) faces of the saints and the poor were relieved in the latter by an easier discipline that focuses on more familiar and attractive figures. The vocations that defined the protocols of chastity are rooted in desire, pulling the whole person ineluctably toward a particular form of life. And the experience of desire, far from making us comfortable, renders us vulnerable and open to hurt in a way that is as potentially destructive of the body of Christ as the exclusion and narrowness of vision addressed by the protocols of *dulia*. In the face of this feature of human existence, the protocols of chastity are not about quenching this desire, but rather about rendering it ecclesiastically (and, inasmuch as the life of the individual is understood to be nourished within the ecclesial body, personally) productive in fostering relationships of mutual support and critique within the wider community of faith. Indeed, the very fact that these relationships are conceived as entailing lifelong commitment highlights the fact that the discernment of the divine image takes time even in those who are familiar to us, precisely because the fact of familiarity makes it easy for our own projections to supervene on the essential, ungraspable mystery of the other. Only when the risks as well as the pleasures of familiarity are taken seriously can our personal knowledge of the other in such vocations contribute to our discerning the image of God.

chapter 7

Discernment in Ecclesial Formation

The Sacraments as Protocols

Discernment in Context

The last two chapters have examined a range of Christian practices in order to evaluate their significance as protocols for discerning the image of God in persons inside and outside the church. I have argued that the protocols of *dulia* and chastity can each be understood as disciplines that can aid Christians in discerning the divine image by working against the ever-present temptation to identify that image with what is most familiar or congenial. In the case of *dulia*, this process takes the form of a communal discipline of discernment whose particular foci are determined through an explicitly political process of debate and negotiation. By contrast, the protocols of chastity, though regulated by the community with respect to form, leave the particular objects of discernment to the vocational sensibilities of the individuals involved.

Both these sets of protocols serve (and are in large part designed) to give shape to the church's life, but they also presuppose an already existing ecclesial context. In other words, they rest on still more fundamental practices that define the church as a particular community in the first place. That neither of these protocols themselves has this defining function is evident from the fact that neither of them, considered as more or less clearly defined, self-conscious, regulated features of communal practice, is coeval with the birth of the church. Each acquired definite form only after many centuries of theological reflection and development. Thus, however valuable various forms of Christian *dulia* and chastity may be in building up the body of Christ, they do not in themselves constitute the church as that body. On the contrary, their main focus is to enhance the capacity for discernment of the body that is already constituted on other grounds.

Two practices that arguably do play this more fundamental role are baptism and the Eucharist. Both show every evidence of having been constitutive practices of Christian communities from the earliest times (see, for instance, Acts 2:38, 46; 1 Cor. 11:23-26). Just as significant for the present argument, both practices are interpreted by Paul in terms of incorporation into Christ's body. Believers are baptized "into one body" (1 Cor. 12:13) that is "Christ" (Rom. 6:3) and have thereby "clothed [them]selves with Christ" (Gal. 3:27). And, still more explicitly with respect to the communion rite, "we who are many are one body, for we all partake of the one bread" (1 Cor. 10:17). Indeed, the one place where Paul speaks specifically of the problem of discerning the body is precisely in the context of the celebration of the Lord's Supper (1 Cor. 11:29; compare v. 31).

This passage in particular is useful for understanding the close relationship between the bodies of individual Christians and the body of Christ in Paul's thought. It is introduced in the context of a critique of several key features of Corinthian eucharistic practice that have come to Paul's attention. The fundamental problem raised by all of them is that of disunity:

> For, to begin with, when you come together as a church, I hear there are divisions among you. . . . When you come together, it is not really to eat the Lord's supper. For when the time comes to eat, each of you goes ahead with your own supper, and one goes hungry and another becomes drunk. What! Do you not have homes to eat and drink in? Or do you show contempt for the church of God and humiliate those who have nothing? (1 Cor. 11:18, 20-22)

There are several points to note here. First, Paul effectively equates the practice of gathering as a church with celebrating the Lord's Supper. Second, his criticism of a situation in which people eat individually clearly indicates that he believes that the Supper should manifest the fundamental unity of the community. Third, the divisions within the community correspond to class lines, with the wealthier members indulging in the common meal without bothering to wait for the arrival of the less well-off (note the admonition in v. 33 to "wait for one another"), who thus wind up both physically hungry (v. 21) and socially humiliated (v. 22). For Paul this is not simply a matter of discourtesy, but indicative of a fundamental misapprehension of what the church is.[1]

It is in this context that the issue of "discerning the body" becomes important. As already noted, Paul has in the previous chapter of this letter argued that the bread and wine of communion, as the body and blood of Christ, join those who partake in them as members of one body (1 Cor. 10:16-17). In light of the disreputable practices at Corinth that have been reported to him, he now proceeds to spell out the implications of this fact:

> Whoever, therefore, eats the bread or drinks the cup of the Lord in an unworthy manner will be liable for the body and blood of the Lord. Examine [*dokimazeto*]

> yourselves, and only then eat of the bread and drink of the cup. For all who eat and drink without discerning [*diakrinon*] the body, eat and drink judgment against themselves. For this reason many of you are weak and ill, and some have died. But if we practiced discernment [*diakrinomen*] with respect to ourselves, we would not be judged. (1 Cor. 11:27-31; translation altered)

Having the right understanding of what is going on in the celebration of communion—and thus of what it means to be a church—is clearly a crucial matter for Paul, so that the solution to the problems experienced at Corinth is evidently a capacity for "discerning the body." But what "body" does Paul have in mind? And what exactly does its discernment entail? Some Greek manuscripts specify "the body of the Lord," but given the multiple references of this phrase in 1 Corinthians, which equates the Lord's body with the eucharistic elements (10:16), the physical body of Jesus (11:27), and the church as a whole (12:27), this addition does not do much to clarify matters.

Dale Martin has plausibly suggested that all three senses of Christ's body should be understood as implied in the act of "discerning the body," along with the believer's proper understanding of her own body.[2] Given the care Paul takes in 1 Cor. 11:23-26 to relate the practice of the Eucharist in the Corinthian church with Christ's words and actions at the Last Supper, it is hard to imagine that his readers would have failed to identify the "body" mentioned in v. 29 with the bread and wine, notwithstanding the fact that Paul does not go into detail about the ontological status of the eucharistic elements. Likewise, the charge of being "liable" for Christ's body and blood in v. 27 points back to the crucifixion and thus to the historical flesh and blood of Jesus of Nazareth. And the idea that the body in question should also be taken to refer to the church is supported not only by Paul's claim in v. 22 that the Corinthians' eucharistic practice betrays a fundamental misunderstanding of what the church is, but also by the extensive discussion of the church as the body of Christ that follows in chapter 12. Finally, Paul's comments in v. 31 about the need to practice discernment with respect to oneself suggests that discerning the body of Christ requires looking within as well as attending to the sacramental and social realities without.

This interweaving of these various dimensions of the term *body* is consistent with Paul's claim in 1 Cor. 10:16-17 that the consumption of the elements integrate the believer into a single, communal body, which is the body of Christ. Interpreting the rite of communion within this broad ecclesial framework leaves no basis for isolating any one dimension of Christ's body over against the others. Because Christ identified himself with the elements "on the night when he was betrayed," they are his body. And in eating them,

Christians take this body into their own and thus become part of that body.[3] In this way, Christians are what they eat in a very literal sense,[4] and it is for this reason that discernment of the body entails a proper understanding of one's own "contingent status as a member of the larger body of Christ."[5] If one fails to understand what the body of Christ is, then eating Christ's body and blood puts one's own life at risk—as proved for Paul by the fact that many at Corinth "are weak and ill, and some have died" (1 Cor. 11:30). While the precise sequence of cause and effect that underlies Paul's inference here is not altogether clear, it seems reasonable to assume once again that the various dimensions of Christ's body are intersecting with one another in his thought. By the lack of respect they show one another in the conduct of communal meals, the Corinthians are dividing the body of Christ—and a body that is divided dies (note again Paul's concern that people are making themselves "liable" for the body and blood of Christ in 1 Cor. 11:27). The rending of a body implicates each of its members, so that if the body as a whole is unwell, it is fully to be expected that this will cause individual members to sicken and die.[6]

The upshot of Paul's reasoning is that the proper discernment of Christ's body is not simply a means of improving ecclesial existence, but a necessary condition of the church existing at all. Where the body is not discerned, the church dies in and through the deaths of its members. The capacity for discernment is, in the first instance, rooted in familiarity with the story of Jesus of Nazareth (and it is worth noting that the recitation of the origin of the eucharistic rite in 1 Cor. 11:23-26 is one of the only places in his extant correspondence where Paul makes mention of the details of Jesus' life). After all, it is *his* body of which the church's members have become part, and the eucharistic rite through whom that participation is both manifested and realized is in itself a proclamation of his death until he comes again (1 Cor. 11:26). At the same time, however, because this body now includes all those who share in the bread and the cup, discerning the body is not merely a historical exercise. Nor can it be limited to the particular sorts of relationships associated with *dulia*, monasticism, and matrimony. It is, rather, an ongoing task that comes to the fore every time the community celebrates the rite that defines it as the body of Christ in the first place. It is therefore necessary to explore the character of the Eucharist in greater detail in order to appreciate the demands of this particular means of discerning the image of God in Christ.

The Politics of Communion

One might think that meaningful analysis of the communion rite would presuppose a discussion of baptism, since Christians regard baptism as a prerequisite to participation in the eucharistic meal. While there is a definite temporal priority of baptism over the Eucharist in the lives of individual believers, however, in ecclesiological terms logical priority belongs to the Eucharist. Baptism brings new members into the body, but the very act of baptizing presupposes the existence of a body into which the grafting of new members is possible. In other words, if baptism gives the body growth, it is the celebration of communion that marks a particular community as the one body of Christ. In principle, after all, one could imagine a Christian community where no baptisms took place (for example, a group of monks stranded on a desert island for many years), but a community in which there was no celebration of communion would not be recognizable as the church.[7] I will therefore begin with an examination of Eucharist before proceeding to a discussion of baptism.[8]

In his theologically profound and humanly moving study *Torture and Eucharist*, William Cavanaugh provides a framework within which to appreciate the Eucharist as a protocol of discernment by characterizing it as a form of politics or, more specifically, as what he calls a "counter-politics" to the violence of the secular police state. To this end, he relates the Pauline themes of participation directly to the political idea of the Eucharist as a subversive form of social practice:

> Eucharist makes real the presence of Christ both in the elements and in the body of believers. The church becomes [in the Eucharist] the very body of Christ. . . . Where torture is an anti-liturgy for the realization of the state's power on the bodies of others, Eucharist is the liturgical realization of Christ's suffering and redemptive body in the bodies of His followers. Torture creates fearful and isolated bodies . . . the Eucharist effects the body of Christ. . . . Torture creates victims; Eucharist creates witnesses, *martyrs*. Isolation is overcome in the Eucharist by the building of a communal body which resists the state's attempts to disappear it.[9]

Cavanaugh's main point here and throughout his book is that the Eucharist makes the body of Christ visible in and through its members. If the church fails to recognize this epiphanic character of its eucharistic practice, he argues, the body of Christ cannot be seen. In a rough parallel with Paul's arguments about the physiological effects of poor eucharistic practice in 1 Corinthians 11, the invisibility that results from poor practice is understood by Cavanaugh in a very literal sense: where the church fails to be a true eucharistic body, its members simply disappear, whether by virtue of being rounded up by agents of the state security apparatus or, just as effectively, because they are so afraid to make themselves visible that they hide away in their homes or some other private refuge.

Cavanaugh argues that the history of eucharistic practice in the Catholic tradition has rendered its political character more difficult to grasp. He traces this process of depoliticization to the increasing focus in the later Middle Ages on the Eucharist as an object of devotion in its own right (for instance, with the introduction of the Feast of Corpus Christi in the thirteenth century) rather than as the means to the end of communion between members of the church.[10] A second step was an increasing conceptual distinction between the ecclesial and political spheres that manifested itself in the idea of the church as Christ's "mystical body" with a specifically spiritual sphere of jurisdiction alongside the increasingly secular state, which was acknowledged to have its own, specifically temporal, area of competence.[11] The effect of these processes, Cavanaugh argues, was that the Pauline work of discernment came to focus exclusively on the eucharistic elements on the one hand and the juridical structure of the church on the other, with the result that the body of Christ became abstracted from the concrete realities of particular human bodies in a way that rendered the life of the church static, timeless, and profoundly *dis*-embodied.

Against these trends, Cavanaugh argues for a renewed emphasis on the political role of the Eucharist in building up and (thereby) exhibiting the concrete social body that is the church. From this perspective, receiving the Eucharist is not an end in itself, any more than Christ's sacrifice was. Rather, it functions as a means of establishing Christ's body as an ongoing, dynamic reality in time and space. This is not to deny either the once-and-for-all character of Christ's sacrifice or the personal benefits of the Eucharist to the individual, but it is to contextualize them in terms of the larger purposes of Christ's ministry. Specifically, the point of Christ's sacrifice is not the establishing of a fund of grace that then is appropriated by individuals through consuming the sacramental elements. Instead, the grace of the Eucharist continually brings the body of Christ into being "by the participation of many in his sacrifice."[12] Cavanaugh draws here on Augustine's idea that our act of sacrifice is not necessary to fill any lack in God, but rather to address our lack as beings who remain unfulfilled until they are joined to God.[13] In short, the Eucharist is the means by which the church makes the body of Christ manifest in the world at large because it is the means by which the church quite literally becomes Christ's body.

Cavanaugh is careful to add that this body is visible only in part in the church on earth.[14] Nevertheless, he insists that a clear understanding of the church's reality as the genuine (if incomplete) body of Christ now is essential if it is to avoid disappearing from public view as a social body. In this context he stresses the importance of excommunication as a discipline that makes the church visible by clearly defining its boundaries: "The Eucharist, as the gift which effects the visibility of the body of Christ, is . . . the church's counter-imagination to that of the state. Formal excommunication makes the church visible, if only temporarily, by bringing to light a boundary between church and world which those who attack the church have themselves drawn.[15]

In illustration of this point, Cavanaugh cites the decrees of excommunication against torturers issued in 1980 by a number of Chilean bishops under the Pinochet regime.[16] While the actual effect of the declaration appears to have been limited at best (at least partly, he avers, because it identified neither torturers nor torture centers by name), it did at least declare the peculiar nature of torture as (in the words of one of the excommunicating bishops) "a sin which produces a significant social effect."[17] As such, it implicitly recognized both the church and its eucharistic protocols as public and political realities calling for public and political monitoring. While a more focused decree (specifically, one that targeted Pinochet himself, as well as other primary instigators of torture in the junta and its security service) would undoubtedly have made the point more forcefully, just raising the specter of excommunication pointed to the epistemological function of the church as the place where the body of Christ is seen and known.

Though Cavanaugh does not put his argument in such specifically epistemological terms, the relationship between church politics and eucharistic meaning is evident in his reference to a Chilean priest who publicly advocated General Pinochet's excommunication on the grounds that (among other things) the Eucharist should not be a scandal to the poor.[18] It became such under the Pinochet regime, Cavanaugh suggests, because the participation in systematic torture by individuals who were overwhelmingly (and often very publicly) Christian made a mockery of the reconciled unity that the Eucharist is supposed to illustrate. Within the terms of the present argument, one might make the same point by arguing that in such a context the eucharistic practice of Christians complicit in torture effectively made it impossible to discern the body of Christ.

The point of all this is not that it takes the presence of torture or some other equally heinous crime to reveal the political character of the Eucharist as communion. At the same time, however, Cavanaugh clearly does suggest that the fact of systematic torture proved particularly effective in showing the untenability of ecclesiologies that located the church on a spiritual plane unconnected with the concrete practices that give shape to human lives. In particular (and in a way remarkably similar to the issues faced by the Confessing Church in Germany half a century earlier), the story of the Chilean church under Pinochet gives testimony to the epistemological significance of the claim that the church is the body of Christ. The practice of excommunication is central to this story because it draws attention to the fact that the church can be known as this particular body over against other social "bodies" only insofar as it is willing to expel those who do violence to it and so make discernment of its identity as this body impossible. In short, excommunication is necessary because where the principle of reconciliation is deliberately violated, the body of Christ is rendered incapable of discernment, and the church is thereby destroyed.

The significance of this point is hard to underestimate, for it means that no amount of formally orthodox preaching or canonically valid sacramental administration in themselves identify the church as the body of Christ apart from more explicitly political means of defining the church's boundaries. In this respect, those traditions that have claimed ecclesial discipline as a distinct mark of the church have a serious claim on the churches' attention.[19] This is not because Christ abandons the sinful church (as argued by the Donatists), as though the church's status as Christ's body were a quality to be secured by human obedience. On the contrary, Paul's warnings to the Corinthians make it clear that the danger faced by a faithless church is caused by Christ's refusal to leave the church to its own devices. The reason many are "weak and ill" in Corinth is not that Christ has ceased to be present in the Eucharist. The fact of illness and death bears testimony rather to the fact that Christ continues to be present in the eucharistic event in power—but insofar as the body is being rent by the Corinthians this presence is manifest as judgment rather than grace. Discernment is impossible not because Christ has abandoned the church, but because Christian rending of the body of Christ causes the members through whom the body is visible to vanish, whether by being left out of the eucharistic feast in first-century Corinth or "disappeared" in twentieth-century Chile. Where the community does not live out the reconciliation the Eucharist both represents and effects, Christ cannot be seen, and God cannot be known.

The Eucharistic Framework of Christology

Paul's critique of Corinthian practice provides solid biblical precedent for framing eucharistic discipline in terms of excluding those whose practices result in the Eucharist becoming a scandal to the poor. If we recall our earlier identification of the poor with those who find themselves on the margins of the effective structures of the church, a Eucharist that is a scandal to the poor is one in which the church fails to communicate the gospel by failing to disclose the God who in Christ identifies with the poor. This does not necessarily mean that the church has spoken propositions that in themselves fail the test of orthodoxy, only that the ecclesial context within which it speaks of them is such that they fail to communicate the gospel.[20] Because the Eucharist is the practice that most fundamentally defines the church as the body of Christ, it provides the basic context within which the church's utterances about forgiveness, justification, eternal life, and so forth acquire their public meaning. Correspondingly, these utterances will point to the Christ rather than the many idols of human (including also Christian) imagination only if that context accurately reflects the shape of Christ's own body. Otherwise, even the most orthodox doctrines will simply fail to pick out the one who was born of Mary owing to a lack of referent (or, more accurately, to the substitution of a false referent for the true). So, in the Corinthian church the fact that the words of institution were (as we may assume) correctly recited was not in itself sufficient to provide a context for discerning Christ's body in face of the self-serving behavior of some of the members of the congregation (compare 1 Cor. 1:10-13).[21]

This relationship between meaning and context provides a useful framework for extending analysis of eucharistic practice beyond the Catholic context examined by Cavanaugh to include the more typically Protestant understanding of the sacraments as visible words.[22] It was a matter of consensus among at least the so-called magisterial Reformers that such words are integral to any full and adequate preaching of the gospel, but—as the sacramental atrophy that has afflicted many Protestant churches in the wake of the Reformation bears witness—it has not always been clear why. The Reformers' sacramentology led them to reject what they saw as the Catholic tendency to view the sacraments in general and the Eucharist in particular as grace-bearing substances whose efficacy was not tied to preaching; but their own position could easily be taken to imply that the sacraments were simply a repetition of what is preached in a less cerebral form. In fact, though sacraments are inseparable from verbal preaching (against the first view), neither are they reducible to it (against the second). Here again, the relationship between speech and context is crucial. Certainly the Eucharist is itself a matter of verbal address (namely, in the words, "This is the body of Christ, given for you"), but it is an address in which the content of what is spoken is inseparable from a particular set of actions that center on the blessing, distribution, and consumption of the elements of bread and wine to all the baptized without distinction. Similarly, the Eucharist as a whole is properly viewed as an inseparable part of the broader piece of communicative action, including especially the sermon, traditionally called the mass. From this perspective, the absence of either component means that the proclamation of the gospel (and the corresponding identification of the proclaiming community as the body of Christ) is deficient. In short, the Eucharist has a central place in the church's life to the extent that it is understood to be a deliberate (as opposed to merely incidental) and nonnegotiable (as opposed to merely customary) dimension of the church's communicative activity.[23]

In short, the Eucharist provides the communal framework for the discernment of Christ's body insofar as it is the act by which that body is identified with the congregation in the act of sharing and eating of the consecrated elements. Nothing could be less justified, however, than to conclude from this that proclaiming Christ is reducible to proclaiming the church. The point is rather to emphasize the interdependence of the spoken and the enacted words as together constitutive of the referential system of Christian discourse. Knowledge of God is mediated through the community for the simple reason that God's speech and presence are inseparable from the mutual encounter of believers (Matt. 18:20).[24] To the extent that the church is through the Eucharist "a place where God locates God's own self,"[25] the church's talk about Christ is inadequate to the extent that is not conditioned by a eucharistic frame of reference that includes the discipline of bodily discernment demanded by Paul. For while the body of Christ invariably exceeds the bounds of the visible church, let alone any particular congregation, it remains the case (as Paul emphasized) that success in discerning Christ's body is as much a matter of ecclesial performance as of individual knowledge.

The idea that the eucharistic action is constitutive of the community's identity as body of Christ raises questions about the relationship between the historically specific body of Jesus and the communal body of the believers. Obviously the two are not the same, and their difference is constituted principally in the asymmetry in their mutual identification suggested by the specification that the church is precisely *his* body, such that he alone is the source and measure of its identity. Christian confession affirms that who Jesus is, is defined by his story as the one who was "born of the virgin Mary . . . suffered under Pontius Pilate . . . crucified, died, and was buried" and then "rose again." This story establishes him as the head in such a way that his identity can never be subsumed under or absorbed by that of his body's many members. The church is not a collective, to the identity of which each member contributes equally; it is specifically the body of *Christ*. At the same time (and as argued in ch. 4 above), the affirmation that it is genuinely his *body* means that Christ cannot be known fully without reference to it, because Christ has in his own story bound his destiny to the community of those who confess him as Lord.

The Eucharist constitutes the linchpin of this asymmetrical relationship insofar as it both stands over against the church as a gift and at the same time establishes the church as the locus of Christ's own ongoing presence in history. If, as I have argued, human beings can be seen as creatures made in the image of God only because they are seen to be part of the body of Christ, the Eucharist is the central practice through which this seeing takes place. Thus, the church is that body insofar as it celebrates the Eucharist. This point has led Robert Jenson to affirm so strong an identification between Christ and the community as to affirm that "there is and needs to be no other place than the church for him to be embodied."[26] Yet while Jenson seems right to highlight the role of the Eucharist as a practice in which Christ's presence is concretely enacted in and to the community rather than as a kind of conduit linking metaphysically distinct planes, his language is not without problems. The direct equation of Jesus' risen body with the eucharistic bread and cup fails to take account of the significance of the ascension and thus gives insufficient attention to Jesus' absence from the church prior to the parousia (see 2 Cor. 5:6; compare Phil. 1:23).[27] In pushing the Pauline imagery of the body to the point of insisting that the church is the only form in which Christ is available to himself or others, Jenson winds up with a situation in which Christ's address to the church becomes indistinguishable from the church talking to itself.

The way in which Paul characterizes the Eucharist to the Corinthians suggests more of a tension between Christ and the church than Jenson allows. For Paul discerning the body is not just a matter of seeing what is already there. Nor is it simply a question of realizing that there is always more to Christ than what is experienced in the present. That sort of eschatological proviso, while certainly not false, too easily mutes the discontinuity between the reality of Christ's body as it is to be unveiled on the last day and as it is experienced in the present. In breaking the bread and sharing the cup the church bears witness to Christ's undeniable absence as well as his sacramental presence. Indeed, insofar as the eucharistic act is the proclamation of "the Lord's death *until he comes*" (1 Cor. 11:26), the theme of Christ's absence is arguably just as strong a note as his presence. In this respect, discerning the body cannot be understood merely as a matter of seeing what is already there, but of recognizing what is *not* there.

This stress on Christ's absence from the assembly highlights the enduring difference between the particular life of Jesus of Nazareth seated at God's right hand and the collective life of the church. Importantly, however, it is more than an affirmation of the enduring distinction between head and body that will remain even in glory. It is also testimony to the fact that the ecclesial body is presently under construction—and therefore incomplete—in a way that will cease with Christ's return. Still more specifically, it reminds the church of its failure to live out its calling as Christ's body. This failure is manifest whenever (as was evidently the case in Corinth) the community is riven by factionalism; but it is also a feature of any particular Christian congregation prior to the eschaton, insofar as every such congregation evidently excludes large numbers of others who are also called to be part of the ecclesial body but who do not seem to acknowledge or answer that call. Even a congregation that has managed to overcome the threat of factionalism will fall short of this eschatological standard; indeed, the situation is arguably more dangerous for a highly unified community, insofar as it is more easily tempted to a triumphalism that is blind to the degree to which Christ's absence is experienced not only in the delay of the parousia, but also in the absence of communion with all those who remain on the outside of the eucharistic assembly.[28]

In short, discerning the body refers not only to the way in which the whole of the gathered community is constituted as one body in the Eucharist (so that divisions in the assembly signal a failure to discern the body), but also to the incompleteness of the body from the perspective of a God who "desires everyone to be saved and to come to the knowledge of the truth" (1 Tim. 2:4). Complacency with respect to this second factor also constitutes a failure to discern the body, precisely because it implies an overrealized eschatology in which the otherness and absence of Christ with respect to the gathered community does not receive due recognition. Here again, excommunication has an important ecclesial function to the extent that its practice is correlated with a strong sense of the community's ongoing responsibility to the excommunicated. For if exclusion from the eucharistic assembly is a means of defending integrity of the community's witness to Christ, it is no less a means of reconciling the sinner to the community in a way that acknowledges the genuine loss to the body that results from the exclusion (however temporary) of even a single member (1 Cor. 12:26). For while it is true that the one excluded from the assembly is by Jesus' own judgment to be viewed "as a Gentile and a tax collector" (Matt. 18:17), this same Jesus characterizes his own ministry as one dedicated to the task of calling "not the righteous but sinners to repentance" (Luke 5:32).[29]

In this way, the act of excommunication both enhances the distinctness of the eucharistic assembly over against the world at large and also problematizes that distinctiveness. The dynamics of eucharistic politics can thus be seen to enact at an ecclesiologically more fundamental level the bivalent character of *dulia* described in chapter 5. Just as the protocols of *dulia* direct the community both to its center (in the shape of outstanding figures from the church's past) and to its margins (in the form of encounter with those whose position on the boundaries of the church renders them "outstanding" in a different sense), so the proclamation of Christ's death in the Eucharist both confirms the church as the body of Christ now and highlights the incompleteness of Christ's body in the church. Moreover, this appreciation of Christ's absence from the community provides the ground for the other great sacramental practice of the church: baptism. For through baptism (and the activities of penance that derive from it) the church gives testimony to its persistent incompleteness by receiving in (or in penance receiving back) those who stand outside the community. It therefore constitutes a sacramental protocol in its own right.

The Politics of Baptism

The political character of baptism depends on that of the Eucharist. As already noted, though Jesus' baptism preceded his Last Supper, Eucharist remains logically prior to baptism, because it is the act that both proclaims and constitutes the community as the body of Christ. Baptism is logically derivative insofar as it is a means of enlarging the fellowship and (through the closely associated rights of penance) monitoring its boundaries. Apart from a properly eucharistic framework, baptism reduces to a rite of passage, whether associated with birth (as in the majority of Christian churches) or coming of age (in the case of those Christian communities that practice believers' baptism). In these decadent forms baptism does little to define the particular character of the church as the body of Christ, however effective it may be in marking the church's boundaries in a purely sociological sense. To be sure, baptism remains the church's rite of initiation whatever the ensemble of broader church practices within and in relation to which it is performed; but where its essential connection with the Eucharist is lost, the political implications of joining this community are muted.[30]

The interpretation of baptism as an act of being engrafted into the body of Christ constitutes an obvious difference between the Christian rite of baptism and the washing of John the Baptist from which it derived and to which it is in many other respects similar (for example, in its association with eschatological repentance and the forgiveness of sin). Though the imagery of physical incorporation into Christ only becomes explicit with Paul, it is at least consistent with what is generally assumed by scholars to be the very early practice of baptism "in[to] the name of Jesus" attested in Acts (2:38; 8:16; 10:48; 19:5).[31] Paul's varied ways of speaking of baptism in his Corinthian correspondence suggests that he may have seen connections between the liturgical language of baptism into Christ's name and incorporation into Christ's body. For example, Paul points indirectly to the practice of baptism into Jesus' name by reminding the Corinthians that they have not been baptized into his own name (1 Cor. 1:13-15; compare 6:11); and he links his interpretation of the exodus as the Israelites' having been baptized "into" Moses at the Red Sea (10:2; compare Acts 19:3) with a reference to Christians' baptism "into one body" that is Christ (12:13; compare Rom. 6:3; Gal. 3:27). Be that as it may, Paul clearly believes that the act of being baptized reconstitutes the individual: having been buried with Christ in baptism (Rom. 6:4), the Christian neophyte is now "in" Christ and, as such, has so been translated from one sphere of existence to another as to constitute "a new creation" (2 Cor. 5:17). As one writer puts it, "the water is the vehicle of the recreation of matter in Christ."[32]

Paul's language would make no sense if baptism were simply a natural correlate of birth. The need for "new creation" clearly implies that there is something wrong with human circumstances demanding the kind of translation from one sphere to another that Paul's dramatic language of burial suggests. The biblical writers give little suggestion that early Christians believed that this process required either an extended period of instruction or an elaborate liturgy. The accounts of baptism in Acts, for example, suggest little in the way of preparation beyond a sudden confrontation with the news of Jesus' resurrection (for instance, 2:37-41; 8:34-38; 16:14-15; compare 19:1-6). As is especially clear in the story of Cornelius (10:44-48), the impression is of a church driven to catch up immediately all who responded to the eschatological work of the Spirit.

Be that as it may, by the third century baptism had become a much more time-consuming and symbolically ramified process with respect both to preparation for it and the conduct of the rite itself. Since the writers of the time give no hint of any consciousness of departure from earlier practice, the motivations behind this shift must remain to some degree speculative. Still, it seems reasonable to see these developments as a function of Christians' increasing sense of the political character and consequences of church membership within the Roman Empire. To be sure, already in the first decades of the church's existence Paul saw Christian confession as a matter of translation from the sphere of "the present age" and its "rulers" to that of Christ (see, for instance, Rom. 12:2; 1 Cor. 2:6-8; 2 Cor. 4:4; 6:14-16; compare Acts 26:16-18), but his own writings tend to support the picture of comparatively informal baptismal practice depicted in Acts.[33] The experience of the practical consequences of church membership, however, ultimately produced baptismal liturgies that included a more elaborate acknowledgment of the church's "countercultural" character. For example, by the fifth century, baptismal candidates were universally required to make some formal renunciation of Satan as a sign both of their rejection of pagan religion and of their dissociation from the social order which that religion underwrote.[34]

This way of formally integrating the political dimension of Christian existence into baptismal practice entailed an equally formal process of communal discernment with respect to the suitability of candidates. One particularly detailed description of this process is found in the *Apostolic Tradition* of Hippolytus, which is generally taken as witness to the practice of the church at Rome in the third century. It assumes a three-year catechumenate and excludes certain categories of persons (including prostitutes, homosexuals, and self-made eunuchs) from the outset as morally unclean.[35] When the catechetical course was completed, candidates were received by the church as *competentes* or *electi* who were subject to an intensified program of preparation in the run-up to the act of baptism itself.[36] Exorcism played a prominent role in this final stage of preparation, reflecting the belief that within a pagan society all non-Christians were captive to the devil.[37] Hippolytus describes an initial examination focusing on the morals of the candidate during the catechumenate, followed by a series of daily exorcisms designed to certify that the candidate was free of demonic influence.[38] In the area around Antioch, the process of rooting out demons appears to have been carried out in a particularly intense and uncompromising fashion:

> . . . once the course of instruction was over, the bishop exorcised each catechumen one by one to see if he were truly clean and not possessed by an unclean spirit. If there was someone who was not clean, his condition would be made evident by the unclean spirit himself (presumably because the spirit would not be able to remain concealed in the face of the bishop's spiritual attack). Such a catechumen was not to be cleansed . . . but was rather to depart . . . in disgrace, "because the evil and alien spirit abided in him."[39]

Only after this process was complete were the candidates in a position to undertake a more active role through their formal renunciation of Satan and his works and the confession of Jesus, followed by the washing of baptism itself.

Immediately after baptism came a ceremony during which the bishop laid hands on each candidate and anointed them with oil, after which the candidates were brought to the table to share for the first time in the body and blood of Christ as full members of the eucharistic fellowship. As that which completed the process of initiation, this episcopal anointing was understood both to symbolize and to effect for the Christian the same "anointing" with the Holy Spirit (John 2:30-33, 41) that defined Jesus as the "Christ," or anointed one.[40] While the precise development of this practice is uncertain,[41] the New Testament bears witness that very early on the gift of the Spirit (conferred by the laying on of hands) was associated with baptism even though distinguished from it (see, for instance, Acts 8:14-17; 10:44-48; 19:4-6; compare John 3:5). The writings of Cyprian of Carthage[42] and Hippolytus[43] show that a close liturgical link between baptism and anointing (or chrismation) was well established by the third century, and the two continue to be performed together in the Orthodox churches. In the West, however, episcopal refusal to delegate anointing to the parish clergy led to the gradual separation of the episcopal unction and laying on of hands ("confirmation") from baptism in the medieval period.[44] While this separation continues to be the practice in the Catholic tradition and many Protestant churches, it has come under criticism as a historical accident with no theological justification.[45]

If Christian initiation is understood in the context of protocols of discernment, then the liturgical conjoining of baptism and chrismation is consistent with the ways in which the overall process has an impact on both the candidate and the community. From the perspective of the candidate, baptism entails a turning from the world to Christ, as captured liturgically in the renunciation of Satan and the confession of faith in the triune God. In the baptismal rites of the early church, this double turning (the literal sense of "conversion") was often enacted quite literally, as the candidate faced west when renouncing the devil and then turned to the east when professing the creed.[46] Whatever the shape of the liturgical drama, however, the aim is to give shape to the candidate's repentance and renunciation on the one hand, and confession of Christ on the other. Both aspects together testify to a fundamental lack on the candidate's part that is made good only through baptismal incorporation into the death (Rom. 6:3-4) and thereby the risen body (1 Cor. 12:13) of Christ.[47]

Less immediately obvious in the form of the rite itself (especially when the actions associated with the gift of the Spirit is divided from the baptismal washing), is the way in which the ceremony of Christian initiation also testifies to the church's lack. A first step in appreciating this dimension of the rite is the recognition that baptism is not a gift of the community to the individual, but rather a gift of God that, in building up the body of Christ, transforms candidate and community alike. To be sure, the transformation is not equal in the two cases: it is not to be expected that the church will be changed in the same way (let alone to the same degree) by the addition of a new member as the new member will be by her incorporation into the life of the community. Nevertheless, in receiving a newly baptized member, the church is affected in a way that testifies to its ongoing need to *be* changed as a condition of its fulfilling the task of building up the body of Christ. For if "each is given a manifestation of the Spirit for the common good" (1 Cor. 12:7), then the church as a whole benefits from the bestowing of the Spirit and, correspondingly, suffers so long as an individual's spiritual gifts are not received.[48]

In this way Christian initiation (including both the washing in water and the subsequent anointing and laying on of hands) gives further testimony to the presence and absence of Christ in the church. In line with Paul's account in Romans 6, the act of baptism presupposes that the church is already the body of Christ; but the same rite stands as a reminder the church is not yet the body of Christ in its fullness. In seeking to be joined to the congregation through a washing that is nothing less than a symbolic drowning, the candidate testifies to her own lack. But in praying that this same candidate may receive the gift of the Holy Spirit for the upbuilding of the community as a whole, the church testifies to its own lack, which is no less serious for the fact that no one knows precisely which spiritual gifts any new member will bring to the church. Indeed, in praying for the gift of the Spirit who "blows where it chooses" (John 3:8), the one who lays hands on the neophyte implicitly surrenders any claim to predict or control what ecclesial lack she will address—as does the neophyte herself in submitting to such a prayer.

Much, if not most, current Christian practice suppresses the countercultural character of the baptismal process as a shock to the individual and the community. With the political triumph of Christianity and the corresponding diminishment of the number of candidates baptized as adults, the more dramatic features of early Christian initiation were either telescoped into a much smaller period or eliminated from the liturgy altogether.[49] Though the Orthodox liturgy continues to include a fairly dramatic ritual of renunciation that features spitting at the devil, even here there is little real suggestion that Christianity might imply the renunciation of anything save "a few obviously sinful and immoral acts."[50] And the difficulty of maintaining baptism as a ministry of discernment is evident not only in communities where all infants are baptized as a matter of course, but also among churches that insist on believers' baptism, since the dynamics of socialization easily conspire to render submission to baptism as "automatic" in Baptist communities as confirmation or first communion is in pedobaptist churches.[51]

As lamentable as the erosion of the processes associated with primitive Christian initiation may be, baptism remains a political act. The problems that have attended the development of baptismal practice merely point to the fact that the character of the baptizing community is decisive for the kind of politics baptism instantiates. Where Christianity is the established religion, baptism will invariably function to confirm the wider social order, whether it is given at birth or at a later age.[52] In this context, the capacity of baptism to render the body of Christ visible will depend on eucharistic practice, which has a more immediate effect in giving shape to the ecclesial economy over against the wider society. Nevertheless, baptism retains its own significance insofar as it bears more direct witness than the Eucharist—both to the world at large and to the church itself—to the fundamental incompleteness of the ecclesial body within history.

The implications of this point for the church's own self-understanding are significant. From a purely ecclesiastical perspective, it means that the church's mission cannot be identified with the project of "saving souls" by bringing them within an ecclesial ark of salvation, nor even with the less overtly imperialistic task of sharing the good news of Jesus. Both perspectives fall short because they suggest a sufficiency or completeness on the church's part that is inconsistent with an adequate understanding of the church as the body of Christ. To be sure, Paul speaks of becoming "all things to all people, so that I might by all means save some" (1 Cor. 9:22; compare 10:33); but he immediately adds that this work redounds to his own benefit (v. 23). And while the immediate context may suggest that this benefit refers to a personal reward for services rendered, such a purely mercenary understanding is belied by the way in which Paul goes on in the same letter to stress both that the well-being of the individual is inseparable from the well-being of the body (12:21-26), and (presumably, for this reason) that the building up of the whole body is of more value than any purely private gain on the part of a single member (14:2-5). In other words, baptism serves the fundamental task of discerning the body both directly, through the acquisition of fresh and unexpected spiritual gifts that serve to "flesh out" the body of Christ, and indirectly, inasmuch as the persistence of persons outside the church serves as a stubborn reminder of the many gifts that the church has yet to experience and apart from which it is not yet fully the church.

Conclusion

The correlation of baptism with the enrichment of the church's life has risks of its own. Models of mission that focus on the benefits to the convert may come across as paternalistic, but they do have the virtue of focusing on the community's obligation to the other. By contrast, focus on the church's need for new members can make the task of proclaiming the good news appear shamelessly self-serving. And at one level this perception is accurate: the baptism of a new member does represent a genuine gain for the church, in the very concrete sense that the church benefits from it. But it is not gain in the same sense that acquiring a piece of land, a new building, or even a seat on a national panel on medical ethics would be. The latter mode of gain is one that does not alter the basic character of the church, but simply represents an extension of its power and prestige. Obviously, the acquisition of new members can also function in this way and, unfortunately, generally has done so during the church's history. A serious appreciation for the church's status as the body of Christ, however, serves to undercut that kind of ecclesiastical triumphalism. For the gains the church makes through baptism serve as a reminder not only that it remains a very incomplete manifestation of the body of Christ, but also that it never has more than a very imperfect understanding of what it means to be Christ's body.

Through baptism the church is "fleshed out" as the body of Christ through the addition of new members—members in the absence of whom the community cannot fully represent that body. As Paul suggests in 1 Cor. 12:21, such partial representations are no more accurate than if one were to conceive of a human body as an eye without a hand, or a head without feet. In the absence of the full complement of members, one's perception of the shape of Christ's body will be deficient. Christians simply cannot know what the body of Christ will look like apart from their actual experience of the way in which the body is "fleshed out" in the concrete particularity of congregations and their members. To be sure, they may and should be confident that the form that emerges will be consistent with the portrait of Jesus they read in the Bible (indeed, where it is inconsistent with this picture, they will be forced to conclude that the form in question is no longer the body of Christ at all). But such judgments are only possible *a posteriori*, in much the same way that a parent's ability to acknowledge that the character of her daughter at the age of twenty-five is consistent with her character as a girl of ten does not imply an ability to extrapolate the former from the latter.

From this perspective, the gains of evangelism can be seen as epistemological. By bringing people into the fellowship of the church through baptism, the church acquires the resources to know Christ better—as do the newly baptized themselves. And to the extent that the church's baptismal practice is embedded in a wider eucharistic economy that makes the church visible, the epistemological benefits extend to those outside the church as well, who (as exemplified in Cavanaugh's analysis of the fate of the church under the Pinochet regime in Chile) will at least recognize that here is a community whose practices distinguish it from society at large.[53] Needless to say, whether or not the church makes use of these resources to enrich its understanding of Christ is another question, but there can be no doubt that the resolution of debates over such issues as the status of Gentile converts and the acceptability of slavery, as well as continuing controversies over the ordination of women and same-sex marriage have had very definite consequences on understanding what it means to be the body of Christ among the baptized and unbaptized alike.

Thus, while the protocols discussed in the previous two chapters focus on discerning the divine image in particular members of the ecclesial body, the sacramental protocols, while by no means lacking this dimension, bring into relief the divine image in the church as a whole. In the words of Jenson, as the body of Christ the church is where "the risen Christ is available to be found, to be responded to, to be grasped."[54] At the same time, however, the sacraments also bear witness to the nonidentity of the church with the body of Christ, as evident in the over-againstness of the eucharistic elements with respect both to every individual in the church and to the church itself. The Eucharist structures the church as the body of Christ (1 Cor. 10:17) but also reminds the church that this body is a gift that the church must always receive and does not control. Likewise, the baptismal incorporation of a new member into the ecclesial body is a reminder that Christ, though fully present in this particular body, also always exceeds its limits. In both cases, proper recognition of Christ's presence in and with the church must be completed by an acknowledgment that he stands over against the ecclesial community.

The role of sacraments as allowing for the discernment of Christ in the community as a whole puts obvious weight on Eucharist and baptism as those two rites that have traditionally served to define the center and the boundaries of communal life, respectively. At the same time, however, there is no particular reason to insist on a strict limit of the sacraments to two. Certain other acts (rites of penance most prominently, but mention might also be made of anointing the sick or setting apart individuals for particular forms of ministry within the community) also play important roles in defining the shape of the church. Nevertheless, Eucharist and baptism retain a distinct place in Christian faith and practice because it is in them that Christians not only perceive but also become the body.[55] By liturgically incorporating individuals into Christ's body, these two protocols define the church as a body and thus establish for every Christian a baseline understanding of what Christ's body looks like. That is certainly not all they do. For those being baptized and communicated, the sacraments are first and foremost the direct address of Christ, in which he claims them as members of his body in the water and affirms that claim in the bread and the wine. But while the sacraments are clearly more than protocols of discernment, they are also this. Indeed, they establish the concrete framework within which all other discernment takes place, since to see someone as a member of Christ's body is finally to see her as someone who has a place at the font and the table.

And yet at this point we come up against the obvious problem that it is precisely in this specifically ecclesial context that discernment seems the most difficult. This is not only because a vision of the whole body is evidently denied us under conditions of time and space, but also (and more seriously) because it is precisely with respect to the sacramental reality of the church that Christians seem to find it impossible to agree among themselves on the shape of the body—thereby raising the question of whether genuine discernment of it is possible. I suspect that few Christians would deny in principle the possibility (or, indeed, the importance) of discerning the image of God in another person. Yet the fact that Christianity is marked by a myriad of divisions with respect to eucharistic and baptismal practice bears not very elegant but intensely practical testimony to the lack of consensus over the form of the divine image, and thus over what it means for a person to be seen as part of it. While this disagreement is no longer as likely to be the occasion for the mutual and often vitriolic denunciations of past centuries, it remains a stubborn fact of church existence that would appear to compromise the discernment of the divine image at its source. After all, how can the church function as the context for discerning the image of God when there is no consensus on where the church is to be found? Can any statements about the body of Christ hold water where the church is divided? And even if these objections can be met, what exactly is the form that believers discern when they follow these protocols? These questions will be the focus of the final chapter.

chapter 8 Seeing the Divine Image

Discernment and Ecclesial Division

The first chapters of this book explored the paradox of affirming simultaneously that God is utterly transcendent on the one hand, and that Jesus Christ is the visible image of God on the other. This apparent contradiction was addressed in two ways. First (and very briefly), it was conceded that the ultimate condition of the infinite God's being known in the finite is simply God's own will that it should be so. Second (and at far greater length), it was argued that the process by which this image is seen and known in the body of Christ is itself suggestive of the fact that God is not reducible to any finite reality even when fully present in it. In the same way that the disciples' eyes were at once drawn to and overwhelmed by the glory of Christ transfigured, so the human encounter with the body of Christ in its individual members bears witness to the fact that the fullness of that body always exceeds any existing conception of it.

Yet if the biblical category of the image of God, made visible in and as the body of Christ, can be used to counter theoretical objections to the human knowledge of God, further, practical objections arise when it comes to exploring how this body is discerned in the life of the church. At one level, such objections have been a central theme of the last three chapters, in which it was found necessary to consider a wide (and by no means exhaustive) range of "protocols of discernment," operating on different levels of ecclesial existence in order to check the distortions and blind spots that characterize the attempts of finite, fallen human beings to identify the contours of the divine image. Yet while it is probably true that the vast majority of Christians regard the protocols we have reviewed as important for the life of faith, in practice churches have not been able to achieve consensus regarding the proper form by which saints may be honored, by which the poor may be served, by which Christians most properly live out their vocation to chastity, or even regarding the central Christian practices of baptism and Eucharist. To the extent that these disagreements have given rise to division within the churches, they reflect significant differences regarding the shape and, perhaps still more importantly, the social location of the body of Christ. Given the biblical insistence that Christ's body is one (Eph. 4:4), it would seem that the whole project of discernment must collapse where the church is divided.

No one has highlighted this problem more forcefully than Ephraim Radner, who contends that the fact of disunity undermines the possibility that common Christian practices might be employed as the basis for the discernment of the body of Christ across ecclesial divisions.[1] In discussing the veneration of saints, for example, he notes that even the seemingly uncontroversial idea that the example of martyrs might constitute a unifying feature across different Christian communities (as proposed by Pope John Paul II in his 1995 encyclical *Ut unum sint*) runs into serious problems in practice, owing to differing judgments regarding where genuine martyrdom is found. Specifically, Radner claims that "the morass of misunderstanding into which the Word is thrust within the divided Church extends to include even the brilliance of the Spirit's human instruments," thus undermining the possibility of "a structure for their encouragement and identification."[2] This line of reasoning calls into question the viability of the protocols outlined over the last three chapters, inasmuch as they were proposed precisely as a set of structures for identifying particular human beings as God's instruments in building up the church. By linking the possibility of such identification to confessional and juridical unity, Radner makes ecclesial division an epistemic barrier to human knowledge of God.

The particular ecclesial divisions Radner has in mind are those originating in sixteenth-century Europe. He argues that a decisive (and heretofore underappreciated) consequence of the Reformation was that it led both Protestants and Catholics to reject the trustworthiness of communal experience as a source of ecclesiological enrichment. Instead (and in sharp contrast to the perspective of earlier generations), the church came to be viewed by both sides as a possible and, indeed, likely locus of demonic activity, and that its integrity as the body of Christ had to be guaranteed externally, either by appeal to an unchanging body of doctrine (among Protestants) or to equally timeless institutional structures (among Catholics). In line with this new perspective, Protestants tended to reject all miracles after the apostolic period as the devil's work, and even Catholics found themselves inclined to deny any significance to miracles until such time as the hierarchy assigned them an official meaning.[3] Likewise, the fact that competing confessional groups were capable of producing martyrs meant (in stark contrast to ancient Christian sensibility) that neither side could view martyrdom as a spiritually glorious or transparent phenomenon in itself.[4]

Radner sees the emphasis on certain unchanging "marks" of the church among both Protestants and Catholics in the post-Reformation period as further evidence of their shared commitment to the idea of the church as an essentially timeless entity.[5] This abstraction of the church from history is crucial to Radner's assessment of its present predicament, insofar as it entails a radical diminishment of any notion that the church actually lives as the body of Christ within history in a way that would make possible believers "completing what is lacking in Christ's afflictions" (Col. 1:24) and thereby allow the body to be seen and celebrated in greater fullness over time.[6] According to Radner, only the Jansenists—precisely because of their refusal to make doctrinal disagreement a cause for condemnation and separation—retained a vigorous notion of ecclesial sin, suffering, and repentance rooted in the lived vicissitudes of the faithful. For the rest of the Western church, the denial by Protestants and Catholics alike that ordinary Christian experience could display the Spirit's presence apart from validation through ecclesiastically approved channels meant that the departure of the Spirit had been effectively conceded by both sides. This pneumatic abandonment of the churches becomes for Radner the defining mark of church life in the modern West, with disastrous implications for the attempt to discern the emerging shape of Christ's body over time.

Radner goes on to argue that any attempt to mitigate or overcome the effects of ecclesial division by appeal to common Christian experience is untenable, since the absence of the Spirit deprives the church of its only theologically secure basis for such an appeal. In answer to the charge that this assessment betrays a "defeatist" lack of confidence in the power of the gospel, Radner counters that the idea of pneumatic absence is fully consistent with biblical characterizations of the Spirit's work in history.[7] Specifically, he argues for a figural reading of Scripture in which the divided church is identified with the divided kingdom of Israel.[8] Just as Israel's division into northern and southern kingdoms led to an "accelerating inability of the nation to right itself, to perceive the truth of God's will and call" and a "deadening confusion of competing and self-deceiving claims to truth," so the state of ecclesial division leads invariably to a "constriction or dulling of the 'senses' by which God's life is known and joyfully received by the Church."[9]

In developing this typological linkage between the church and Israel, Radner stresses the fact that both the northern and southern kingdoms suffered the sentence of divine rejection in the form of defeat and exile prior to any promise of restoration and redemption.[10] Viewing ecclesial division in these terms, he argues, undermines the two most popular interpretations of division in the post-Reformation West. On the one hand, it renders untenable the attempt (characteristic of traditional interconfessional polemics and still the official position of the Catholic magisterium) to defend the validity of one's own church by denying full ecclesial status to other groups; on the other, it also leaves no space for the view (more typical of contemporary ecumenical Protestantism) that division is only a surface phenomenon that does not touch the essence of the church.[11] In place of these options, Radner argues that a more responsible theological appraisal of the situation leads to the conclusion that division simply undermines the church's capacity for discernment of the body of Christ in history.[12]

Severe as this judgment may appear, Radner is careful to add that it does not amount to a denial that the divided church is still the church, any more than divided Israel is any less Israel in the perspective of 1 and 2 Kings. Nevertheless, this fact does little to mitigate Radner's overall assessment of Christian division: "The divided Church is still Christ's Body; and it is a Body for which the life of God is given and given with the promise of indelibility. But as a divided Church, it is a dead body, no less Christ's and no less taken up by a living God, but dead for all that."[13]

In short, the continuing identity of the divided church as the body of Christ does not provide a basis for discernment in spite of disunity, but rather forces a confession of incapacity and confusion. With respect to the Eucharist in particular, Radner asks tough questions regarding how it is possible to speak credibly of discerning the body when the body is rent by divisions of much longer duration and correspondingly more intractable than anything Paul faced in Corinth.[14] Certainly the attempt to follow Radner's own hint and speak of the discernment of a dead body simply highlights the basic problem; namely, that a divided church undermines genuine encounter with the living Christ and, a fortiori, with the God of whom that Christ is the image.[15]

The Enduring Need for Protocols

The problems identified by Radner are important, but his imagery of pneumatic abandonment rests on a false picture of the Spirit's relation to the church. Although his analysis is predicated on a firm rejection of the understanding of the Spirit as a principle of divine immanence within the church,[16] the opposition between pneumatic presence and absence, in which terms he structures his depiction of the current state of the church, has the effect of suggesting just such a situation as the ideal. This is not to deny his claim that the division of Israel provides an appropriate framework within which to interpret the present situation of ecclesial division in the West, but it is to argue that even in the time of the divided kingdom the dichotomy of presence and absence is not as stark as he implies. The fact that the writers of Kings (let alone Chronicles) displays no hesitation when it comes to identifying Jerusalem rather than Bethel as the proper site for worship belies an all-or-nothing characterization of the Spirit's presence. Moreover, the New Testament characterization of the Spirit as a power that "blows where it chooses" (John 3:8), even to the extent of falling upon the unbaptized (Acts 10:44), suggests that the category of "presence" may not be the most appropriate for characterizing the Spirit's relation to the church. Arguably, it is more in keeping with the tenor of the biblical witness to conceive the Spirit as a gift that always breaks in upon the church from without, and for which it must always pray anew.[17]

This theological point regarding the relationship between pneumatology and ecclesiology leads to further questions regarding Radner's claim that the divisions of the Reformation era represent an unprecedented crisis in the history of Christianity. Certainly the sociopolitical context of the Reformation brought the practical ramifications of ecclesial division to the fore in a way that the earlier break between the geographically and culturally separated Eastern and Western branches of the church did not. But it is hard to see how the divisions that afflicted North African Christians at the time of the Donatist schism, or Alexandrian Christians in the aftermath of Chalcedon, were any less serious than those that have afflicted Protestants and Catholics since the sixteenth century. In those cases, too, both sides could produce martyrs, suggesting that problems of discerning the body identified by Radner are not limited to the modern West. Indeed, one would be hard pressed to identify *any* period where there has been a clear consensus among all those who identified themselves as Christians about the church's proper form. And if the pre-Reformation church displayed a confidence on such questions that is lacking in the modern period, one might well question whether that is necessarily to be seen as a good thing.[18]

All of this is not to deny the extent to which ecclesial division problematizes the work of discerning the body of Christ, but it is to point out that such problems have been present for the church from the beginning. Moreover, the consciousness of these problems that Radner rightly identifies as characteristic of the post-Reformation West at least has the merit of highlighting the inherent difficulty fallen human beings have in seeing Christ's body. In this context, Radner's final assessment of martyrdom (which he rightly identifies with those events in the life of the community in which the contours of Christ's body should be most clearly visible) is worth quoting:

> Doubtless Protestant and Catholic Christians have "died for the faith." . . . Doubtless, too, the lives of these and other Christian saints embody some real holiness. But to *see* this purity, to *see* this holiness, as the Spirit's life unveiled

> and resplendent in its "power" and "authority" is no longer something any one of us could dare affirm before the eyes of the Church, let alone the world.[19]

Radner's sensitivity to the implications of claiming to see the Spirit's life shine forth in the life of another is surely well founded, but again, it might be asked whether the onus assumed by those making such declarations is in fact any greater now than in the past. Indeed, if experience has forced on the churches a certain modesty in affirming that the Spirit's life can be seen as "unveiled and resplendent" in any human life, it may be that this state is more consistent with the often far from resplendent ways in which the Spirit proved to be visible in Christ's own life.

Radner contends that the effect of the Reformation was a narrowing of ecclesiological vistas and a correspondingly greater reliance on doctrinal and political structures that he views as evidence of a loss of confidence in the Spirit's guidance of the church. His documentation of this loss of confidence is meticulous and might be extended far beyond the numerous examples he cites. It is probably no accident, for example, that the current, highly formalized process for vetting candidates for canonization in the Catholic Church is a post-Reformation development characterized precisely by the suspicion of the miraculous that Radner shows to have been typical of the period. But insofar as this change in procedure seems also to reflect an implicit recognition that the absence of formal procedures had on occasion produced less than ideal results, it is probably not to be lamented in principle, whatever its defects in practice.[20] In this respect, the fact of ecclesial division would seem less grounds for rejecting the concept of protocols of discernment than reason for appreciating their inherent limitations as protocols, whose use within the church is not based on the presumption that they guarantee discernment, but rather that they provide appropriate structures for its being undertaken.

These considerations take nothing away from the point that deep-seated disagreements regarding the locus and shape of Christ's body in a divided church render discernment problematic in a way that would not be the case if unity prevailed. They do, however, cast doubt on the thesis that visible unity is a necessary condition of discernment. Insofar as the light of the Spirit always shines on the church from without, the Spirit's presence or absence cannot be correlated with any particular ecclesiastical state of affairs, whether the fact of unity, the presence of a particular polity, or even devotion to Scripture. Viewed from this perspective, the definition of protocols of discernment should not be taken as an implied declaration of confidence in the abilities of Christians, whether considered individually or collectively. On the contrary, such protocols are necessary precisely in recognition of the partial and broken character of Christian perception of Christ's body at every point in the church's history. Where unity is lacking, a given community must operate from the position where it finds itself, in the hope that its own efforts at discernment may perhaps provide a basis for overcoming division. Radner himself suggests as much in his own concluding appeal for ecclesial penitence, advocating "the struggle to apprehend the unity of the church as the suffering of dispute, within which the figure of Jesus emerges and controls."[21] But this, of course, brings us back to the essential question of what it means to recognize and surrender control to the figure of Jesus where consensus on what this figure looks like is absent. Given that the accounts of protocols of discernment offered in this book have been as heavy on procedural descriptions of how to look for the divine image as they have been light on the detail when it came to the content of what was seen, it is time to ask precisely what is gained for the church by their use.

The God Who Is Known in Christ

In order to answer this question, it is necessary to locate the protocols in terms of the wider context of Christian talk about God. As a first step in this process, it is important to recognize that if the second half of this book has focused more on how the divine image is discerned than on what is learned through discernment, the first half arguably suffered from just the opposite problem. There a number of definite statements were made about the Christian God. By and large, these statements served as an epistemological foundation, describing God in order to identify the one to be recognized through the use of the protocols. From this perspective, the first and second parts of this book stand in a definite relation to one another that corresponds roughly to Reinhard Hütter's distinction between catechetical and intratextual theology: the first part of the argument provided a "catechetical" description of who God is and the second a more "intratextual" account of the implications of this identity for the practice of the Christian faith.[22] This sequence is necessary because in the same way that I cannot look for a person in a crowd until I have some description of the person for whom I am to look, so meaningful discussion of protocols for discerning God presupposes some account of what God is like (and, correspondingly, where God is likely to be found).

Abstracting from the details of the argument in the first four chapters, four theological claims anchor the "catechetical" description of God found there.

1. God is absolutely transcendent over the world.

The Christian doctrine of creation is fundamentally an assertion that the world and all that is in it are at once from God and other than God. Thus, while everything created depends upon God exclusively and completely for its existence, everything created is for that reason radically distinct from God. In short, God is not part of the world—and thus is said to transcend it. It follows that no creature has any inherent capacity to serve as an ontological or epistemological link to God, because every creature is utterly different from God. Indeed, by virtue of its status as created, any creature differs from God far more than it does from any other creature. Though large portions of the Christian tradition have resisted the implications of the fact, they are clear: angels are no more "like" God than mud is.

Belief in divine transcendence raises serious problems for human (or, for that matter, any creature's) knowledge of God, because such knowledge is itself a feature of created reality and thus is inherently cut off from a God who transcends the creation. We know particular entities as we encounter them in space and time and relate them to other entities using conceptual categories that are themselves products of our creaturely intellects. Inasmuch as God transcends space and time, however, God evidently cannot be encountered in a creaturely context. Moreover, all of the conceptual categories with which creatures are equipped (for instance, size, shape, color, location, and so forth) are relative to space and time and thus could not be applied to a being outside the space-time continuum.[23] Indeed, even the seemingly modest claim that we might acquire at least the knowledge that there is a God by reasoning from the effect of creation to its ultimate cause finally fails, because (as Kant argued) the very principle of causation is inner-worldly, and thus provides no basis for the inferential leap to a transcendent cause outside of the world.

2. God has an image.

The claim that God has an image seems at first glance to stand in the strongest possible tension with the assertion that God is transcendent. After all, God's transcendence means that God cannot be known, because God cannot be mapped on to any conceivable material or conceptual grid. By contrast, images are arguably the medium of human knowledge, precisely insofar as an image is the translation of some reality into just such a grid. So, for example, one way in which it is possible to convey knowledge of entities like the Parthenon, the hydrogen atom, or Ted Williams is to form images of them; and (in a more temporally extended sense) one may even speak of having an "image" of a baseball game or of the American Civil Rights Movement. This is certainly not to argue that all knowledge can be reduced to pictures, but it is to note that an image is a means by which an entity may be apprehended in such a way as to be conceived and known in its particularity over against other things.

Before jumping to the conclusion that God's having an image means that God can be known by creatures, however, it is important to note that if this image is truly God's, then it would seem to follow that it, too, must be transcendent and, indeed, itself nothing less than God. Anything else would fail to reflect God's transcendence and thus would necessarily fail to qualify as an image of *God*. In this way, the confession that God has an image is, in the first instance, less a statement about the possibility of God being known by creatures than a recognition that God is not a prisoner of God's transcendence. To be God is not to be trapped in ontological isolation, inherently cut off from and oblivious to all that is not God (as is seemingly the case, for example, with Aristotle's unmoved mover). That God has an image means that God incorporates otherness within God's own life, and (because this otherness cannot, without violating the very terms of God's transcendence, be anything other than God) that God communicates the fullness of God's own being to this other, who thereby has and is all that God has and is. In short, the affirmation of a divine image means, in the first instance, that God's life is intrinsically self-communicating and, indeed, may itself be conceived as an eternal process of God fully communicating God's own being so as to be fully known.

3. Jesus Christ is the image of God.

Crucially, the claim that knowledge of God is a feature of God's own life does not in itself say anything about how or whether God is known outside of that life. God might have been content to be eternally self-communicating within God's own life without any relation to nondivine existence. Yet the assertion that God has an image (and, for that matter, that God is transcendent), can be known to be true only because God has in fact extended the internal process of divine self-communication to include that which is not God. In other words, human beings can affirm that God has an image only because that image has in fact been disclosed to them as the basis for human knowledge of God. We do not start from the principle that God has an image and then go about looking for it; rather, we infer from the fact that the image of God has been shown to us in such a way that God is known by us that God has an image by which God may be known. Specifically, Christians confess that the human being Jesus of Nazareth is God's image. On this basis they go on to confess that Jesus is himself fully God, eternally begotten of the one he called Father and nothing less than God's own Word made flesh.

And yet as they confess that God's image has been revealed in Jesus Christ, Christians are also bound to affirm that God's having an image is not dependent on that revelation and, indeed, is logically prior to and independent of it. On the basis of Christ's coming, it can and must be said that it is God's nature to have an image that is also God eternally. That this image should be shown to human creatures, however, is a matter of grace. In this respect, to confess that Jesus Christ is the image of God is to recognize that the knowledge of God made possible in him is to be received as a gift rather than as an entitlement: we know God only because God has chosen to come among us and communicate the divine self to us in time as God does within the divine life in eternity.[24]

And yet even if God should wish to share God's life with creatures, there seem insuperable barriers to God's doing so. As already noted, if God is transcendent, then God's image—if it is to be genuinely the image of *God*—must also be transcendent. But Jesus of Nazareth is evidently not transcendent: he is a human being with a particular, clearly definable spatio-temporal location ("... born of the Virgin Mary ... suffered under Pontius Pilate ...") that allows him to be identified in the same way as any other human being might be. In short, at the same time that this life is confessed as God's own and thus as fully divine (to the extent that whatever may be predicated of Jesus may also be predicated of God),[25] it is also acknowledged to be fully human and thus subject to all the limitations of creaturely existence. It is therefore unclear how Jesus can possibly be the "image of the invisible God," since his very visibility would seem *eo ipso* to render such a claim impossible.

The only Christian response to this contradiction is simply to affirm that what is impossible for creatures is possible for God. Thus, while Karl Barth recognized that the "primary objectivity" by which God knows God's self from eternity is evidently different from the "secondary objectivity" by which God is known by creatures in Christ, he immediately added that the latter differs from the former "not by a lesser degree of truth, but by its particular form suitable for us."[26] This is not to deny that Jesus, too, may be made into an idol (a possibility Jesus himself seems to acknowledge in, for instance, Matt. 7:21-23), but it is to insist that this happens only to the extent that people fail to recognize Jesus for who he is and regard him instead "from a human point of view" (2 Cor. 5:16). *How* it is that people are able to see Jesus as the image of God is as little susceptible to explanation or justification as the claim that he is the image: as noted in chapter 1, the confession of Jesus as God's image is analytic, and its acceptance is, correspondingly, a matter of faith. At most, the church can point to an event like the transfiguration, where the divine glory both exceeds and yet remains utterly inseparable from Christ's human form, as suggestive of what it means for the infinite God to be fully present in, without being contained by, finite humanity.

4. Jesus Christ lives as a body incorporating an indefinite number of human beings.

If the *possibility* of Jesus being truly the image of God is finally explicable only by reference to the power of God, still the *shape* of this image and the way in which it encounters human beings is subject to investigation and explication by reference to the particular features of Jesus' story. Thus, the fact that the glory revealed on Mount Tabor is at once specifically Jesus' and yet also radiates beyond the limits of his person intimates that seeing and knowing Jesus as the image of God is not accomplished by limiting one's gaze to his physical body. This intimation can be substantiated by noting what happens to his body. Jesus' status as God's image is established only once his body, which had been put to death, is raised from the dead by the power of the Holy Spirit (1 Tim. 3:16; compare Rom. 1:4) and thereby revealed in a new richness. While it is still without question Jesus' body (see, for instance, Luke 24:38-40; John 20:27), in its resurrected form this body is now revealed to have been made in the Spirit "one flesh" (Eph. 5:31-32) with those Jesus has claimed as his own by delivering them from the power of sin and death. In this way, the body of Christ, though defined as Christ's body by Jesus, is not exhausted by Jesus: rather, to see Jesus in his identity as the image of God is to see him as the head of a body with many members (Col. 1:18; compare 1 Cor. 12:12-27).

That Jesus remains the *head* of the body rules out any dissolution of his identity into that of humanity as a whole or the church in particular. The body of Christ is not a collective personality in which the particular identity of Jesus is on the same level as that of the other members; rather, Jesus remains the one "from whom the whole body, nourished and held together by its ligaments and sinews, grows with a growth that is from God" (Col. 2:19; compare Eph. 4:16). For this reason, only he is the *imago dei* in the strict sense, because he alone of all the members of the body is fully divine as well as fully human. Nevertheless, insofar as all the other members share in his life as part of his body, they are rightly described as creatures made "in" that image. Because they remain distinct from the head, they do not define the identity of the image; rather, they disclose its shape as those whom Jesus has desired and claimed for his own. In this subsidiary role, the epistemological significance of human beings as creatures made in God's image is crucial, because in order truly to see Jesus as the image of God in the face of the ever-present temptation to replace him with an idol of our own construction, it is necessary to look again and again at *this* body, with its many members. This point puts the problem of human knowledge of an infinite God in a new light by suggesting that divine transcendence is both modeled and mediated socially through the presence of the neighbor.

The Discipline of Scripture

These four "catechetical" statements provide the ground for the use of protocols of discernment by establishing the identity of the God to be known by means of these protocols. This preliminary work of establishing the divine identity is important, because it is only after the church knows who God is that it can begin to shape its actions in such a way as to know this God, in much the same way that it is only possible for me to get to know Jane Doe once I know who she is (that is, in such a way that I know where to look for her and how to recognize her when I see her). In short, any claim I make to know God needs to be tested against a body of publicly available knowledge about God.

In order to pick an individual human being out of the crowd, I need some sort of identifying description that allows me to distinguish her from other people. Where God is concerned, Christians claim that such an identifying description is found in Scripture, which presents Jesus of Nazareth as the image of God. Once again, this claim is not a synthetic judgment arrived at by comparing Jesus with some previously known reality. Because only God can determine the terms on which God is known, the statement that Jesus is God's image is analytic and thus a matter of definition.[27] This is not to say that its truth is self-evident, but only that for Christians there is no reality other than that identified by the name "Jesus of Nazareth" to which one might refer to define the phrase "image of God."[28] Human beings do and can know that Jesus is the image of God only because God vouches for that fact; and for Christians God does so through the prophetic and apostolic witness of Scripture.

Needless to say, the biblical witness is not exhausted by the proposition "Jesus is the image of God." That statement is a summary that by itself does not give much direction when it comes to knowing who Jesus is or where he is to be found. The Gospels and the texts that surround them provide this information by telling Jesus' story in such a way as to make it possible to distinguish this particular individual (as opposed to Moses or Priscilla or Genghis Khan) as the one to be confessed as the image of God.[29] For Christians the biblical canon contains what is sufficient for this identification. This affirmation of sufficiency does not mean that there is nothing more to be said about Jesus, but rather reflects the church's conviction that the biblical texts are reliable—in a way others, however otherwise helpful, are not—as the source for authoritative knowledge about God in their cumulative (and, outside of the four Gospels, largely indirect) depiction of Jesus.[30] Needless to say, it is possible to ascribe such reliability to Scripture only to the extent that it is understood to be God's own chosen means of self-attestation. In light of this acknowledgment, however, the biblical canon both can and should serve as the basis and touchstone for all further claims to be made about Jesus.

In line with this last point, I have argued that the church finds itself both authorized and required to develop protocols of discernment as a necessary condition of knowing the God whose identity is self-attested in Scripture. This shift marks a move from "catechetical" to "intratextual" theology, as the church supplements its understanding of Christ's body as recorded in the Bible with the work of discerning that body in the world. In this way, the church gives evidence of its desire to encounter the Jesus of Scripture—that is, the Jesus who is Lord—and not a historical or confessional phantom of its own making. Nevertheless, it remains the case that the church's *seeing* the image of God in the world depends on a prior divine *speaking* in (and a corresponding human hearing of) Scripture: we can see the divine image only because we have first been taught to see, because seeing is in this case a matter of recognition, and we can recognize (literally, "know again") someone only if we already know something about whom we are looking for.

Because the church's use of protocols of discernment presupposes definite knowledge of the divine identity derived from Scripture, Scripture enjoys a logical priority with respect to the protocols and to this extent is not to be classed among them. Yet if reading Scripture is in this way distinguished from protocols of discernment, this is emphatically not because it represents a kind of activity that is somehow insulated from the political messiness of ecclesial existence (as in some more naïve understandings of *sola scriptura*). In practice, any reading of Scripture will be a function of interaction with the traditions and practices of the community as a whole and with the opinions of individuals within it. Even where the clarity of Scripture is accepted as an article of faith, it should not be taken to imply that there is no occasion for exegetical debate within the church, but only as an expression of the conviction that Scripture remains the highest court of appeal in adjudicating such disputes.

It follows that the meaning of Scripture will be no more self-evident in any given instance than any other aspect of the community's understanding of the image of God, and will be subject to the same need for persistent review and correction to overcome the effects of human short-sightedness and self-interest. The reading of Scripture therefore does not differ from the protocols of discernment in a methodological sense (that is, that its procedures are in themselves more certain, or its results less subject to distortion), but rather in the *kind* of knowledge that derives from it. Scripture provides definite and unsubstitutable knowledge *about* God. But acquiring knowledge about God, however accurate it may be, is not the same as *knowing* God. By identifying Jesus as the divine image, Scripture tells us that he is the one to whom we must look if we are to know God. But Scripture also bears witness that if we are to see him, if we are to discern his body in a way that signals a decisive refusal of the ever-present temptation to settle for something less than God, we must look to those whose lives he has claimed for his own to form one flesh, one body in and with him. For this (scriptural!) reason, reading Scripture must be viewed as a necessary, but not a sufficient condition for knowing Jesus. One does not know Jesus in a book, even if that book is the Bible. Where knowledge is a matter of persons rather than facts, any third-person description finally falls short.[31] We know Jesus as he confronts us, and he confronts us concretely in other people's bodies.

Knowing God in Christ

It might be objected at this point that the distinction between knowing about God and knowing God seems both to underemphasize the role of the biblical word and to overemphasize the role of interhuman encounter in mediating knowledge of God. In answer to this concern, it needs to be stressed that discernment of Christ's body through protocols of discernment is not the only way in which God is known. If the biblical concept of the divine image means that God confronts us through the particularity of other human lives, God also confronts us through word and sacrament in the mode of direct address.[32] Yet even the ministry of the word, though based on the text of Scripture, entails that this text be proclaimed publicly. In this context, it is worth remembering that Luther once went so far as to argue that the gospel ought never to have been written down, in order that its third-person description of Christ be bound as closely as possible to the fact that the gospel is preeminently Christ's address to us in the second person.[33] For as much as I may learn the content of the gospel by reading Scripture, its objectivity as Christ's speech to me (rather than my speaking to myself) is ineluctably linked with its coming from the mouth of another person. As Dietrich Bonhoeffer put it, "the promise of forgiveness becomes fully certain to me only when it is spoken by another believer in God's name."[34]

Needless to say, there is no question here of identifying the other human being who encounters me with God. The preacher's role is to draw attention to God rather than herself. Indeed, in terms of the content of her speech, her whole task is simply to bear witness to the identity of God communicated in Scripture. She directs me to God by pointing away from herself—and yet it remains crucial that it is she rather than I who does the pointing. Thus, although it need not be the case that she furnish me with any new information about God, her mediation is nevertheless crucial if the knowledge *about* God that is the presupposition of her speaking is to be for me the basis for my *knowing* God. This is certainly not to deny that I may and should read the Bible (or other devotional literature) on my own.[35] But though it is through such means that I present myself to God, it is not through them that God is presented to me: I can no more preach to myself than I can baptize or absolve myself. Indeed, insofar as I am attentive to the God who is the subject of Scripture, I will be referred to the other through whom God will confront me.

The objectivity of the human other as the mediator of God's otherness is no less fundamental to the logic of the protocols of discernment. There are, of course, crucial differences that, again, reflect the difference between the catechetical and intratextual modes of theology. Thus, the protocols are features of an already established life of faith and thus presuppose that the gospel message has been spoken and heard.[36] Further, the protocols are not a matter of the other pointing to God explicitly by speaking in God's name. On the contrary, the reference to God is implicit, being grounded in the simple facticity of the other's status as a person who, as a member of Christ's body, has been called to an unsubstitutable and irreplaceable relation to the head. In this respect, her status as a creature made in God's image is established precisely as she speaks—and is heard—in her own name, and thereby challenges and corrects any vision of the divine image in which she is included only at the price of having her particularity occluded.

In this way, the task of seeing others in Christ must be kept quite distinct from that of seeing Christ in others. The latter unavoidably reduces the divine image to a set of properties and the other's particular identity to a mask, so that seeing the divine image becomes a matter of engaging some mode of spiritual vision capable of penetrating this outer shell to disclose some deeper, Christlike reality. Such an approach, however well intentioned, effectively renders the particularity of the other indifferent, since anyone at any time could serve equally well as the occasion for this process. By contrast, the need for protocols of discernment is predicated on the thesis that the identity of the other in whom the body is discerned is *not* indifferent. God's image is not visible in just anyone, but in the particular one in whom God summons me to see it. Luther once observed, "If I profess with the loudest voice and clearest exposition every portion of the truth of God except precisely at that little point which the world and the devil are at that moment attacking, I am not confessing Christ, however boldly I may be professing him."[37] An analogous point may be made here: however inclusive my own vision of the divine image may be, I have missed God's own particular visibility—the visibility of the body of Christ—if I fail to look for and see it at that point where God calls me to do so.

In short, Christ is visible not somewhere *behind* the particularity of my neighbor, but *in* it, as the one who claims and confirms it in the face of sin and death. This point is crucial if the confession of Christ as the image of God is to avoid the critique leveled against it by Feuerbach:

> Man is to be loved for man's sake. . . . Love should be immediate, undetermined by anything else than its object;—nay, only as such is it love. But if I interpose between my fellow-man and myself the idea of an individuality, in whom the ideal of the species is supposed to be already realised, I annihilate the very soul of love, I disturb the unity by the idea of a third [namely, Christ] external to us; for in that case my fellow-man is then an object of love to me only on account of his resemblance or relation to this model, not for his own sake.[38]

Feuerbach sees Christianity as promoting love of the neighbor only in an instrumental sense. The neighbor is loved as a substitute for God, with the result that love of God comes at the expense of the neighbor. Although this concern is in principle entirely legitimate, it rests on what for Christians can only be regarded as the false assumption that there is a "unity between me and my fellow man" that exists independently of Jesus and which the introduction of Jesus somehow disrupts. It is precisely such a primordial unity that the gospel denies by painting a picture of humanity so riven by divisions of gender, age, race, class, and nation that claims to unity in the spirit of Feuerbach's can only be interpreted as a pretense for subsuming the neighbor's particularity to the interests of some normative self. Far from disrupting a preexistent unity, Christ "has broken down the dividing wall" of hostility between persons (Eph. 2:14) and grafted the opposing parts into one body (Gal. 3:28; Col. 3:11, 15). In short, Christ is not some anthropological ideal that *I* introduce as a means justifying my behavior toward those around me. Quite the contrary, in biblical perspective it is *Christ* who interposes himself between myself and my neighbor—and does so precisely so that I may see my neighbor as and for the person she is.[39]

Because Christians are as subject to the temptations of idolatry as anyone else, Feuerbach is right to worry that they will seek to assimilate their neighbors to their own personal image of Christ as a means of determining for themselves the terms of their relationship with them, and he is right to protest against this. Yet if this urge is checked, it will not be, as Feuerbach supposes, because I find myself able through the exercise of my own insight to break through to some more fundamental unity of heart or mind that renders the mention of Christ superfluous. It will be, rather, because Christ himself blocks it by taking my neighbor's part over against me and claiming precisely that in which my neighbour differs from me (and which I am thus most reluctant to acknowledge as fully or genuinely human) as his own.[40]

Humanity in the Image of God

The Bible prohibits the construction of any image of God because such images represent a denial of God's essential invisibility. The manufactured image is an idol: an attempt to bring God into conformity with some human ideal; but the God whom "no one has ever seen" (John 1:18; compare 1 John 4:12) cannot and will not be limited in this way. And yet the Bible records that this same God has been seen in Jesus Christ, who is "the image of the invisible God" (Col. 1:15). There seems to be a contradiction here, inasmuch as God's having become visible would appear to contradict the divine invisibility in such a way as to open the door to and, indeed, legitimate idolatry. But the story does not end here, for it turns out that Jesus' visibility is inseparable from his having a body composed of an indefinite number of creatures who have been made in the divine image. These images, made by divine rather than human hands, resist this tendency to idolatry by constantly presenting aspects of the divine image that destabilize and fracture the finely honed contours of the idol. In them the divine image is truly visible—but in such a way as to remind the faithful observer that the divine image is a product of God's ongoing construction and thus cannot be equated with any image of human manufacture.

It is on this basis that it is possible to claim that seeing and knowing Jesus as the image of God means looking at those who have been created in his image. This is not because of any inherent qualities or attributes that constitute human beings as creatures made in God's image. Human beings can be said to be in God's image simply and exclusively because they have been incorporated as members of Christ's body. Indeed, so little is the *imago dei* an inherent property of humanity as such that it is described biblically as a state into which we are gradually transformed as the same Spirit that raised Jesus from the dead raises us to life with Christ by binding our lives ever more closely to his (see, for example, Rom. 8:29; 1 Cor. 15:49; 2 Cor. 3:18; Col. 3:10). Human creation in the image of God thus refers, in the first instance, to the fact that God has chosen to relate to human beings in a particular way. Specifically, it means that God wills for us to live in Jesus and, through Jesus, to become sharers in God's own triune life.

It follows that seeing the divine image—and thereby knowing God—is not a matter of trying to isolate certain qualities that Jesus and the rest of humankind have in common. This is certainly not to deny that there are such qualities, or even that they are subject to continual perfecting by the power of the Spirit until that day when "we will be like [Christ], for we will see him as he is" (1 John 3:2; compare Col. 3:4). But it is to argue that the image of God is rightly regarded not as something that we have, but rather as something God does to us by grafting us into the life of Christ. Having said this, however, it is important to add that this engrafting, this being conformed to the image of Jesus (Rom. 8:29), is not a matter of our being transformed into so many carbon copies of the risen rabbi from Nazareth. Instead, it should be understood in terms of each of us being enabled to fulfill our own callings within the body of Christ. When this process is complete, we shall indeed be "like him," not because we are indistinguishable from him, but precisely because we will be distinct but inseparable parts of his risen and glorified body.

Because God is the source of our existence as free and responsible creatures, what God does to us in grafting us into Christ's body cannot be separated from what we are called to be and do as members of that body. To live in the body is to see oneself as one member among others under the head. Seeing my neighbor as a creature made in God's image is nothing more or less than to see her in this relationship: as someone who is quite literally "in" Christ. Because we are still in the process of being transformed into the likeness of Christ, still being shaped (and thus revealed) as the particular member God has predestined us to be, the process of discernment is not a straightforward task. Every person's place in the body is still in the process of being worked out. In many cases, it may not even be clear that a given person or class of people has a place there. That is why protocols of discernment are necessary.

Yet the difficulty of discerning the divine image is not solely a product of the fact that Christ's body is still in the process of being revealed. An even greater threat is posed by the fact that human beings are so good at identifying God with themselves in a way that leads them to ignore the other. Protocols are also helpful here, though they certainly do not provide guaranteed results. The capacity of institutional inertia to stifle the challenge of any practice should never be underestimated: one need only consider the routinized character of baptism, Eucharist, marriage, veneration of the saints, and even attempts to exercise the preferential option for the poor in much of Western Christianity.[41] Yet these and other protocols remain sources of genuine insight to the extent that they are reclaimed by the church as expressions of its commitment to find in the other clues to its own life in God's image.

At the same time, as much as protocols serve a critical function within the life of the church as forms of Christian ascesis, something has gone badly wrong when they are promoted or experienced as a kind of penitential burden. The protocols that have been identified in this book—the practices of venerating the saints, serving the poor, living chastely, sharing the eucharistic bread and wine—are properly occasions of joy and celebration, to the extent that one test of the propriety of other possible protocols is whether they may be lived out with similar exuberance. The plurality of protocols is necessary to check the pervasive human tendency to idolatry, but it is also an expression of the richness of the life God intends for us in and as Christ's body. Their proliferation in the life of the church should thus be viewed not as an ever more wearisome accumulation of bureaucratic checks and balances, but rather as a sign of the always unexpected richness of God's image, which Christians find themselves called to glimpse in ever new and unexpected ways.

Because the content of that image on this side of the eschaton remains open-ended, nothing more than a glimpse should be expected. And from this perspective, the doctrine of the *imago dei* may prove in practice as much as a source of consternation as of celebration. It gives to every human being the assurance that he or she has a place in God's life; but in forcibly turning the attention of the individual and the community alike to the particularity of those who they would otherwise be tempted to ignore, it reveals the defects and distortions in their present understanding of what that life includes. In this way, the church's appreciation of Christ's richness may only be purchased at the price of submission to judgment over its resistance to God's own peculiar form of visibility in the body of Christ and the ever fuller vision of God to be seen therein. Yet if we are now limited to glimpses, if our knowledge remains partial and our sight dim, we have every incentive to seek to sharpen our gaze in the confidence that whatever we see now draws us on toward that ever greater and inexhaustible splendor that will be revealed on that day when we will know fully, even as we are and have been fully known.

Notes

1. The Image of God as a Theological Problem

1. For example, it is central to the anthropologies of theologians as otherwise dissimilar as Rosemary Radford Ruether (*Sexism and God-Talk: Toward a Feminist Theology* [Boston: Beacon, 1984], chap. 4) and Wolfhart Pannenberg (*Systematic Theology*, vol. 2 [Edinburgh: T. & T. Clark, 1994], chap. 8).

2. Unless otherwise indicated, all biblical quotations are taken from the New Revised Standard Version.

3. While there are undoubtedly echoes of Genesis 1 in Ps. 8:5-8, comparison with the more pessimistic views found in Job 7:17-19 and Eccl. 3:18-21 illustrates the tentative character of the cumulative Old Testament reflection on human distinctiveness.

4. In the passage from 1 Corinthians the language of the image is applied exclusively to males in a way that contradicts the wording of Genesis 1.

5. ". . . for the perfect man consists in the commingling and the union of the soul receiving the spirit of the Father, and the admixture of the fleshy nature which was moulded after the image of God." Irenaeus of Lyons, *Against Heresies* V.vi.1, in *The Apostolic Fathers with Justin Martyr and Irenaeus*, vol. 1 of *The Ante-Nicene Fathers*, ed. Alexander Roberts and James Donaldson (Grand Rapids, Mich.: Eerdmans, 1985).

6. E.g., Thomas Aquinas, *Summa Theologiae* [hereafter *ST*], 61 vols., Blackfriars ed. (London: Eyre & Spottiswood, 1964–1981), Ia, qu. 93, art. 2; cf. art. 6. The equation of the *imago dei* with reason is found already in Philo of Alexandria, *De opificio mundi*, 69, in *Philo*, vol. 1, Loeb Classical Library (Cambridge, Mass.: Harvard University Press, 1929).

7. E.g., Reinhold Seeberg, *Christliche Dogma*, vol. 1 (1924): 499. Cf. Gregory of Nyssa, "On the Making of Man," XVI.11, in *Gregory of Nyssa: Dogmatic Treatises, etc.*, vol. 5 of *A Select Library of Nicene and Post-Nicene Fathers*, Second Series, ed. Philip Schaff and Henry Wace (Boston: Hendrickson, 1995), 405.

8. E.g., Reinhold Niebuhr, *Human Nature*, vol. 1 of *The Nature and Destiny of Man* (London: Nisbet, 1941), 176–77. Cf. Robert W. Jenson, *Systematic Theology*, 2 vols.(New York: Oxford University Press, 1997–1999), 2:73. Though Jenson earlier (p. 58) speaks against understanding *imago dei* as "a complex of qualities, supposedly possessed by us and not by other creatures," he proceeds to develop his anthropology along just such lines (see esp. pp. 64–65), though he warns against a "reified self-transcendence" conceived as a personal "power" (p. 74).

9. E.g., Emil Brunner, *Man in Revolt: A Christian Anthropology* (London: Lutterworth, 1939), 102–5.

10. Karl Barth, *Church Dogmatics* [hereafter *CD*], 13 vols., ed. Geoffrey W. Bromiley and T. F. Torrance (Edinburgh: T. & T. Clark, 1956–1974), III/1, 193.

11. John Chrysostom, "Homilies on the Statues," VII.3, in *Saint Chrysostom: On the Priesthood, Ascetic Treatises, Select Homilies and Letter, Homilies on the Statues*, vol. 9 of *A Select Library of Nicene and Post-Nicene Fathers*, First Series, ed. Philip Schaff (Grand Rapids, Mich.: Eerdmans, 1984). Cf. Douglas John Hall, *Imaging God: Dominion as Stewardship* (Grand Rapids, Mich.: Eerdmans, 1986), and Hans Walter Wolff, *Anthropology of the Old Testament* (London: SCM, 1974), chap. XVIII.

12. Barth makes this point in *CD*, III/1, 194.

13. See Francis Watson, *Text and Truth: Redefining Biblical Theology* (Edinburgh: T. & T. Clark, 1997), 293.

14. Barth, *CD*, III/1, 195.

15. Phyllis Trible, *God and the Rhetoric of Sexuality,* Overtures to Biblical Theology (Philadelphia: Fortress, 1978), 15–23; cf. Colin E. Gunton, *The Promise of Trinitarian Theology* (Edinburgh: T. & T. Clark, 1991), chap. 6, and *The Triune Creator: A Historical and Systematic Survey* (Edinburgh: T. & T. Clark, 1998), chap. 9.

16. The NRSV's translation of *'adam* as "human" in the first half of the verse and "humankind" in the second obscures the fact that the writer clearly has the individual in mind throughout.

17. Aquinas, *ST*, Ia, qu. 93, art. 7.

18. Claus Westermann, *Genesis 1–11: A Commentary,* Continental Commentaries (Minneapolis: Augsburg, 1984), 156.

19. Ibid., 157.

20. See, e.g., Aquinas's claim that the *imago dei* is to be found in men in a way that it is not in women (*ST*, Ia, qu. 93, art. 4, ad 1). Aquinas defends this claim by reference to Paul's arguments about the relative preeminence of men and women in 1 Cor. 11:7-9; but given his identification of the *imago* with humanity's intellective nature, it is hard not to connect his judgment with his belief that men's rational powers are superior to women's (*ST*, Ia, qu. 92, art. 1, ad 2).

21. "For in times long past, it was *said* that man was created after the image of God, but it was not *shown*; for the Word was as yet invisible after whose image man was created." Irenaeus of Lyons, *Against Heresies*, V.xvi.2; cf. Aquinas, *ST*, Ia, qu. 93, art. 1, ad. 2.

22. Pliny the Younger, *Epistles* 10.96.7; cited in Jaroslav Pelikan, *The Emergence of the Catholic Tradition (100–600)*, vol. 1 of *The Christian Tradition: A History of the Development of Doctrine* (Chicago: University of Chicago Press, 1971), 173.

23. See John D. Zizioulas, *Being as Communion: Studies in Personhood and the Church* (Crestwood, N.Y.: St. Vladimir's Seminary Press, 1985), 34–41.

24. See Colin E. Gunton, *The Promise of Trinitarian Theology* (Edinburgh: T. & T. Clark, 1991), 106–10.

25. See also the references to rabbinic characterization of Gentile depravity in Eugene F. Rogers, Jr., *Sexuality and the Christian Body: Their Way into the Triune God* (Oxford: Blackwell, 1999), 63.

26. Patricia Ranft's attempts to argue that the abolition of division confessed in Galatians 3 and Colossians 3 is rooted in a "common spiritual nature" that is

humanity's "most essential characteristic" (see her *Women and Spiritual Equality in the Christian Tradition* [London: Macmillan, 2000], 3–5) are unconvincing and run counter to the explicitly christological shape of both passages.

27. Watson, *Text and Truth*, 283.

28. Ibid., 300.

29. Ibid., 285.

30. See Iain Torrance, "Is Christianity Irredeemably Sexist?" in *Who Needs Feminism? Male Responses to Sexism in the Church*, ed. Richard Holloway (London: SPCK, 1991), 75–84.

31. See, for example, Elizabeth A. Johnson, "Redeeming the Name of Christ," in *Freeing Theology: The Essentials of Theology in Feminist Perspective*, ed. Catherine Mowry LaCugna (San Francisco: HarperCollins, 1993), 120.

32. Watson, *Text and Truth*, 292.

33. Here, too, our knowledge is primarily negative. The disciples' experience of the risen Lord tells us that the resurrection life is not bodiless, but Paul's affirmations regarding the exchange of physical for spiritual bodies (1 Cor. 15:44-49) does little more than amplify this point: our bodies will not be as they are now—but what they will be is not subject to precise description.

34. Mary McClintock Fulkerson, "Contesting the Gendered Subject: A Feminist Account of the *imago dei*," in *Horizons in Feminist Theology: Identity, Tradition, and Norms*, ed. Rebecca S. Chopp and Sheila Greeve Davaney (Minneapolis: Fortress Press, 1997), 99–115.

35. Ibid., 108–9. For a more thorough discussion of the exclusionary dynamics at work in white feminist discourse, see Ellen T. Armour, *Deconstruction, Feminist Theology, and the Problem of Difference: Subverting the Race/Gender Divide* (Chicago: University of Chicago Press, 1999), especially chap. 1.

36. See Fulkerson, "Contesting the Gendered Subject," 115.

37. Ibid., 114.

38. Ibid.

39. Gunton promisingly suggests that "the doctrine of the image of God . . . has its primary reference to God," but insofar as he goes on to explain this as meaning that "God constitutes a particular being among all other created beings to subsist in a particular and unique kind of relation with him" (Gunton, *The Triune Creator*, 207), the focus appears to be on human beings after all.

40. "All images reveal and make perceptible those things which are hidden." John of Damascus, *On Divine Images*, III.17 (Crestwood, N.Y.: St. Vladimir's Seminary Press, 1980).

41. Origen, *De Principiis*, I.ii.8, in *Fathers of the Church*, URL: http://www.newadvent.org/fathers/04122.htm [24 June 2005].

42. Origen departs from the biblical witness in distinguishing Jesus' status as image from his embodied humanity (which he regards as "insignificant") and identifying it instead with "the resemblance of His works and power to the Father." *De Principiis*, I.ii.8. Cf. I.ii.6, where he emphasizes that the Son is the image of the Father precisely insofar as he, too, is essentially invisible, since "the Son is the

Word, and therefore we are not to understand that anything in Him is cognisable by the senses."

2. The Ambiguity of Images

1. Thus, the early form of the commandment found in Deut. 27:15 seems to refer specifically to the practice of making an image of YHWH and not to the worship of foreign deities. See Gerhard von Rad, *The Theology of Israel's Historical Traditions*, vol. 1 of *Old Testament Theology* (Philadelphia: Westminster, 1962), 215–16.

2. See, e.g., "Definition of the Holy Great and Ecumenical Council, the Second in Nicea," in Daniel J. Sahas, *Icon and Logos: Sources in Eighth-Century Iconoclasm* (Toronto: University of Toronto Press, 1986), 179. Though the Council took this distinction from John of Damascus, it seems to have originated in the West, with Augustine (*City of God*, X.i) being among its earliest witnesses. See Jaroslav Pelikan, *Imago Dei: The Byzantine Apologia for Icons* (Princeton: Princeton University Press, 1990), 137–40.

3. "Already in Greek religious usage, the image always bears the character of that which it represented, that is, the person represented becomes present in the image." Eduard Schweizer, *The Letter to the Colossians: A Commentary* (London: SPCK, 1982), 66.

4. See, e.g., Vladimir Lossky, "Apophasis and Trinitarian Theology," in *In the Image and Likeness of God* (London and Oxford: Mowbray, 1974), 14: "The apophasis of the Old Testament, which expressed itself in the prohibition of all images, was suppressed by the fact that 'the image of the substance of the Father' . . . assumed human nature."

5. See the discussion of the eighth-century iconoclastic controversy below, pp. 25–29.

6. Among Christians, Catholics and Lutherans read the prohibition against the making of images as part of the first commandment's prohibition of the worship of other gods. My decision to follow the practice of the Orthodox, Reformed, and Anglican communions in treating it as a distinct (second) commandment is largely pragmatic: it makes it easier to isolate image making as a distinct theological issue, and it also reflects the phrasing in most English translations of Exodus 20, where a paragraph break is normally put between verses 3 and 4.

7. See K. H. Bernhardt, *Gott und Bild* (Berlin: Evangelische Verlagsanstalt, 1956), 69–109; cited in Wolfhart Pannenberg, *Systematic Theology*, vol. 1 (Edinburgh: T. & T. Clark, 1991), 181.

8. "The religious criticism of Judaism which developed in conjunction with the prohibition of idols . . . is not directed against . . . the aesthetics of depicting deity in and of itself, but against the perversion of the religious relation in magical control over the deity." Pannenberg, *Systematic Theology*, vol. 1, 182.

9. *The Catechism of the Catholic Church* (Dublin: Veritas, 1994), §2130.

10. It should be noted, however, that at least one later Jewish interpreter did think it possible to interpret the serpent as "a token of deliverance" made "to remind [the people] of the law's demand" (Wis. 16:6).

11. It is true that Jacob speaks of having seen God "face to face" (Gen. 32:30), but the tenor of the narrative supports the traditional interpretation of the stranger with whom he wrestles as a divine emissary rather than God's own self.

12. Cf. Irenaeus of Lyons, *Against Heresies*, IV.xx.10, in *The Apostolic Fathers with Justin Martyr and Irenaeus*, vol. 1 of *The Ante-Nicene Fathers*, ed. Alexander Roberts and James Donaldson (Grand Rapids, Mich.: Eerdmans, 1985). Note that even this periphrasis seems to have claimed too much for the later rabbinic tradition, which forbade the reading of "the chapter about the Chariot" in the synagogue (*Megilloth* 4.10; cited in Francis Watson, *Text and Truth: Redefining Biblical Theology* [Edinburgh: T. & T. Clark, 1997], 289).

13. While conceding that some classical pagans doubtless "naïvely believed that the very image they were worshipping . . . was indeed the God itself. . . . the dominant quality in the ancient attitude to images of gods was a certain ambiguity." Moshe Barasch, *Icon: Studies in the History of an Idea* (New York: New York University Press, 1992), 40.

14. One might add here the Philistines' respect for the power of divinity in the captured ark (1 Samuel 6) or the importance Cyrus attached to reconstructing the Jerusalem temple (Ezra 1) as further evidence of this general sensibility.

15. "In the last analysis, even the prohibition of images and the ever increasing awareness of God's essential invisibility serve to keep this eschatological dimension open." Hans Urs von Balthasar, *Seeing the Form*, vol. 1 of *The Glory of the Lord: A Theological Aesthetics* (San Francisco: Ignatius, 1982), 336. Cf. Irenaeus of Lyons, *Against Heresies*, IV.xx.10, "The prophets . . . did not openly behold the actual face of God, but the dispensations and the mysteries through which man should afterwards see God."

16. See, e.g., Hans Walter Wolff, *Anthropology of the Old Testament* (London: SCM, 1974), 160–61.

17. In this context, von Rad notes that insofar as the plural "let us" of Gen. 1:26 may be supposed to refer to God acting in concert with a heavenly court of angelic beings (as in, e.g., 1 Kings 22:19; Job 1:6; cf. Ps. 82:6), it prevents the divine image in human beings "being referred directly to God alone." Von Rad, *Old Testament Theology*, I, 145.

18. John Calvin, *Institutes of the Christian Religion*, I.i.3, ed. John T. McNeill (Philadelphia: Westminster, 1960), p. 39.

19. At the same time, the presence of the divine image in humankind is clearly connected with the status of Wisdom as the primordial image of God, since the writer, in an obvious echo of Gen. 1:26, prays to God as the one who "by your wisdom have formed humankind to have dominion over the creatures" (Wisd. 9:2).

20. That Wisdom is in herself supremely knowable has already been made clear in 6:12-13: "Wisdom is radiant and unfading, and she is easily discerned by those who love her, and is found by those who seek her. She hastens to make herself known to those who desire her."

21. Note that even before the advent of Christianity, the Jewish exegete Philo of Alexandria had already equated Wisdom (as the means by which God is active and present in sustaining creation) with Greek philosophical concept of the Logos, which had been introduced by Heraclitus and developed by the Stoics to refer to the underlying principle that orders and structures to the cosmos. Philo of Alexandria, *Legum allegoriae* 1:43 (in vol. 1 of *Philo*, Loeb Classical Library [New York: G. P. Putnam's Sons, 1929]) and *De confusione linguarum* 146–47 (in vol. 4 of *Philo*, Loeb Classical Library [New York: G. P. Putnam's Sons, 1932]).

22. As James Dunn notes, "'image' could . . . bridge the otherwise unbridgeable gulf between the invisible world and God on the one side and visible creation and humanity on the other. . . . [thereby] safeguarding the unknowability of God by providing a mode of speaking of the invisible God's self-revelatory action." James D. G. Dunn, *The Epistles to Colossians and to Philemon: A Commentary on the Greek Text* (Grand Rapids, Mich./Carlisle, UK: Eerdmans/Paternoster, 1996), 87.

23. See, e.g., Stephen's speech in Acts 7:44-50, which suggests that even the highly restricted use of images associated with the temple cult was inconsistent with proper worship of God (cf. also John 4:21-24). Writing perhaps half a century later, Justin Martyr not only charges the Jews with persistent idolatrous tendencies, but also claims they teach that "the unbegotten God, has hands and feet, and fingers, and a soul, like a composite being." Justin Martyr, *Dialogue with Trypho*, chap. 114, in *The Apostolic Fathers with Justin Martyr and Irenaeus*, vol. 1 of *The Ante-Nicene Fathers*, ed. Alexander Roberts and James Donaldson (Grand Rapids, Mich.: Eerdmans, 1985), 256; cf. chaps. 46, 67, 130.

24. Origen, *Contra Celsum*, VII.64, ed. Henry Chadwick (Cambridge: Cambridge University Press, 1953); cited in Pelikan, *Imago Dei*, 2.

25. For the complexity of Christian attitudes toward images of Christ in the period surrounding Constantine's conversion, see the discussion of Eusebius's varying assessment of different kinds of images in Barasch, *Icon*, 143–55.

26. John of Damascus, *Exposition of the Orthodox Faith*, IV.xvi, in *Hilary of Poitiers, John of Damascus*, vol. 9 of *Nicene and Post-Nicene Fathers*, Second Series, ed. Philip Schaff and Henry Wace (Boston: Hendrickson, 1995), 88.

27. "Despite their theological speculations based on the psychology of sense-perception, on the metaphysics of light, and on the aesthetic implications of the Incarnation, even the later defenders of icons never gave up also employing the far simpler method of argumentation based on the didactic use of icons." Pelikan, *Imago Dei*, 118. See also the discussion of Dionysius the Areopagite's view that images are God's "concession to the nature of our own mind" (*The Celestial Hierarchy*, 2.1) in Barasch, *Icon*, 172–79.

28. "The Sixth Session of the Seventh Ecumenical Council (787), containing the Definition of the Council of Constantinople (754) and its refutation," in Sahas, *Icon and Logos*, 98. Cf. John of Damascus, *On the Divine Images* (Crestwood, N.Y.: St. Vladimir's Seminary Press, 1980), III.12: "Since we are fashioned of both soul and

body, and our souls are not naked spirits, but are covered . . . with a fleshy veil, it is impossible for us to think without using physical images."

29. "Definition of the Holy Great and Ecumenical Council, the Second in Nicea," in Sahas, *Icon and Logos*, 179.

30. "Sixth Session," in Sahas, *Icon and Logos*, 145.

31. See Basil of Caesarea, *On the Holy Spirit*, xviii.45, in *Basil: Letters and Selected Works*, vol. 8 of *Nicene and Post-Nicene Fathers*, Second Series, ed. Philip Schaff and Henry Wace (Boston: Hendrickson, 1995), 28. The same argument is used by Athanasius in *Four Discourses against the Arians*, III.5, in *Athanasius: Select Works and Letters*, vol. 4 of *Nicene and Post-Nicene Fathers*, 396.

32. In this context, Barasch observes that a crucial distinction between iconoclasts and iconodules was that the latter (as exemplified by the Emperor Constantine V) seem to have understood the idea of a "true" image as requiring an exhaustive and correspondence between image and prototype. By contrast, iconodules like John of Damascus insisted that an icon remained capable of "showing in itself what it depicts" all the while remaining distinct from its prototype (*On the Divine Images*, III.16). See Barasch, *Icon*, 196–98, 271–73.

33. In stressing the distinction between this one legitimate "icon" and painted images, the iconoclasts noted that Christ "commanded that the substance of bread be offered which does not yield the shape of a man's form, so that idolatry may not be introduced indirectly." The iconodules, in their turn, responded that the iconoclasts were here diminishing the significance of the Eucharist, since "nowhere did either the Lord, or the Apostles, or the Fathers" call the eucharistic elements "'an icon,' but rather 'this very body' and 'this very blood.'" "Sixth Session," in Sahas, *Icon and Logos*, 93–95.

34. "Symbol of Chalcedon," (DS 615) in *The Christian Faith in the Doctrinal Definitions of the Catholic Church*, ed. J. Neuner, S.J., and J. Dupuis, S.J. (New York: Alba House, 1982), 154.

35. This point acquired dogmatic status at the Second Council of Constantinople in 553.

36. In the words of one contemporary theologian, this development of Chalcedonian Christology (which later came to be called the doctrine of *enhypostasia*) "simply means that what Jesus does is attributed to the Word in the same way the Word's own properly divine predicates are attributed to the Word; the human being Jesus acts but these are God's own works." Kathryn Tanner, *Jesus, Humanity and the Trinity: A Brief Systematic Theology* (Minneapolis/Edinburgh: Fortress Press/T. & T. Clark, 2001), 26.

37. In the words of the iconoclast council of 754, "From those . . . who think that they are drawing the icon of Christ, it must be gathered either that the divinity is circumscribable and confused with the flesh or that the [human] body of Christ was without divinity and divided." "Sixth Session," in Sahas, *Icon and Logos*, 90.

38. Quoted by Nicephorus of Constantinople, *Refutation of the Iconoclasts*, II.1; cited in Pelikan, *Imago Dei*, 74.

39. John of Damascus, *On the Divine Images*, I.4.

40. "[T]he fact that the Lord has been iconographed in so far as he became a perfect man is not a cause of separation and individualization, or of any kind of division, or again . . . of confusion. . . . For the icon is one thing and the prototype another. No one of sound mind looks in any way to the icon for the qualities of the prototype. In the icon the true discourse knows nothing else but how to communicate in name, not in essence, with the one who is in the icon." "Sixth Session," in Sahas, *Icon and Logos*, 89.

41. A second wave of iconoclasm was to intervene before the final political and ecclesiastical triumph of the iconodule party in 843.

42. Thus, the conciliar "Definition" of 787 holds that icons may be "of our Lord and Saviour Jesus Christ, or of our pure Lady the holy Theotokos, or of honourable angels, or of any saint or holy man." Cited in Sahas, *Icon and Logos*, 179.

43. "I boldly draw an image of the invisible God, not as invisible, but as having become visible for our sakes by partaking of flesh and blood." John of Damascus, *On the Divine Images*, I.4.

44. "These are they who have become likenesses of God as far as is possible, since they have chosen to cooperate with divine election. Therefore God dwells in them . . . [and] they are to be venerated, not because they deserve it on their own account, but because they bear in themselves Him who is by nature worshipful." Ibid., *On the Divine Images*, III.33; cf. II.36.

45. Ibid., I.7; cf. II.7–8.

46. Ibid., I.16.

47. In this context, Robert Jenson has made a distinction between *icons* that depict Jesus' hypostasis as a "narrated identity" within the Gospels and *portraits* of Jesus that "if intended to have a religious function, will necessarily try to show his divinity by features of his countenance and expression" and thereby will invariably run afoul of the Second Commandment. See Robert W. Jenson, *Systematic Theology*, 2 vols. (New York: Oxford University Press, 1997–1999), 2:287.

48. John of Damascus, *On the Divine Images*, III.24.

49. Ibid., III.37.

50. Ibid., III.25.

51. Von Balthasar, *Seeing the Form*, 40–41.

52. Alain Besançon, *The Forbidden Image: An Intellectual History of Iconoclasm* (Chicago: University of Chicago Press, 2000), 134.

53. He claims that there are no icons at all of the wedding at Cana (John 2), or of the meals in the house of Matthew/Levi (Matthew 9; Luke 5) and Simon the leper (Matthew 26 and pars.). Ibid., 393.

54. See ibid., 136; cf. 139, where he cites Leonid Ouspensky's argument (*Essai sur la théologie de l'icône* [Paris: Édition de l'Exarchat patriarchal, 1960], 216) for the superiority of a Russian icon of Mary over a Madonna of Raphael because the former alone "communicates to us by its adequate symbolism the teachings of the Church on the Incarnation of God and divine Maternity."

55. Besançon, *The Forbidden Image*, 144.

56. Witness the following words of John of Damascus: "I honor and venerate angels, and men, and all matter which partakes of divine power, for these things have assisted in my salvation, and God has worked through them. I do not honor the Jews, for they refused to partake of the divine power. . . . They crucified my God, the Lord of glory; they attacked God their benefactor with envy and hatred." John of Damascus, *On Divine Images*, III.34.

57. See, e.g., the "Revelation through Acts, Words and Images," in Dumitru Staniloae, *Theology and the Church* (Crestwood, N.Y.: St. Vladimir's Seminary Press, 1980), 109–54.

3. The Image of God in Christ

1. Dumitru Staniloae, *Theology and the Church* (Crestwood, N.Y.: St. Vladimir's Seminary Press, 1980), 152.

2. Once again, Besançon is fairly critical of Orthodoxy on this score: "The theological self-assurance blinds one to the practical laxness: because the divine image was possible, people incautiously believed it existed." Alain Besançon, *The Forbidden Image: An Intellectual History of Iconoclasm* (Chicago: University of Chicago Press, 2000), 145.

3. "If we attempted to make an image of the invisible God, this would be sinful indeed. It is impossible to portray one who is without body: invisible, uncircumscribed, and without form." John of Damascus, *On Divine Images* (Crestwood, N.Y.: St. Vladimir's Seminary Press, 1980), II.5.

4. Maximus the Confessor, *Centuries on Love*, IV.7, in *The Philokalia*, vol. 2, ed. G. E. H. Palmer, Philip Sheridan, Kallistos Ware (London: Faber and Faber, 1981), translation altered. Note that alterations in the translation have been made with reference to the Greek text in Migne, *Patrologia Graeca*, vols. 90–91.

5. Maximus, *Centuries on Love*, II.27 (translation altered). Cf. I.100 for a similar assessment of the theological task.

6. Thus Luther famously insisted, "That person does not deserve to be called a theologian who looks upon the invisible things of God as though they were clearly perceptible in those things which have actually happened." Martin Luther, "Heidelberg Disputation," in *The Career of the Reformer: I*, vol. 31 of *Luther's Works*, American ed., ed. Harold J. Grimm (Philadelphia: Fortress Press, 1957), 52.

7. Maximus, *Centuries on Love*, II.100; cf. I.86. Vladimir Lossky concurs that for Maximus "[God's] attributes or energies are known through created beings." Vladimir Lossky, *The Vision of God* (Leighton Buzzard, UK: Faith Press, 1963), 107.

8. Karl Barth was sensitive to this problem and answered it by developing the distinction between the "primary objectivity" whereby God is known to Godself and the "secondary objectivity" whereby God is known to creatures, insisting that the latter is distinguished from the former "not by a lesser degree of truth, but by its particular form suitable to . . . the creature." Karl Barth, *Church Dogmatics*, 13 vols., ed. G. W. Bromiley and T. F. Torrance (Edinburgh: T. & T. Clark, 1956–1974), II/1, 16. See chapter eight below for further discussion of this distinction.

9. See, e.g., Maximus, *Centuries on Love*, II.15.

10. See *Centuries on Theology and the Incarnate Dispensation of the Son of God, Written for Thalassius*, I.82–83, in *The Philokalia*, vol. 2. Cf. II.2: "Intellection and intelligibility (*to noein kai to noiesthai*) appertain by nature to what is subsequent to God" (translation altered).

11. Maximus, *Centuries on Love*, III.24.

12. Thus, Maximus describes participation as a state in which the creature's "natural energy" (*phusike energeia*) is suspended in such a way that God "establishes [the creature's own] natural energy within God Himself" (*Centuries on Theology*, I. 47).

13. Maximus calls it "hyperknowing" in *Centuries on Love*, III.99 and "unknowing" in *Centuries on Love*, III. 45.

14. "When the intellect receives conceptual images (*noemata*) of things, it becomes conformed to each image. If it contemplates these objects spiritually, it is transformed in various ways according to that which is contemplated. But once it is established (*genomenos*) in God, it loses form and configuration altogether, for by contemplating Him who is simple it becomes simple itself and wholly filled with spiritual radiance." Maximus, *Centuries on Love*, III.97 (translation altered); cf. II.62.

15. In *Centuries on Love*, III.23–24, Maximus notes that though concepts are internal to the intellect, the (created) realities they represent are external to it.

16. See Maximus, *Centuries on Love*, II.6; III.97.

17. In this context it is worth noting that Maximus generally uses periphrastic expressions to speak of the divine attributes. In addition to *hoi peri auton* (the phrase used in the passages quoted at the beginning of this chapter), he employs the more fulsome *hoi peri tes ousias autou* in *Centuries on Love* I.100, and *hosa peri auton ousiodos* in *Centuries on Theology*, I.48. The language of *Centuries on Love*, IV.8 suggests that he avoids speaking more directly of divine properties (*hexeis*) or attributes (*epitedeiotes*) as a means of blocking any suggestion that God's essence is composite.

18. "Participable beings . . . such as goodness . . . are perhaps works of God which did not begin to be in time. Briefly, these include all life, immortality, simplicity, immutability, infinity and all other qualities that contemplative vision perceives as substantively appertaining to God. These are works of God, yet not begun in time." Maximus, *Centuries on Theology*, I.48; cf. I.50.

19. "God who is above all leads us through the historical nature, so to speak, of the appearances of created things to amazement and a kind of ascent through contemplation and knowledge of them . . . and then introduces the contemplation of the more spiritual meaning (*logos*) within these things." Maximus the Confessor, "Difficulty 71," in Andrew Louth, *Maximus the Confessor* (New York: Routledge, 1996), 167.

20. Andrew Louth, *Wisdom of the Byzantine Church: Evagrios of Pontus and Maximos the Confessor*, ed. Jill Raitt (Columbia, Mo.: Department of Religious Studies, University of Missouri, 1998), 16. Staniloae notes that patristic writers "sometimes distinguished the meaning of a thing from its inner principle or 'reason' strictly so

called, giving the name *logos* to the latter and *noema* to the former," but adds that in patristic perspective it is also impossible "to make a separation between the rationality implied in the repetition of things [*viz.*, their *logos*] and their deeper meaning." Dumitru Staniloae, *The World: Creation and Deification*, vol. 2 of *The Experience of God: Orthodox Dogmatic Theology*, ed. Ioan Ionita and Robert Barringer (Brookline, Mass.: Holy Cross Orthodox Press, 2000), 29, 42.

21. Maximus, *Centuries on Love*, IV.45. For the importance of separating passion from concepts, see ibid., II.4, 15, 17, 71–74, 78, and *passim*.

22. "The world, bounded by its own inner principles (*logoi*), is called both the place and age of those dwelling in it. There are modes of contemplation natural to it which are able to engender in created beings a partial understanding of the wisdom of God that governs all things. So long as they make use of these modes to gain understanding, they cannot have more than a mediate and partial apprehension." Ibid., I.70.

23. "A soul can never attain the knowledge of God unless God Himself in His condescension takes hold of it and raises it up to Himself. For the human intellect lacks the power to ascend and to participate in the divine illumination, unless God Himself draws it up." Ibid., I.31.

24. In ibid., I.98–99, Maximus argues that the dispassionate intellect is driven first to seek out the creature's "natural principles" (*phusikoi logoi*) and then to the cause (*aitia*) or providence (*pronoia*) that determines their place in the cosmos. For a fuller account of the intellect's search for the ultimate cause of created being, see Maximus, "Difficulty 10," in Louth, *Maximus the Confessor*, 137–38.

25. See *Centuries on Love*, II.6, where Maximus contrasts the state of the one "abandoning all conceptual images of the world, concentrates itself and prays without distraction or disturbance as if God Himself were present" with the more exalted state of the one who actually experiences God. The first state corresponds to the limit of the intellect, which at most can only act as if God were present; the second corresponds to the intellect to which God has revealed God's self.

26. Ibid., II.75.

27. Lars Thunberg suggests the importance of the distinction between "natural" contemplation of the *logoi* in creatures and knowledge of the Logos through the *logoi* as follows: "The outward impression suggests the *logoi* of things to an attentive soul, so that they—and the Logos in them—may be spiritually contemplated. The reasonable part of the human soul may gain an analytical knowledge of things through the *logoi*. But this knowledge of the *logoi* is as such a divine gift." *Microcosm and Mediator: The Theological Anthropology of Maximus the Confessor* (Chicago: Open Court, 1995), 78.

28. Maximus, *Centuries on Theology*, I.67.

29. Ibid., II.4. Cf. "Difficulty 10," 154.

30. Maximus, *Centuries on Love*, I.95.

31. In this context, David Yeago has argued that Maximus's opposition to monenergism and monothelitism centered on a refusal to see in Christ an exemplification of a natural tendency toward union with God built into the cosmos. David

S. Yeago, "Jesus of Nazareth and Cosmic Redemption: The Relevance of St. Maximus the Confessor," in *Modern Theology* 12, no. 2 (April 1996): 163–93.

32. Maximus, *Centuries on Theology*, II.83.

33. "[R]edemption is *what happens in the story of Jesus*, impossible to characterize without constitutive reference to . . . that particular narrative." Yeago, "Jesus of Nazareth and Cosmic Redemption," 177.

34. "There is already a natural coinherence or copenetration between the sensible and intelligible dimensions of creation, and the tension thus established is a creative tension, resolved only by the Logos himself." Paul M. Blowers, *Exegesis and Spiritual Pedagogy in Maximus the Confessor: An Investigation of the Quaestiones ad Thalassium* (Notre Dame, Ind.: University of Notre Dame Press, 1991), 99.

35. Maximus the Confessor, "Difficulty 10," 107.

36. Ibid., 154; cf. *Centuries on Theology*, II.4.

37. "Created things reveal their meaning above all because their rationality is seen . . . as having its source in the personal God. . . . Thus it is through created things that we grow, inasmuch as through them we come to know God's loving intentions for us more completely. As created things are better known, the wisdom of God and his love for human beings are consequently also better known, and as these in turn come to be known more completely, so too the deeper meanings come to be seen within the things themselves." Staniloae, *The World*, 40–41.

38. Maximus, "Difficulty 10," 109.

39. "The knowledge of all that has come to be through Him is naturally and properly made known together with Him. For just as with the rising of the sensible sun all bodies are made known, so it is with God, the intelligible sun of righteousness, rising in the mind: although He is known to be separate from the created order, He wishes the true meanings of everything, whether intelligible or sensible, to be made known together with Himself." Ibid., 125–26.

40. Ibid., 109. A similar point was made in a very different historical and intellectual context by Jonathan Edwards: "[T]he whole universe, heaven and earth, air and seas, and the divine constitution and history of the holy Scriptures, [are] full of images of divine things, as full as language is of words." Jonathan Edwards, *The Works of Jonathan Edwards*, vol. 11 (New Haven: Yale University Press, 199), 152; cited in Amy Plantinga Pauw, *The Supreme Harmony of All: The Trinitarian Theology of Jonathan Edwards* (Grand Rapids, Mich.: Eerdmans, 2002), 191.

41. "Thus . . . we shall behold the garments of the Word, by which I mean the words of Scripture, and the manifestations of creatures, which are radiant and glorious by the dogmas that penetrate them, rendered splendid by the divine Word for exalted contemplation." Maximus, "Difficulty 10," 112.

42. "Christian contemplation (*theoria*) may see the Logos in the *logoi*, but on the other hand, the eternal presence of the Logos in the *logoi* is one which in this world of time and space is to be perceived by faith and in a strictly Christological perspective." Thunberg, *Microcosm and Mediator*, 75.

43. Maximus, *Centuries on Theology*, II.39; cf. 27, 38. Louth (*Wisdom of the Byzantine Church*, 27–29) notes that the *Centuries on Theology* exude a far more spiritualized

Christology than some of Maximus's other writings and suggests that this is due to the fact that in this work Maximus is attempting to appropriate themes from Origen.

44. Maximus explicitly cites 2 Cor. 5:16 in this context in *Centuries on Theology*, II.61.

45. Ibid., II.18; cf. 73.

46. In this context, Blowers has argued that for Maximus "the transcendent Logos is never conceptually separate from the *historically* incarnate Christ." Blowers, *Exegesis and Spiritual Pedagogy*, 118; cf. Lars Thunberg, *Man and the Cosmos: The Vision of St. Maximus the Confessor* (Crestwood, N.Y.: St. Vladimir's Seminary Press, 1985), 166.

47. Maximus, *Centuries on Theology*, I.97; cf. "Difficulty 10," 109, where Maximus again draws the same contrast between the christological significance of Isaiah 53 and Psalm 45.

48. Maximus, "Difficulty 10," 131–32.

49. Ibid., 132.

50. "From what they [Moses and Elijah] said to the Lord and their speaking of the exodus that was about to be fulfilled in Jerusalem, they were taught . . . an apprehension of providence and judgment of the whole nature of visible things, and the modes through which the end of this present harmony naturally consists, and is well-nigh expressly proclaimed." Ibid., 133–34.

51. Maximus, "Difficulty 10," 132. Cf. *Centuries on Theology*, II.73.

52. "After the incarnation, then, the *logoi* and *tupoi* of creation and scripture do not suddenly lose their force but continue to be the effective instrument of Christ's self-communication in the Church and in individual souls." Blowers, *Exegesis and Spiritual Pedagogy*, 252.

53. Note the following claim from the *Quaestiones ad Thalassium*, 25: "Through himself, the Logos conducts the mind led by devout contemplation of created beings to th[e] divine Mind and supplies it with intellectual reflections of the divine realities *proportionate to its knowledge of visible things*." Cited in Blowers, *Exegesis and Spiritual Pedagogy*, 201.

54. For a particularly striking illustration of the way in which Jesus exemplifies God's knowability and unknowability alike, see Maximus's interpretation of Christ's body in *Quaestiones ad Thalassium*, 35, where the flesh and blood (which we are enjoined to consume) are interpreted as referring to the knowledge of the *logoi* of sensible and intelligible things, respectively, while the bones (unbroken and thus unconsumed) refer to "the principles of his divinity that transcend our intelligence." Cited in Blowers, *Exegesis and Spiritual Pedagogy*, 147.

55. There is here an interesting parallel to Luther, who states that "sun, moon, heaven, earth, Peter, Paul, I, you, etc., are all words of God, or perhaps syllables or letters in context of the whole creation." Martin Luther, *Ennaratio in Genesis*, 17; cited in Robert W. Jenson, *Systematic Theology*, 2 vols. (New York: Oxford University Press, 1997–1999), 2:159.

56. Vladimir Lossky, *The Mystical Theology of the Eastern Church* (London: James Clarke, 1957), 238.

57. Louth, *Wisdom of the Byzantine Church*, 24.

58. Ibid., 42.

59. See Maximus, *Centuries on Theology*, II.41.

60. See n. 39 above.

61. Thus, it is "in the honour shown [Jesus] by Moses and Elijah" as the symbols of God's providential government of creation that the disciples on Mount Tabor "recognized his great awesomeness." Maximus, "Difficulty 10," 108–9.

62. "[T]here is no lack of 'spirit' in other religious world-views. The distinctive Christian factor is that here we not only 'start from' the corporeal and the sensory as from some religious material on which we can then perform the necessary abstractions; rather, we abide in the seeing, hearing, touching." Hans Urs von Balthasar, *Seeing the Form*, vol. 1 of *The Glory of the Lord: A Theological Aesthetics* (San Francisco: Ignatius, 1982), 313–14.

63. Von Balthasar, *Seeing the Form*, 302.

64. Maximus, "Difficulty 5," in Louth, *Maximus the Confessor*, 173. Note that in the combined collection of "Difficulties" found in the *Patrologia Graeca*, vol. 91, numbers 1–5 (the *Ambigua ad Thomam*) were written after the remainder of the series (the *Ambigua ad Ioannem*). For a brief reflection on the history of the combined collection, see Polycarp Sherwood, O.S.B., *The Earlier Ambigua of St. Maximus the Confessor and his Refutation of Origenism* (Rome: Herder, 1955), 39–40.

65. See Irenaeus: "And for this reason did the Word become the dispenser of the paternal grace for the benefit of men, for whom He made such great dispensations, revealing God indeed to men, but . . . preserving at the same time the invisibility of the Father, lest man should at any time become a despiser of God, and that he should always possess something towards which he might advance." Irenaeus of Lyons, *Against Heresies*, IV.xx.7, in *The Apostolic Fathers with Justin Martyr and Irenaeus*, vol. 1 of *The Ante-Nicene Fathers*, ed. Alexander Roberts and James Donaldson (Grand Rapids, Mich.: Eerdmans, 1985).

66. Von Balthasar himself recognizes the need for this sort of qualification: "Christ's existence and his teachings would not be a comprehensible form if it were not for his rootedness in a salvation-history that leads up to him. Both in his union with that history and in his relief from it, Christ becomes for us the image that reveals the invisible God. Even Scripture is not an isolated book, but rather is embedded in the context of everything created, established, and effected by Christ—the total reality constituted by his work and activity in the world. Only in this context is the form of Scripture [and thus of Christ] perceivable." Von Balthasar, *Seeing the Form*, 32.

67. In the words of Dumitru Staniloae, the finality of Christ "does not mean, however, that the integral Christ needs no further explanation or that further dimensions of his significance and other effects produced by him in the souls of men cannot be brought to light." Thus, as the church "experiences . . . pressure from the active presence of Christ. . . . It is not something essentially new which is always communicated to her, but instead the endless riches of one and the same Christ in whom the whole of revelation is concentrated and brought to an end." Dumitru

Staniloae, *Revelation and Knowledge of the Triune God*, vol. 1 of *The Experience of God: Orthodox Dogmatic Theology*, ed. Ioan Ionita and Robert Barringer (Brookline, Mass.: Holy Cross Orthodox Press, 1994), 47, 64.

4. The Image of God in Human Beings

1. Hans Urs von Balthasar, *Seeing the Form*, vol. 1 of *The Glory of the Lord: A Theological Aesthetics* (San Francisco: Ignatius, 1982), 216.

2. "The Bible is the concrete means by which the Church recollects God's past revelation . . .[but]is not in itself and as such God's past revelation. . . . Purely formally, the revelation to which the biblical witnesses direct their gaze . . . is to be distinguished from the word of the witnesses in exactly the same way as an event itself is to be distinguished from even the best and most faithful account of it." Karl Barth, *Church Dogmatics* [hereafter *CD*], ed. G. W. Bromiley and T. F. Torrance (Edinburgh: T. & T. Clark, 1956–1974), I/1, 111 and 113. See chap. 8 for further discussion of the role of Scripture in the Christian discernment of the divine image.

3. See *CD*, I/2, 601–2.

4. "As One and Unique, and yet as one who is to be understood only in the context of mankind's entire history and in the context of the whole created cosmos, Jesus is the Word, the Image, the Expression and the Exegesis of God." Von Balthasar, *Seeing the Form*, 29.

5. It is not a matter of theological consensus, however, and is explicitly rejected by, e.g., Augustine. See his *On the Trinity*, VII.6, in *St. Augustine: On the Holy Trinity, Doctrinal Treatises, Moral Treatises*, vol. 3 of *The Nicene and Post-Nicene Fathers*, ed. Philip Schaff (Grand Rapids, Mich.: Eerdmans, 1956).

6. While Wayne Meeks argues for the metaphorical character of Paul's imagery on the grounds that the language of 1 Corinthians 12 "is not materially different from the use by Cicero or Seneca or Plutarch" (Wayne A. Meeks, *The Origins of Christian Morality: The First Two Centuries* [New Haven: Yale University Press, 1993], 134), E. P. Sanders defends "the realism of Paul's view" (E. P. Sanders, *Paul and Palestinian Judaism: A Comparison of Patterns of Religion* [Minneapolis/London: Fortress Press/SCM, 1977], 522–23).

7. See Dale B. Martin, *The Corinthian Body* (New Haven: Yale University Press, 1995), 94–96, for an analysis of how Paul's use of body imagery in 1 Corinthians 12 subverts the conservative force this image normally carries in classical rhetoric.

8. In this respect the present argument differs from Robert Jenson's proposal that Jesus' body is "risen into the church and sacraments" (Robert W. Jenson, *Systematic Theology*, 2 vols. [Oxford: Oxford University Press, 1997–1999], 1:229). As he develops this theme in the second volume of this work, Jenson does invoke the head-body distinction, but in such a way that Jesus' headship refers to his status as "the subject whose objectivity is this community" rather than to his freedom as the church's Lord and Judge (see *Systematic Theology* 2:214–15; cf. 1:206). It is hard to see how this level of identification of Jesus with the community (which is more redolent of the relationship between soul and body than head and members) preserves a sufficiently robust sense of Jesus' "over-againstness" with respect to the church.

9. This kind of corporate interpretation of the divine image is proposed by Gregory of Nyssa, who maintains: "Our whole nature . . . extending from first to last, is, so to say, one image of Him Who is." Gregory of Nyssa, *On the Making of Man*, XVI, in *Gregory of Nyssa: Dogmatic Treatises, Etc.*, vol. 5 of *Nicene and Post-Nicene Fathers*, Second Series, ed. Philip Schaff and Henry Wace (Boston: Hendrickson, 1995), 406.

10. "Their forms . . . are not imitations or repetitions of Christ's form, but the form of Christ that takes form in human beings." Dietrich Bonhoeffer, *Ethics*, vol. 6 of *Dietrich Bonhoeffer Works*, ed. Clifford J. Green (Minneapolis: Fortress Press, 2005), 96.

11. In this respect, Peter Brunner's description of the church as an "epiphany" of Jesus, whose own human body has ascended to heaven and is seated at God's right hand, is to be preferred to Jenson's perspective. See Peter Brunner, *Worship in the Name of Jesus* (St. Louis: Concordia, 1969), 72.

12. This kind of encounter can also happen in my physical absence, as when, for example, someone sees my footprints long after I have passed by.

13. It is important to note that because both forms of encounter relate specifically to persons, they do not correspond to Martin Buber's distinction between I-Thou and I-it relationships.

14. A situation in which such address is taken as a complete misrepresentation constitutes a limiting case. It is logically equivalent to the failure to recognize a given sequence of sounds or actions as an address at all—in which case they can only be taken as the physical data of a third-person encounter.

15. If it is asked where the head is located, the claim that it is in heaven and that heaven, as "the place of God," is "inconceivable" and "inaccessible," to the extent that it "cannot be explored or described" (Barth, *CD*, III/3, 437; cf. Jenson, *Systematic Theology* 2:120) seems consistent with what little the Bible has to say about the ascension: namely, that the risen Jesus was taken up into heaven, and that heaven, whatever its other characteristics is "out of [our] sight" (see Acts 1:9-11; cf. Mark 16:19; Luke 24:51; 1 Thess. 4:16).

16. "Jesus would not be Christ without his relation to those who are 'in Christ'; he would not be himself." Francis Watson, *Agape, Eros, Gender: Towards a Pauline Sexual Ethic* (Cambridge: Cambridge University Press, 1999), 140.

17. Because human beings fulfill this function only indirectly, insofar as they point to the head who is the exclusive locus of God's ontological union with the creation, Paul Evdokimov's claim that the incarnation makes "of humanity a Theophany, the beloved ground of [God's] presence" must be judged an overstatement. Paul Evdokimov, *The Sacrament of Love* (Crestwood, N.Y.: St. Vladimir's Seminary Press, 1985), 50.

18. "In the beginning with God . . . the very first thing is the decree whose realisation means and is Jesus Christ." Barth, *CD* II/2, 157.

19. "But in this primal decision God does not choose only Himself. In this choice of self He also chooses another, the other which is man." Barth, *CD*, II/2, 169.

20. This assessment of the Spirit's role in constituting the body of Christ closely parallels that found in Dietrich Bonhoeffer's *Sanctorum Communio*, where "the

reality of the new humanity in Christ is *actualized* among people by the Holy Spirit." Clifford J. Green, *Bonhoeffer: A Theology of Sociality*, rev. ed. (Grand Rapids, Mich.: Eerdmans, 1999), 53.

21. This argument is made by Thomas Aquinas, *Summa Theologiae*, Blackfriars ed. (London: Eyre & Spottiswood, 1964–1981), IIIa, qu. 8, art. 3; cf. Ia, qu. 93, art. 4. According to Thomas, non-Christians are, strictly speaking, members only potentially.

22. N. A. Nissiotis, *Die Theologie der Ostkirche im ökumenischen Dialog. Kirche und Welt in orthodoxer Sicht* (Stuttgart: Evangelisches Verlagswerk, 1968), 75. Cited in Reinhard Hütter, *Suffering Divine Things: Theology as Church Practice* (Grand Rapids, Mich.: Eerdmans, 2000), 114; emphasis added.

23. Compare Irenaeus's famous remark that "the glory of God is a living human being, and the life of a human being consists in beholding God." Irenaeus, *Against Heresies*, IV.xx.7.

24. Rowan Williams, *On Christian Theology* (Oxford: Blackwell, 2000), 172–73.

25. Von Balthasar, *Seeing the Form*, 215.

26. Bruce D. Marshall, *Trinity and Truth* (Cambridge: Cambridge University Press, 2000), especially 191–203; cf. George A. Lindbeck, *The Nature of Doctrine: Religion and Theology in a Postliberal Age* (Philadelphia: Westminster, 1984), 63–69.

27. The phrase "technology of desire" represents Bell's conflation of Michel Foucault's idea of "technologies of the self" (see especially Michel Foucault, "Technologies of the Self," in *Technologies of the Self: A Seminar with Michel Foucault*, eds. Luther H. Martin, Huck Gutman, Patrick H. Hutton [Amherst, Mass.: University of Massachusetts Press, 1988]); and Gilles Deleuze's analysis of desire (as expounded in, e.g., Gilles Deleuze and Félix Guattari, *Anti-Oedipus: Capitalism and Schizophrenia* [Minneapolis: University of Minnesota Press, 1983]). Bell defines Christianity itself as "an ensemble of technologies of desire" in order to emphasize its socially embedded and material (as opposed to merely ideological) character. Daniel M. Bell, Jr., *Liberation Theology after the End of History: The Refusal to Cease Suffering* (London: Routledge, 2001), 86–87; cf. 40.

28. See Miroslav Volf, "*Liberation Theology after the End of History*: An Exchange," in *Modern Theology* 19, no. 2 (April 2003): 264–65.

29. In his response to Volf's review, Bell concedes that his rhetoric may sometimes give a misleading impression without conceding that the language of technology is inappropriate. Daniel M. Bell, Jr., "What Gift Is Given? A Response to Volf," in *Modern Theology* 19, no. 2 (April 2003): 276–77.

30. It is important to note that Rawls himself insists that his theoretical construct of the original position is just that—a "model-conception" designed solely to get reflection off the ground and not a full-blown anthropology (see John Rawls, "Kantian Constructivism in Moral Theory: The Dewey Lectures 1980," in *The Journal of Philosophy* 77 [9 September 1980]: 520). Nevertheless, insofar as this "model-conception" locates the essence of persons in their being free, rational, and mutually autonomous, it imposes profound limits on the Rawlsian vision of humanity, especially with respect to its power to include those who are dependent on the care of

others for their survival. See Eva Feder Kittay, *Love's Labor: Essays on Women, Equality, and Dependency* (New York: Routledge, 1999), 75–82.

31. Notwithstanding Protestant rejection of a formal cult of the saints, martyrologies were extremely common among Protestants in the early modern period. Alongside Foxe's *Acts and Monuments* and the Anabaptist *Martyrs' Mirror* can be listed numerous parallels from Reformed (though not so much the Lutheran) Protestants on the Continent. See Ephraim Radner, *The End of the Church: A Pneumatology of Christian Division in the West* (Grand Rapids, Mich.: Eerdmans, 1998), 126–28. Radner notes, however, that Protestant martyrologies tend to focus on the details of the doctrine confessed by the victims rather than on the particular character of their lives.

32. "We may behold the Divine image in men by the medium of those who have ordered their lives aright." Gregory of Nyssa, *On the Making of Man*, XVIII.7, in *Gregory of Nyssa: Dogmatic Treatises, etc.*, vol. 5 of *Nicene and Post-Nicene Fathers*, Second Series, ed. Philip Schaff and Henry Wace (Boston: Hendrickson, 1995).

33. This parallel also includes a difference, since in Catholic theology a further distinction is drawn between "dulia in the absolute sense, the honour paid to persons, and dulia in the relative sense, the honour paid to inanimate objects, such as images and relics. With regard to the saints, dulia includes veneration and invocation; the former being the honour paid directly to them, the latter having primarily in view the petitioner's advantage." See E. A. Pace, "Dulia" in vol. 5 of *The Catholic Encyclopedia* (New York: Robert Appleton, 1909). Cf. Aquinas, *Summa Theologiae*, IIa IIae, qu. 103, art. 4, ad 3.

34. Peter Brown notes that in late antique reliquaries the martyr was "often shown in the pose of the Crucified." Peter Brown, *The Cult of the Saints: Its Rise and Function in Latin Christianity* (Chicago: University of Chicago Press, 1981), 72.

35. "What distinguishes the martyrdom of a Christian from similar acts of heroism recorded of Jewish witnesses for the law, or of pagan philosophers . . . is that the Christian suffered not merely for the sake of loyalty and obedience to the beliefs and practices that he held to be true and inviolable, or because of a principle of world renunciation. Christian martyrdom was . . . nothing less than a mystic communion and conformation with the One who died for our sins." Massey Hamilton Shepherd, Jr., "Introduction" to *The Martyrdom of Polycarp, Bishop of Smyrna, as Told in the Letter of the Church of Smyrna to the Church of Philomelium*, in *Early Christian Fathers*, ed. Cyril C. Richardson (New York: Collier, 1970), 141.

36. Significantly, textual evidence suggests that Jesus' prayer for the forgiveness of his executioners (Luke 23:34) may not be original to Luke but was rather retrojected back into the passion narrative in imitation of the parallel prayer attributed to Stephen in Acts 7:60. If so, the New Testament itself would bear indirect witness to the idea that the image of God revealed in Christ is not exhausted by him and can be perceived in its fullness only with reference to the lives of other human beings. For a succinct review of the textual problems associated with this passage, see Joseph A. Fitzmyer, S.J., *The Gospel According to Luke (X–XXIV): Introduction, Translation, and Notes* (New York: Doubleday, 1985), 1503–4.

37. *Martyrdom of Polycarp*, 149.

38. Ibid., 155.

39. Ibid., 156. The connection between such anniversary celebrations and the written records of martyrdom appear to have been strong: where accounts of a martyr's sufferings were not available, the strength of the cult declined, since "it is the custom of the man in the street to give more attentive veneration to those saints of God whose combats are read aloud." Cited in Brown, *Cult of the Saints*, 82.

40. Brown, *Cult of the Saints*, 72. Again, already the writer of *The Martyrdom of Polycarp* describes how church members "took up his bones, more precious than costly stones and more valuable than gold, and laid them away in a suitable place." *Martyrdom of Polycarp*, 156.

41. See Brown, *Cult of the Saints*, 3–8, 41–46.

42. Athanasius of Alexandria, *Life of St. Antony of Egypt*, 85, in *Medieval Hagiography: An Anthology*, ed. Thomas Head (New York: Routledge, 2001).

43. Athanasius, *Life of St. Antony*, 46, cf. 55, where Athanasius writes that through his own discipline Antony taught others "to remember the actions of the saints so that the soul . . . might be brought into harmony with their zeal."

44. David Brown, *Discipleship and Imagination: Christian Tradition and Truth* (Oxford: Oxford University Press, 2000), 64.

45. Athanasius, *Life of St. Antony*, 47. Note that while an earlier author like Origen recognized that there were "those, known to God alone, who are already martyrs by the testimony of their conscience," he added that the fact that God never calls upon such people to make the supreme sacrifice means that there is no ground for their veneration. Origen, *Homily on Numbers*, X.2, cited in Henri Crouzel, *Origen* (Edinburgh: T. & T. Clark, 1989), 238.

46. Athanasius, *Life of St. Antony*, 94.

47. See, e.g., ibid., 48, 58, 71, 86, 93.

48. See ibid., Preface.

49. "Saints are, broadly speaking, saints in the eyes of the whole community of the Church, but this reference to the whole Church is usually tenuous and inexplicit. In effect, saints are first and foremost local saints." Pierre Delooz, "Towards a Sociological Study of Canonized Sainthood," in *Saints and Their Cults: Studies in Religious Sociology, Folklore and History*, ed. Stephen Wilson (Cambridge: Cambridge University Press, 1983), 194.

50. In line with its polity, the Orthodox process of canonization is considerably less formal and more decentralized, with responsibility for vetting candidates falling to local synods of bishops.

51. A detailed sociological study of patterns of veneration from the Middle Ages through the early modern period concludes that "no single act established sanctity; behavior initially perceived as bizarre by parents and friends only gradually came to be seen as divinely inspired." Donald Weinstein and Rudolph M. Bell, *Saints and Society: Two Worlds of Western Christendom, 1000–1700* (Chicago: University of Chicago Press, 1982), 143.

52. Indeed, David Brown shows how the popular appeal of even purely fictional saints like Catherine of Alexandria and Margaret of Antioch provided innovative models of sanctity capable of inspiring real-life figures like Catherine of Siena and Joan of Arc. Brown, *Discipleship and Imagination*, 83–93.

53. See Weinstein and Bell, *Saints and Society*, 197.

54. Weinstein and Bell's figures do indicate a decline in saints from royal or noble lineage in favor of those classified as from the rising urban elites and of "good family," but there is no shift from rich to poor: "Among the ranks of saints, counts and bishops were joined by merchants, and serfs by cobblers, but the well-to-do continued to dominate all others to a degree essentially unchanged." Ibid., 198.

55. "Canonization documents make it clear that the formation of a cult brought together people of distinct classes. The local noble joined his peasants on his knees at the tomb of the saint and secured the help of the bishop in documenting the wonders performed by someone who in life may have been his bondsman." Ibid., 207.

56. "The lesser prominence of supernatural activity among saints of upper-class backgrounds suggests not that miracles and visions were unimportant among those classes, but that highborn saints had alternative paths to recognition. . . . Canonization required cult; cult depended upon visibility; and visibility came with social position." Ibid., 209.

57. Women make up less than 20 percent of the total number of saints over Weinstein and Bell's seven-century survey period, and, again, lack of access both to education and to the majority of publicly visible social roles meant that the majority of female saints fall in the category of ascetic visionaries (as opposed to teachers, evangelists, or prominent political leaders). See ibid., 220–38.

58. Elizabeth A. Johnson, *Friends of God and Prophets: A Feminist Theological Reading of the Communion of Saints* (London: SCM, 1998), 27–28.

59. Joan of Arc is an outstanding example of a woman of non-noble background who defied the conventions of gender and class alike, though it is worth noting that in spite of the enthusiasm with which she was venerated by French people of all classes, she was not officially canonized until the twentieth century.

60. For example, Elisabeth Schüssler Fiorenza recalls that the stories of female saints on which she was raised "stressed suffering, sexual purity, submission, outmoded piety, and total obedience. They were anti-intellectual and anti-erotic; they told about many nuns and widows and some queens, but rarely did they speak about ordinary women. While we desired our independence and love, the glorification of the saints demanded humble feminine submission and fostered sexual neuroses." Elisabeth Schüssler Fiorenza, *Discipleship of Equals: A Critical Feminist Ekklesia-logy of Liberation* (London: SCM, 1993), 40.

61. Athanasius, *Life of Antony*, 84; cf. note 38 above.

62. See Johnson, *Friends of God and Prophets*, 86. Johnson notes (pp. 78 and 87) that the effects of this shift are especially clear in relation to the cult of the Virgin Mary: whereas in the earliest period the fact that she was not a martyr meant that she was not a prominent object of public veneration, with the rise of a patronage

model she tended to gravitate to the top of the hierarchy of saints as having the best access to the ascended Lord.

63. "Men suppose that Christ is more severe and his saints more approachable; so they trust more in the mercy of the saints than in the mercy of Christ and they flee from Christ and turn to the saints." *Apology of the Augsburg Confession*, XXI.15, in *The Book of Concord: The Confessions of the Evangelical Lutheran Church*, ed. Theodore G. Tappert [Philadelphia: Muhlenburg Press, 1959); cf., however, XXI.4–7, where it is affirmed that the saints are worthy of honor as occasions for thanksgiving, the strengthening of faith, and imitation.

64. The phrase "preferential option for the poor" became the standard form of expression for this principle after its incorporation in the final document of the Third General Conference of Latin American Bishops held at Puebla, Mexico, in 1979. For a discussion of its significance that in many respects parallels that given here, see John E. Thiel, *Senses of Tradition: Continuity and Development in Catholic Faith* (New York: Oxford University Press, 2000), 144-47.

65. Gustavo Gutiérrez, *A Theology of Liberation: History, Politics and Salvation*, rev. ed. (Maryknoll, N.Y.: Orbis, 1988), xx.

66. "Liberation theology was born when faith confronted the injustice done to the poor." Leonardo and Clodovis Boff, *Introducing Liberation Theology* (Tunbridge Wells, UK: Burns & Oates, 1987), 3. Cf. Rosemary Radford Ruether, *Sexism and God-Talk: Toward a Feminist Theology* (Boston: Beacon, 1984), xviii: "The starting point for feminist theology . . . is cognitive dissonance. What is, is not what ought to be."

67. Gutiérrez, "Renewing the Option for the Poor," in *Liberation Theologies, Postmodernity, and the Americas*, ed. David Batstone, Eduardo Mendieta, et al. (London: Routledge, 1997), 75.

68. "The radical originality of the theology of liberation lies in the *insertion of the theologian in the real life of the poor*, understood as a collective, conflictive, and active . . . reality." Clodovis Boff, "Methodology of the Theology of Liberation," in *Systematic Theology: Perspectives from Liberation Theology*, ed. Jon Sobrino and Ignacio Ellacurîa (Maryknoll, N.Y.: Orbis, 1996), 7.

69. "The eternal salvation [God and Christ] offer is mediated by the historical liberations that dignify the children of God and render credible the coming . . . kingdom of God in the midst of humankind." Ibid., 8–9.

70. Ibid., 23; cf. Juan Luis Segundo, *Liberation of Theology* (Maryknoll, N.Y.: Orbis, 1976), 75–90.

71. "There is a hermeneutical circle, then, or 'unceasing interplay' between the poor and the word of God. . . . The primacy in this dialectic, however, belongs undeniably to the sovereign word of God—the primacy of value, at any rate, if not necessarily methodological priority." Boff, "Methodology," 16.

72. So James Cone argues that because Jesus is "an event of liberation . . . there can be no knowledge of Jesus independent of the history and culture of the oppressed." James H. Cone, *God of the Oppressed* (San Francisco: Harper & Row, 1975), 34; cf. Segundo, *Liberation of Theology*, chap. 1.

73. Gutiérrez, *Theology of Liberation*, 118.

74. Ibid., 110.

75. Matt. 25:31-46 is the classic proof text cited by liberation theologians to establish this point, though the degree to which this text supports an identification of Christ with all—as opposed to merely Christian—poor has been questioned on historical-critical grounds (as acknowledged by Gutiérrez himself in *Theology of Liberation*, 112–15).

76. Leonardo Boff, *Good News to the Poor: A New Evangelization* (Tunbridge Wells, UK: Burns & Oates, 1992), 44–48, where, in addition to the poor, the general history of humanity and other religions are listed as sources of the church's own evangelization; cf. the same author's qualified defense of syncretism in *Church: Charism and Power: Liberation Theology and the Institutional Church* (New York: Crossroad, 1985), chap. 7

77. Jon Sobrino, *Jesus the Liberator* (Maryknoll, N.Y.: Orbis, 1993), 267; cf. Leonardo Boff, "Martyrdom: An Attempt at Systematic Reflection," *Concilium* 163 (1983): 9.

78. William T. Cavanaugh, *Torture and Eucharist: Theology, Politics, and the Body of Christ* (Oxford: Blackwell, 1998), 61–62; see also 13, where Cavanaugh makes an analogous argument against liberationist attempts to expand the notion of sacrament to include the physical stimulus of any subjectively significant experience on the grounds that "if God always stands 'behind' the signs, then signs become interchangeable, and God never truly saturates any particular sign."

79. Gutiérrez, *Theology of Liberation*, 116. On pp. 117–18 Gutiérrez himself concedes that "encounter with the Lord under these conditions can disappear by giving way to what he himself brings forth and nourishes: love for humankind." Yet the most he can offer in response to what he acknowledges is "a real difficulty" is the empirically rather dubious claim that "where oppression and human liberation seem to make God irrelevant . . . there must blossom faith and hope in him who came to root out injustice and to offer, in an unforeseen way, total liberation."

80. Cavanaugh, *Torture and Eucharist*, 62.

81. Bell, *Liberation Theology*, 70.

82. In this context, Joerg Rieger has argued persuasively against attempts to interpret liberation theologies as forms of theological liberalism, maintaining that the liberationist turn to others militates equally against liberalism and conservatism by making it clear that "neither the self nor the texts of the church are in a position to usurp the place of God." Joerg Rieger, *God and the Excluded: Visions and Blindspots in Contemporary Theology* (Minneapolis: Fortress Press, 2001), 113.

83. Bell, *Liberation Theology*, 72.

84. Even Leonardo Boff's radical proposals for the transformation of power and responsibility in the Catholic Church recognizes a "charism of unity," exercised by those "who occupy positions of leadership within the community" as being "of prime importance." Boff, *Church: Charism and Power*, 163.

85. "Paradigmatic saints . . . correct or enlarge the community's moral vision, challenging the hardening of heart and loss of creative response." Johnson, *Friends of God and Prophets*, 238.

86. Marshall, *Trinity and Truth*, 203–4.

87. For an interpretation of the a posteriori character of these judgments, see Thiel, *Senses of Tradition*, 181-86.

88. "For instance, the anonymous *Life of Cuthbert* borrows verbatim the first chapter of Sulpicius [Severus's *Life of Martin of Tours*] and describes Cuthbert in language drawn straight from Athanasius." Brown, *Discipleship and Imagination*, 78. Even more remarkable is the fact that the African martyrs Perpetua and Felicity, though both nursing mothers at the time of their deaths, were persistently characterized in the liturgy as virgins until the reforms of Vatican II. See Maureen A. Tilley, "The Passion of Perpetua and Felicity," in *Searching the Scriptures*, ed. Elisabeth Schüssler Fiorenza (London: SCM, 1994), 2:851–52.

89. So Ruether, who concedes that the chief reasons for retaining Christian symbols are pragmatic and concludes that they are but "one cultural resource among others in the struggle for liberation that can meet and converge around the world only by being authentically rooted in many local contexts." *Women and Redemption* (London: SCM, 1998), 281; cf. 277.

90. See, e.g., Cone, *God of the Oppressed*, 33: "Jesus Christ is the Truth and thus stands in judgment over all statements about truth." Cf. Jacqueline Grant, *White Woman's Christ and Black Woman's Jesus: Feminist Christology and Womanist Response* (Atlanta: Scholars Press, 1989).

91. Rieger, *God and the Excluded*, 169.

92. Ibid., 173.

5. Discernment as Communal Discipline

1. Hans Urs von Balthasar, *Seeing the Form*, vol. 1 of *The Glory of the Lord: A Theological Aesthetics* (San Francisco: Ignatius, 1982), 215. See p. 61 above.

2. The importance of the turn to others in the shape of the saints and the poor should not be taken to imply that one's own experiences cannot be a source of knowledge of God, only that theologically productive exploitation of the self's experiences is more indirect than is supposed in, e.g., classic liberal theology: "Encountering its limits in relation to others . . . the process that Schleiermacher mistakenly assumed would be natural happens last: experience is opened up and led beyond itself" (Joerg Rieger, *God and the Excluded: Visions and Blindspots in Contemporary Theology* [Minneapolis: Fortress Press, 2001], 179).

3. It is this point rather than a counsel of social conservatism that lies at the heart of Paul's injunction that each should "remain in the condition in which you were called" (1 Cor. 7:20). See my discussion of this passage in *Difference and Identity: A Theological Anthropology* (Cleveland: Pilgrim, 2001), 108–9.

4. Gustavo Gutiérrez, "Option for the Poor," in *Systematic Theology: Perspectives from Liberation Theology*, ed. Jon Sobrino and Ignacio Ellacuría (Maryknoll, N.Y.: Orbis, 1996), 22; cf. Gutiérrez, *A Theology of Liberation: History, Politics, and Salvation* (Maryknoll, NY: Orbis, 1988), xx.

5. Gutiérrez identifies the preferential option for the poor as a response to Vatican II's call for the faithful to attend to the "signs of the times." Gutiérrez, "Option for the Poor," 23.

6. Ada María Isasi-Díaz, "*Mujerista* Narratives: Creating a New Heaven and a New Earth," in *Liberating Eschatology: Essays in Honor of Letty M. Russell*, ed. Margaret A. Farley and Serene Jones (Louisville: Westminster John Knox, 1999), 231.

7. Even in Catholicism the significance of canonization is understood as a matter of "sustain[ing] the hope of believers by proposing the saints to them as models and intercessors" (*Catechism of the Catholic Church* [Dublin: Veritas, 1994], §828)—a form of language that appears to suggest something less than absolute necessity.

8. The *Catechism of the Catholic Church* (§2448) speaks instead of a "preferential love" for the poor that appears designed to focus attention on the need of the poor for the help of the church rather than the converse. Cf. John Paul II's remarks in the encyclical *Sollicitudo Rei Socialis*, 42 (though compare the rather favorable interpretation by Gutiérrez in "Option for the Poor," 27).

9. Eva Feder Kittay, *Love's Labor: Essay on Women, Equality, and Dependency* (New York: Routledge, 1999. Kittay's spelling of the term is determined by the source from which she appropriates the Greek root. See p. 84 below.

10. Ibid., 92; cf. 29–30.

11. Specifically, she roots human equality in the fact that "we are all some mother's child." Ibid., 66; cf. 69.

12. Ibid., 62.

13. Ibid., 39–40, 55–57.

14. "The dependence of dependent persons obligates dependency workers in ways that situate them unequally with respect to others who are not similarly obligated." Ibid., 76.

15. "For the dependency worker, the well-being and thriving of the charge is the primary focus of the work." Ibid., 31.

16. Ibid., 132–33; cf. 107.

17. Although in 1 Cor. 9:3-12 and 1 Thess. 2:7-9 Paul makes much of not posing an economic burden on the communities he serves (while at the same time noting that he would be within his rights to do so), it remains the case that his ministry would have been impossible without the conscious decision of those communities to receive him hospitably and encourage him in his work. First Thessalonians in particular is testimony to the importance of this sense of being welcome for Paul's determination to persevere in his ministry.

18. Elizabeth Johnson suggests that without some model of care for the dead "who have been overcome and defeated in history . . . the movement for justice turns into a vicious mark of progress that just piles up more victims," but the idea that such care would actually benefit the dead (rather than just help to shape the understanding of the living) would seem to depend on the theologically questionable idea that the future of the dead "is still outstanding." Elizabeth A. Johnson, *Friends of God and Prophets: A Feminist Theological Reading of the Communion of Saints* (London: SCM, 1998), 176.

19. Augustine of Hippo, *City of God*, 10.1.

20. Thomas Aquinas, *Summa Theologiae* [hereafter *ST*] (London: Eyre & Spottiswood, 1964–1981), IIa IIae, qu. 101, art. 1.

21. *ST*, IIa IIae, qu. 102, art. 1.

22. *ST*, IIa IIae, qu. 102, art. 2.

23. Ibid.

24. *ST*, IIa IIae, qu. 102, art. 3, in both the reply and the response to Objection 2. Note, in this context, that piety is distinguished from distributive, legal justice insofar as it is rooted in a debt of obligation that cannot be reciprocated (as justice demands). See IIa IIae, qu. 101, art. 3.

25. *ST*, IIa IIae, qu. 102, art. 2.

26. *ST*, IIa IIae, qu. 103, art. 1.

27. Ibid.

28. *ST*, IIa IIae, qu. 103, art. 2.

29. "In every person there is some basis why another can look on him as superior. . . . It follows that we should all excel each other in showing honour." *ST*, IIa IIae, qu. 103, art. 2, ad 3 (translation slightly altered).

30. "God's dominion is absolute and primary over all creation and every creature in it, since everything is completely subordinated to his power. A man shares a limited likeness to God's control, inasmuch as he holds some particular power. . . . Therefore *dulia*, which pays the service due a man because he is master, is a virtue different from *latria*, with its offering of the service due to God's lordship over all." *ST*, IIa IIae, qu. 103, art. 3.

31. See *ST*, IIa IIaeI, qu. 103, art. 1.

32. Thus, Thomas argues that *dulia* must be given even to wicked rulers in as much as "in them honour is shown to the whole community over which they rule." *ST*, IIa IIae, qu. 103, art. 2, ad 2 (translation slightly altered).

33. *ST*, IIa IIae, qu. 103, art. 3.

34. *ST*, IIa IIaeI, qu. 58, art. 1.

35. *ST*, IIa IIaeI, qu. 58, art. 5, 7; cf. Ia IIae, qu. 60, art. 4, ad. 2

36. "Justice as a general virtue arises in the midst of the effort to articulate the relation between the common good of society and the particular good of the individual. According to Aquinas, the common good is not an 'alien good' juxtaposed with the particular good of the individual person. . . . Rather, society's common good, rightly understood, is at the same time the proper good of its particular members." Daniel M. Bell, Jr., *Liberation Theology after the End of History: The Refusal to Cease Suffering* (London: Routledge, 2001), 102–3.

37. *ST*, IIa IIae, qu. 103, art. 3.

38. See, e.g., Gutiérrez, *A Theology of Liberation*, 116.

39. Thus, the fact that God chooses the poor (Matt. 11:5 and par.; Luke 4:18; cf. 1 Cor. 1:26-28) is not a sign of their merit, but precisely of God's disregard of merit in pouring forth the blessings of the kingdom.

40. Former students of Union Theological Seminary, New York, will recognize that the inspiration for the following piece of exegesis comes from the Rev. Dr. James A. Forbes' sermon, "Hannah Rose."

41. The meaning of v. 5 is uncertain. The Hebrew reads literally "one portion to the face [*appayim*] ," and there is no convincing explanation of what this phrase

means (for thorough discussions of the grammar that come to opposite conclusions, cf. S. R. Driver, *Notes on the Hebrew Text and the Topography of the Books of Samuel* [Oxford: Clarendon, 1913], 7–8 and P. Kyle McCarter, *1 Samuel: A New Translation with Introduction, Notes & Commentary*, Anchor Bible [Garden City, N.Y.: Doubleday, 1980], 51–52). A number of commentators hold that the context implies Hannah received some sort of special treatment (cf. the NRSV's "a double portion"), but such material signs of favor do not seem narratively consistent with Peninnah's taunts. I follow the RSV on the grounds that its "one portion" highlights the main theme of the passage: Hannah's objective lack of status at family gatherings.

42. "Hannah's barrenness overrides the power of Elkanah's love." Walter Brueggemann, *First and Second Samuel* (Louisville: John Knox, 1990), 13. It takes no great stretch of the imagination to draw a parallel with the way that the church has consistently protested its love for the poor while generally avoiding open resistance to the forces that keep them in misery.

43. Ronald Thiemann, *Constructing a Public Theology: The Church in a Pluralistic Culture* (Louisville: Westminster/John Knox, 1991), 57. Among the examples Thiemann cites are the following characters from Matthew: a leper (8:2), a centurion (8:10), a paralytic (9:2), the woman with the hemorrhage (9:22), two blind men (9:29), the Canaanite woman (15:28), and the woman who anoints Jesus in the house of Simon (26:13). One could add to this list Luke's rather different account of the woman who anoints Jesus (Luke 7:36-50), the Samaritan leper (Luke 17:16), Zacchaeus (Luke 19:8), the repentant thief (Luke 23:42), the Samaritan woman (John 4:39), and Martha of Bethany (John 11:27).

44. In an analogous, if converse, fashion, the *dulia* that affirms the christoform life of the canonized needs also to involve a willingness to recognize and reject those features of every saint's life that are judged not to be conformed to Christ.

45. "Feminist theology's commitment to the marginalized is complex . . . not only because it will inevitably be difficult to say who the marginalized might be in any given situation, but also because my identification of the marginalized is an act of the privileged that is inevitably bound to fail." Mary McClintock Fulkerson, *Changing the Subject: Women's Discourses and Feminist Theology* (Eugene, Ore.: Wipf and Stock, 2001[1994]), 386.

46. For example, it seems doubtful that the lives of many of the canonized warrior-kings of the early Middle Ages embody the kind of commitment to the vulnerable that is decisive for the practice of *dulia* outlined here.

47. Hans Frei identifies the problem here succinctly: "To have a limit-language expressing a limit-experience is to reach beyond ourselves to where we hope to espy transcendence but may well end up discerning our own mirror image." Hans W. Frei, "Conflicts in Interpretation: Resolution, Armistice, or Co-existence?" in *Theology and Narrative: Selected Essays*, ed. George Hunsinger and William C. Placher (New York: Oxford University Press, 1993), 163.

48. Fulkerson, *Changing the Subject*, 156.

49. "If social practices such as ecclesial discipleship are embedded and constituted in other social relations, for instance the mode of production, civil, and cultural

processes . . . then it is highly problematic to conceive of a purely theological (or philosophical) construal of textual or biblical meanings." Ibid., 149.

50. Ibid., 374.

51. In this respect, there is good theological ground for the Catholic Church's refusal to canonize anyone before they have died.

6. Discernment as Personal Discipline

1. Nicholas Healy stresses the need to "broaden [the] scope and change [the] orientation" of traditional forms of inquiry "so that they include *explicit* analysis of the ecclesiological context as an integral part of properly *theological* reflection on the church." Nicholas M. Healy, *Church, World and the Christian Life: Practical-Prophetic Ecclesiology* (Cambridge: Cambridge University Press, 2000), 39.

2. Thomas Aquinas, *Summa Theologiae* [hereafter *ST*], Blackfriars ed. (London: Eyre & Spottiswood, 1964–1981), IIIa, qu. 8, art. 3.

3. See Augustine of Hippo, *City of God*, XIV.17-19, in *St. Augustine's City of God and Christian Doctrine*, vol. 2 of *Nicene and Post-Nicene Fathers*, First Series, ed. Philip Schaff (Grand Rapids, Mich.: Eerdmans, 1993).

4. Eugene F. Rogers, Jr., *Sexuality and the Christian Body: Their Way into the Triune God* (Oxford: Blackwell, 1999), 227. Erich Fuchs identifies an anticipation of Rogers's more positive evaluation of sexual desire (though, unlike Rogers's, one keyed to the end of procreation) in Lactantius, who argues (in his *Divine Institutes*, VI.23) that God "placed in bodies the most ardent desire of all living things, so that they might rush most avidly into these emotions and be able by this means to propagate." Quoted from Eric Fuchs, *Sexual Desire and Love: Origins and History of the Christian Ethic of Sexuality and Marriage* (New York: Seabury, 1983), 248.

5. Rowan Williams illustrates this point with reference to the way the character Ronald Merrick's recognition and rejection of his own homosexual desires lead him to ever-increasing levels of violence in Paul Scott's *The Raj Quartet* (San Francisco: HarperCollins, 1984). See Rowan Williams, "The Body's Grace," in *Our Selves, Our Souls and Bodies: Sexuality and the Household of God*, ed. Charles Hefling (Cambridge, Mass.: Cowley, 1996), 58.

6. Augustine of Hippo, *Confessions*, I.i.1.

7. Rogers, *Sexuality and the Christian Body*, 225.

8. See p. 2 above.

9. Paul's advice in 1 Corinthians 7 was understood to imply the superiority of celibacy to marriage throughout the patristic and medieval periods. It was not until the Reformation that the normative status of this judgment was effectively challenged.

10. Linda Woodhead, "Sex in a Wider Context," in *Sex These Days: Essays on Theology, Sexuality and Society*, ed. Jon Davies and Gerard Loughlin (Sheffield: Sheffield Academic Press, 1997), 114. See also, in this context, the evidence for ecclesiastically sanctioned same-sex unions in John Boswell, *The Marriage of Likeness: Same-Sex Unions in Pre-Modern Europe* (London: Fontana, 1996).

11. "Marriage bears an analogy to the trinitarian life in that it grants ungrudging if not unlimited space and time to human love" (Rogers, *Sexuality and the*

Christian Body, 201). The same point could be made of celibate vocations within the church.

12. Karen Labacqz, "Appropriate Vulnerability," in *Sexuality and the Sacred: Sources for Theological Reflection*, ed. James B. Nelson and Sandra P. Longfellow (Louisville: Westminster John Knox, 1994), 256–61.

13. Compare Robert Jenson: "Who devalues the body? Those for whom its gestures make no commitments, or those for whom they can make irrevocable commitments? Those who find freedom in casual nakedness, or those who reserve this most visible word for those to whom they have something extraordinary to say?" Robert W. Jenson, *Visible Words: The Interpretation and Practice of Christian Sacraments* (Philadelphia: Fortress Press, 1978), 24–25; cited in Rogers, *Sexuality and the Christian Body*, 213.

14. "The conclusion to which the reader is drawn is that Christ himself is defiled by fornication and that fornication is a form of infidelity to Christ." Woodhead, "Sex in a Wider Context," 111.

15. Labacqz, "Appropriate Vulnerability," 259.

16. As Maximus the Confessor insists, "We do not become this body [of Christ] through the loss of our own bodies." St. Maximos the Confessor, *Centuries on Theology and the Incarnate Dispensation of the Son of God, Written for Thalassius*, II.84, in *The Philokalia*, vol. 2, ed. G. E. H. Palmer, Philip Sheridan, Kallistos Ware (London: Faber and Faber, 1981).

17. Dale B. Martin, *The Corinthian Body* (New Haven: Yale University Press, 1995), 177. Martin draws here on the work of John Winkler, *The Constraints of Desire: The Anthropology of Sex and Gender in Ancient Greece* (New York: Routledge, 1990), 37–41.

18. That later Christians were not altogether comfortable with Paul's emphasis on the power of the body here is suggested by the fact that a number of Greek manuscripts (including the *textus receptus*) append "and in your spirit" to the end of v. 20.

19. Most commentators, including C. K. Barrett (*A Commentary on the First Epistle to the Corinthians*, 2nd ed. [London: Adam & Charles Black, 1971], 151), Hans Conzelmann (*1 Corinthians: A Commentary on the First Epistle to the Corinthians*, Hermeneia [Philadelphia: Fortress Press, 1975], 112), Richard B. Hays, (*First Corinthians* [Louisville: John Knox, 1997], 106), Jean Héring (*La première épitre de Saint Paul aux Corinthiens* [Neuchâtel: Delachaux & Niestlé, 1949], 49), and Christophe Senft (*La première épitre de Saint Paul aux Corinthiens* [Neuchâtel: Delachaux & Niestlé, 1979], 85) understand Paul to be speaking of individual bodies in these two verses, but Orr and Walther rightly note that the grammar suggests otherwise (William F. Orr and James Arthur Walther, *I Corinthians: A New Translation*, Anchor Bible [Garden City, N.Y.: Doubleday, 1976], 200; see also Roy A. Harrisville, *1 Corinthians*, Augsburg Commentary on the New Testament [Minneapolis: Augsburg, 1987], 103–4). Given that Paul shows himself perfectly capable of using the plural when he wants to (cf. v. 15), and that the language echoes the unambiguously collective imagery of 1 Cor. 3:16-17 ("you [pl.] are God's temple, and God's Spirit dwells

in you [pl.] . . . for God's temple is holy, and you [pl.] are that temple"), there seems every reason to take seriously Paul's use of the singular here.

20. In reflecting on this passage, however, Paul Evdokimov argues that there is no good theological (versus historical-critical) reason to refer the text to physiological virginity, since the "Church absolutely forbids viewing the marriage union as a defilement." Paul Evdokimov, *The Sacrament of Love: The Nuptial Mystery in Light of the Orthodox Tradition* (Crestwood, N.Y.: St. Vladimir's Seminary Press, 1985), 66.

21. Ignatius of Antioch, *Polycarp* 5.2, in *Early Christian Fathers*, ed. Cyril C. Richardson (New York: Collier, 1970).

22. See, e.g., Clement of Alexandria, *Stromateis*, III.71–72, in *Alexandrian Christianity*, ed. Henry Chadwick and John E. L. Oulton (London: SCM, 1954). Note that this position did not prevent Clement from praising marriage as superior to celibacy on the grounds that the unmarried person "is in most respects untried" and "takes thought only for himself" (*Stromateis*, VII.70); but he explicitly opposed married love and sexual desire, arguing that a "man who marries for the sake of begetting children must practise continence so that it is not desire he feels for his wife, whom he ought to love, that he may beget children with a chaste and controlled will" (*Stromateis*, III.58).

23. Tertullian, *To His Wife*, II.8, in *Fathers of the Third Century*, vol. 4 of *The Ante-Nicene Fathers*, ed. Alexander Roberts and James Donaldson (Grand Rapids, Mich.: Eerdmans, 1985).

24. Fuchs, *Sexual Desire and Love*, 97.

25. Jerome's position is set out in his two treatises *Against Helvidius* and *Against Jovinian*, as well as in his Letters XXII, "To Eustochium," and CXXX, "To Demetrias." Gregory of Nyssa's *On Virginity*, though lacking the polemical edge of Jerome's work, is all the more remarkable because the author himself may well have been married at the time he wrote it.

26. Speaking of the patristic era, Fuchs notes: "There is no such thing during this whole period as a 'religious marriage'. Marriage remains essentially a familial and earthly affair, even if it is acknowledged as a gift from God. Anything to do with marital rights comes from civil legislation." Fuchs, *Sexual Desire and Love*, 93. Cf. Boswell, *The Marriage of Likeness*, 111: "In the West the church made very little effort to regulate marriage before the tenth century, and only declared it a sacrament and required ecclesiastical involvement in 1215."

27. "The absence . . . in the patristic tradition generally of a positive theology of marriage is probably due both to their monastic training and to their instinctive opposition to the sexual cults that characterized ancient culture." John Meyendorff, *Christ in Eastern Christian Thought* (Washington, D.C.: Corpus, 1969), 196–97.

28. As Boswell points out, celibacy was "viewed as morally questionable by mainstream Judaism, and as impractical and pointless by the vast majority of pagans." Boswell, *The Marriage of Likeness*, 110.

29. In addition to the reference to the married state of "the other apostles" in 1 Corinthians 9, the New Testament contains other indications that husband and wife teams were prominent among early Christian evangelists. In addition to Priscilla

and Aquila, who worked closely with Paul (Acts 18:1-3; 18-19) and whom the latter credits with having saved his life (Rom. 16:3-4), Andronicus and Junia (Rom. 16:7), Philologus and Julia, and (possibly) "Nereus and his sister" (Rom. 16:15) may be representatives of this phenomenon.

30. 1 Cor. 7:14 mentions children in passing, but only as a typical feature of married life and not as its purpose. 1 Tim. 2:15 avers that a woman "will be saved through childbearing," but that is rather different from the claim that childbearing is the purpose of marriage. The evangelists' report of Jesus' debate with the Sadducees (Matt. 22:23-32 and pars.) does correlate marriage and procreation (following the provisions for levirate marriage in Deut. 25:5, the surviving brother marries "in order to raise up children" for the deceased). But, as all three versions make clear, the point of Jesus' teaching here is the doctrine of the resurrection, not the character of marriage.

31. "Here the good of the species comes before that of the individuals. Society is only interested in the sociological and biological content of nuptial unions." Evdokimov, *The Sacrament of Love*, 41.

32. "In both Latin- and Greek-speaking Europe the lack of celerity in developing an official Christian liturgy [for marriage] doubtless reflected the persistent ambivalence Christians—especially ascetic leaders—felt about the mostly worldly purposes of matrimony." Boswell, *The Marriage of Likeness*, 168.

33. Ibid., xx; cf. 171–72, where Boswell suggests that it was only in the twelfth century—virtually the same time at which the church began to take a more active role in the solemnization of unions—that people expressed the expectation that love was the foundation of marriage.

34. "In premodern Europe marriage usually began as a property arrangement, was in its middle mostly about raising children, and ended about love." Ibid., xxi. Boswell goes on to note that in the contemporary United States the situation is precisely the reverse: most marriages begin with love and end with formal arrangements for the distribution of property.

35. Thus, when in his *On the Making of Humankind* Gregory of Nyssa "asserts that, had we retained . . . equality with angels, 'neither should we have needed marriage that we might multiply' (17.2), he is contrasting [the legitimate] use of our God-given sexuality with the 'dynastic' form of marriage characteristic of late antique society." John Behr, "The Rational Animal: A Rereading of Gregory of Nyssa's *De hominis opificio*," in *Journal of Early Christian Studies* 7, no. 2 (1999): 246.

36. Indeed, among the literate classes of Greco-Roman society, it was pretty much taken for granted that such needs would be met outside of marriage, at least for men.

37. Evdokimov, *The Sacrament of Love*, 43.

38. Ibid., 67; cf. 83, where chastity is defined as both enabling and including "the full consecration of one's life."

39. See, e.g., Justin Martyr, *The First Apology*, XXIX, in vol. 1 of *The Ante-Nicene Fathers*, ed. Alexander Roberts and James Donaldson (Grand Rapids, Mich.: Eerdmans, 1985); Clement of Alexandria, *Stromateis* III.95-97, in *Alexandrian Christology*; Ambrose of Milan, *In Lucam*, I.45, in *Patrologia Latina* 15:1632B. A variant on this theme is found in Methodius of Olympus (*De Castimonia*, in *Patrologia Graeca*

18:49C) and Jerome (Letter XXII, "To Eustochium," 20, in *Jerome: Letters and Select Works*, vol. 6 of *Nicene and Post-Nicene Fathers*, Second Series, ed. Philip Schaff and Henry Wace (Boston: Hendrickson, 1995), who praise marriage on the ground that it produces martyrs and virgins for the church.

40. See, e.g., *De Genesi ad litteram*, III.xxi.33. In *Contra Julianum*, IV.xi.57, however, Augustine appears to imply that the sacramental character of marriage is present even outside the church. Both texts are cited in Fuchs, *Sexual Desire and Love*, 117–18.

41. Saint Augustine, *The Good of Marriage*, chap. 24, in *St. Augustine: Treatises on Marriage and Other Subjects*, vol. 27 of *The Fathers of the Church* (Washington, D.C.: Catholic University of America Press, 1955), 48. In light of this proviso, Eugene Rogers's contention (in *Sexuality and the Christian Body*, 74n18) that Augustine actually "favors the sanctifying good of marriage from the way he contrasts it with the other two" goods of progeny and faithfulness strikes me as doubtful.

42. S. Thomae Aquinatis, *Summa Theologica*, 6 vols., ed. Rubeis, Billuart, et al., *Supplementum* IIIae, qu. 49, art. 3 (Turin: Marietti, 1927).

43. Thus, it is because "the conjugal act is destined primarily by nature for the begetting of children" that those who make use of contraceptive devices "sin [*agunt*] against nature and commit a deed which is shameful and intrinsically vicious." Pius XI, *On Christian Marriage*, §55, in *The Church and the Reconstruction of the Modern World: The Social Encyclicals of Pius XI*, ed. Terence P. McLaughlin, C.S.B. (Garden City, N.Y.: Image Books, 1957). The same point is made in less harsh language by Paul VI in *Humane vitae*, §13.

44. Evdokimov, *The Sacrament of Love*, 67; but cf. 25: "Although marriage is an ecclesial institution, the perfect are called nevertheless to limit the usage of it and to direct themselves toward complete continence."

45. John Chrysostom, *Homily III on Marriage*, 3; cited in Evdokimov, *The Sacrament of Love*, 68.

46. Evdokimov, *The Sacrament of Love*, 67; cf. 114.

47. Ibid., 80.

48. "Evdokimov argues forcefully that it is not the case that marriage is for satisfaction, monasticism for sanctification, marriage for sexuality, monasticism for celibacy. Rather both marriage and monasticism are for sanctification." Rogers, *Sexuality and the Christian Body*, 78. See note 56 below.

49. Ibid., 72–73.

50. So for Evdokimov the relationship of spouses is grounded in the fact that "the one through the other they look at Christ, and it is 'the Other,' His love, that is the gift of grace." Evdokimov, *The Sacrament of Love*, 80; cited in Rogers, *Sexuality and the Christian Body*, 83.

51. Williams, "The Body's Grace," 63, partially quoted in Rogers, *Sexuality and the Christian Body*, 71.

52. ". . . marriage does not merely ratify a pre-existing relationship, but establishes this relationship by placing it before the face of God, friends, family, church, and state." Woodhead, "Sex in a Wider Context," 109.

53. Stanley Hauerwas, *A Community of Character: Toward a Constructive Christian Social Ethic* (Notre Dame, Ind.: University of Notre Dame Press, 1981), 172.

54. "The primary problem morally is learning how to love and care for this stranger to whom you find yourself married." Ibid., 172.

55. "The wedding rite symbolically summarizes the entire married life." Evdokimov, *The Sacrament of Love*, 70.

56. "The married as well as the monastic state are two forms of chastity, each one appropriate to its own mode of being." Ibid., 67.

57. Woodhead, "Sex in a Wider Context," 108–10.

58. To the extent that reproductive technology (as well as practices of adoption) work to ensure greater "control" here, the church has reason to ask whether such practices are consistent with the confession of a Christ who prefers to confront us in a form we do not expect.

59. "The Christian family today, in nourishing the human capacity for compassion and solidarity, can provide a school for and support to Christian commitment which was once much more easily embodied in the renunciation of kin ties and of the bondedness to social structures represented by marital, procreative sexuality." Lisa Sowle Cahill, *Sex, Gender and Christian Ethics* (Cambridge, UK: Cambridge University Press, 1996), 182.

60. For an excellent discussion of these issues in the context of the wider Christian (and more specifically Catholic) tradition of teaching on marriage, see ibid., chaps. 5–7.

61. "The Christian normalization of permanency and sexual fidelity in marriage has, over the centuries, tended . . . to decrease the usefulness of marriage as a tool to secure political and economic goods. With these developments came a proportionate rise in the companionate value of marriage." Ibid., 196–97.

62. Rogers, *Sexuality and the Christian Body*, 248.

63. This is not to imply that the benefits of the protocols of chastity redound only to the individual concerned. While their aim is certainly to provide a framework for individual cultivation of discernment, these individuals also serve the community in their callings insofar as they draw attention to such persons' destiny of eschatological union with Christ and thereby stand as witness for the community of the fact that they are the objects of God's desire.

7. Discernment in Ecclesial Formation

1. In v. 22 Paul says that the wealthier Corinthians *kataphronein* the church. This word is normally (and quite justifiably) rendered "show contempt" or "despise," but it literally refers to "disordered thinking" (see Rom. 2:4, where it is best translated "to misunderstand" or "to have wrong ideas about").

2. For what follows in this paragraph, see Dale B. Martin, *The Corinthian Body* (New Haven: Yale University Press, 1995), 194–96; cf. 74, where Martin interprets this verse in slightly narrower terms, arguing that by "body" Paul means "both the body of the crucified Christ represented by the bread and the communal body of Christ represented by the gathered church."

3. Note that Paul makes his claim that "we who are many are one body, for we all partake of the one bread" (1 Cor. 10:17) in the context of admonishing the Corinthians to avoid meat sacrificed to idols, lest they wind up in communion with demons (1 Cor. 10:20).

4. Augustine imagines Christ speaking to him in graphic terms: "I am the food of strong men; grow, and thou shalt feed upon me; nor shall thou convert me, like the food of thy flesh, into thee, but thou shall be converted into me." Augustine of Hippo, *Confessions*, VII.x, in *St. Augustine: Confessions, Letters*, vol. 1 of *Nicene and Post-Nicene Fathers*, First Series, ed. Philip Schaff (Grand Rapids, Mich.: Eerdmans, 1886).

5. Martin, *The Corinthian Body*, 196.

6. "In Paul's logic, one puts one's own body in a state of vulnerability to disease by dissecting the body of Christ. By opening Christ's body to schism, they open their own bodies to disease and death" (Ibid., 194). Note in this context that Paul does not imply that the ill effects of the Corinthian eucharistic practice affect only those responsible for the schism. Rather, the dissolution of the body puts all the members at risk.

7. This claim would be rejected by, e.g., Quakers, who claim Christian identity while practicing neither baptism nor communion. Given that assessing the ecclesial status of such groups lies beyond the scope of the present work, suffice it to note that my claim does cover all Christian groups that view practice baptism and communion.

8. Robert Jenson characterizes the Eucharist as the church's "only . . . fully developed, clearly contoured and solidly instituted visible word of the gospel simply as such and as a whole." Robert W. Jenson, *Visible Words: The Interpretation and Practice of Christian Sacraments* (Philadelphia: Fortress Press, 1978), 62. Cf. Eugene Rogers's observation that in the Orthodox churches "marriage derives its sacramentality from the eucharist celebrated during the Eastern matrimonial rite." Eugene F. Rogers, Jr., *Sexuality and the Christian Body: Their Way into the Triune God* (Oxford: Blackwell, 1999), 254.

9. William C. Cavanaugh, *Torture and Eucharist: Theology, Politics, and the Body of Christ* (Oxford: Blackwell, 1998), 205–6.

10. "The individual Christian relates not to other Christians but directly to Christ. . . . Furthermore, the increased localization of the sacred in the Eucharistic host in effect secularized all that lay beyond it." Ibid., 214.

11. Ibid., 216–20.

12. Ibid., 229.

13. ". . . not because God needs anything, but simply because it is good for us to belong to God alone." Augustine of Hippo, *City of God*, XIX.23, ed. Vernon J. Bourke (Garden City, N.Y.: Image Books, 1958); cf. X.5.

14. "Until Christ comes again, His body on earth is always a body under construction." Cavanaugh, *Torture and Eucharist*, 233.

15. Ibid., 251.

16. He also notes that back in the seventeenth century the Synod of Santiago excommunicated slave traders, while in the immediate aftermath of the First Vatican

Council the archbishop of Santiago issued a statement of excommunication against Chilean legislators who had voted for laws forbidding clerics from enacting pontifical decrees judged injurious to state security. See ibid., 254.

17. Bishop Carlos Camus, cited in ibid., 256.

18. Ibid., 263.

19. Certain lines of Reformed thinking (e.g., the *Scots Confession*) identify discipline as a mark of the church, as do the Mennonites and other groups that trace their origins to the "radicals" of the Reformation era. Nor were such sentiments entirely absent from Luther. See, e.g., *The Sermon on the Mount and the Magnificat*, vol. 21 of *Luther's Works*, American ed., ed. Jaroslav Pelikan (Philadelphia: Fortress Press, 1955), 56.

20. See Bruce D. Marshall, *Trinity and Truth* (Cambridge, UK: Cambridge University Press, 2000), 192–204; see especially 198n22: "while the sense of any utterance is surely that which the speaker intends it to have, it does not have that sense *because* the speaker intends it to."

21. "In such instances of denial and exclusion from the table, despite the propriety of word and gesture, Eucharist is rendered empty ritual." M. Shawn Copeland, "Body, Race, and Being: Theological Anthropology in the Context of Performing and Subverting Eucharist," in *Constructive Theology: A Contemporary Approach to Classical Themes*, ed. Serene Jones and Paul Lakeland (Minneapolis: Fortress Press, 2004), 112.

22. As Robert Jenson points out, as originally coined by Augustine, the phrase "visible words" was opposed not to audible but to invisible words, and referred to "God's own knowledge and intention of himself and his works." Jenson, *Visible Words*, 4–5.

23. Needless to say, this is not to argue that the mass is the only legitimate form of corporate Christian worship, but only to note that it is the defining act of specifically Christian worship, as seems to have been the case in Corinth (cf. 1 Cor. 11:20; 14:26) and was clearly the case in, e.g., the Roman church of Justin Martyr's day (see Justin Martyr, *First Apology*, LXVII, in *The Apostolic Fathers with Justin Martyr and Irenaeus*, vol. 1 of *The Ante-Nicene Fathers*, ed. Alexander Roberts and James Donaldson (Grand Rapids, Mich.: Eerdmans, 1985).

24. "The whole object reality of our community is the body of Christ. When we pray, we properly look right at each other. When we gather, we gather around the bread and cup. . . . When we seek Christ's peace, it is in the kiss of the fellow believer." Jenson, *Visible Words*, 46; cf. 39.

25. Rogers, *Sexuality and the Christian Body*, 240.

26. Robert W. Jenson, *Systematic Theology*, 2 vols. (New York: Oxford University Press, 1997–1999), 1:206; cf. Jenson, *Visible Words*, 111–12.

27. Douglas Farrow characterizes this problem (though with reference to Barth rather than Jenson) as one of "too much real presence" in which Jesus' "absence is more apparent than real." Douglas Farrow, *Ascension and Ecclesia: On the Significance of the Doctrine of the Ascension for Ecclesiology and Christian Cosmology* (Edinburgh: T. & T. Clark, 1999), 250. For an analogous critique focused specifically on Jenson,

see Douglas Farrow, et al., "Robert Jenson's *Systematic Theology*: Three Responses," in *International Journal of Systematic Theology* 1, no. 1 (March 1999): 92–93.

28. While Paul seems in most respects unconcerned about the situation of those outside the church (see, e.g., 1 Cor. 5:12), his remarks about non-Christian Jews in Rom. 9:1-3 and 10:1 express something of the position I describe here.

29. See the stories of the calling of Matthew (Matt. 9:9-13 and pars.) and Zacchaeus (Luke 19:1-10) for Jesus' treatment of tax collectors in particular.

30. For a brief account of the way in which the reception of the Eucharist came to be separated from baptism in the Western church, see J. D. C. Fisher, *Christian Initiation: Baptism in the Medieval West* (London: SPCK, 1965), chap. 6.

31. Based on Hebrew and Aramaic parallels, Hartman argues that the "into the name" phraseology originally referred to the Christian understanding that Jesus provided "the referential frame which dictates the meaning of the rite" (Lars Hartman, *'Into the Name of the Lord Jesus': Baptism in the Early Church* [Edinburgh: T. & T. Clark, 1997], 44), though even this fairly schematic view suggests some sort of transition from one sphere of existence to another.

32. Raymond Burnish, *The Meaning of Baptism: A Comparison of the Teaching and Practice of the Fourth Century with the Present Day* (London: Alcuin Club/SPCK, 1985), 115.

33. See especially Paul's rather nonchalant references to his own baptismal practice in 1 Cor. 1:14-17 which, while certainly not to be taken as any denigration of baptism itself, does suggest a relatively informal process of Christian initiation. Cf. also the theologically indifferent reference to baptism on behalf of the dead later in the same letter (1 Cor. 15:29).

34. For the development of a formal renunciation of Satan into the baptismal liturgy, see Henry Ansgar Kelly, *The Devil at Baptism: Ritual, Theology, and Drama* (Ithaca, N.Y.: Cornell University Press, 1985), chap. 6.

35. Hippolytus, *Apostolic Tradition*, 16; cited in Kelly, *The Devil at Baptism*, 85.

36. Fisher, *Christian Initiation*, 6–7, 30–31. *Competentes* was the normal Latin designation for those who had been received for baptism; *electi* appears to have been a peculiarly Roman term.

37. The elaboration of prebaptismal exorcistic rites (perhaps via certain forms of Gnosticism) under the influence of the kind of speculation on the presence of "sin demons" in the unbaptized is found in works like the *Testaments of the Twelve Patriarchs* and the *Shepherd of Hermas*. Though the rites persisted, however, the notion of literal demonic possession of the unbaptized was not characteristic of orthodox circles. See Kelly, *The Devil at Baptism*, chaps. 3–4.

38. See ibid., 85–86.

39. Ibid., 140, with reference to the fifth-century Syrian text *The Testament of Our Lord* 2.1-6.

40. See Cyril of Jerusalem, *Mystagogical Cathechesis* 3.1, in *The Works of St. Cyril of Jerusalem*, vol. 2, ed. A. A. Stephenson and L. P. McCauley (Washington, D.C.: Catholic University of America, 1970), 169. Cf. *Catechism of the Catholic Church* (Dublin: Veritas, 1994), §1289.

41. Some have taken the fact that Justin Martyr fails to make any mention of postbaptismal anointing when describing baptism in his *First Apology* as evidence that the rite was not being practiced in Rome in the mid-second century. For a review of the arguments on both sides of the debate, see J. D. C. Fisher, *Confirmation: Then and Now* (London: SPCK, 1978), 11–21.

42. "It is also necessary that he should be anointed who is baptized; so that, having received the chrism, that is, the anointing, he may be anointed of God, and have in him the grace of Christ." Cyprian, *Epistle LXIX* in *Fathers of the Third Century: Hippolytus, Cyprian, Caius, Novatian, Appendix*, vol. 5 of *The Ante-Nicene Fathers*, ed. Alexander Roberts and James Donaldson (Edinburgh: T. & T. Clark, n.d.), 376; cf. 378 (*Epistle LXXI*): "For then finally can they be fully sanctified, and be the sons of God, if they be born of each sacrament."

43. Hippolytus, *The Apostolic Tradition*, 21; cited in J. D. C. Fisher, *Confirmation*, 52–55. Hippolytus records the Roman postbaptismal anointing was divided into a presbyteral unction followed by an episcopal one. As noted in the *Catholic Catechism* (§1291), this fact facilitated the subsequent disjunction of the latter from baptism in Western practice.

44. For a historical summary of this development, see Fisher, *Christian Initiation*, chap. 8. Cf. Fisher, *Confirmation*, chap. 9.

45. "If prayer for the coming to individuals of the Spirit simply *as such*, with the laying on of hands, anointing, or some other profound gesture, is offered otherwise than as the conclusion of baptism, either this prayer is not meant seriously or baptism is effectively repudiated" (Robert W. Jenson, "The Sacraments," in *Christian Dogmatics*, 2 vols., ed. Carl E. Braaten and Robert W. Jenson [Philadelphia: Fortress Press, 1984], II, 329). In defense of Western practice, the *Catholic Catechism* avers (§1292) that it "more clearly expresses [than the Eastern custom] the communion of the new Christian with the bishop as the guarantor and servant of the unity . . . of the church."

46. See, e.g., Cyril of Jerusalem, *Mystagogical Cathechesis* 1.4–9, in *The Works of St. Cyril*, vol. 2, 155–59.

47. See Fisher's suggestion that the presbyteral postbaptismal unction described by Hippolytus relates to the "Second rather than the Third Person of the Trinity" as a symbol "of the union of the baptized with Christ and incorporation into his Messianic body." Fisher, *Confirmation*, 52.

48. As Alexander Schmemann puts it, "the whole Church is charged, enriched and fulfilled when another child of God is integrated into her life, and becomes a member of Christ's body." Alexander Schmemann, *Of Water and the Spirit: A Liturgical Study of Baptism* (Crestwood, N.Y.: St. Vladimir's Seminary Press, 1991), 18.

49. Note, for example, the fate in the Western church of the prebaptismal "scrutinies," which presumably originated as examinations of a candidate's character and knowledge of the faith, but which by Augustine's time seem to have been merged with the prebaptismal exorcisms. See Kelly, *The Devil at Baptism*, 114–18, 204–10; cf. Fisher, *Christian Initiation*, 8–9.

50. Schmemann, *Of Water and the Spirit*, 29.

51. This point is acknowledged by even a staunch supporter of believers' baptism like James McClendon, whose own rather tentative suggestion that baptism be reserved for adolescence or even adulthood (on the grounds that a "'Yes' to God and faith and church is hardly meaningful unless a 'No' is psychologically possible") merely highlights the sociological difficulties attending any attempt to preserve the confessional character of baptism in a situation of *de facto* ecclesiastical "establishment." James Wm. McClendon, Jr., *Doctrine*, vol. 2 of *Systematic Theology* (Nashville: Abingdon, 1994), 394.

52. "If the church means expectation of the eschaton, baptism will mean a radical break with the past. If the church is, at a time and place, the dominant social group at prayer, baptism will be a religious addition to name-giving." Jenson, *Visible Words*, 149.

53. Here it is worth recalling Tertullian's classic remark on the defining "peculiarities" of the church recognized by his pagan contemporaries: "it is mainly the deeds of a love so noble that lead many to put a brand upon us. 'See,' they say, 'how they love one another', for themselves are animated by mutual hatred; 'how they are ready even to die for one another,' for they themselves will sooner put to death." Tertullian, *Apology*, 39, in *Latin Christianity: Its Father, Tertullian*, vol. 3 of *The Ante-Nicene Fathers*, ed. Alexander Roberts and James Donaldson (Edinburgh: T. & T. Clark, n.d.).

54. Robert W. Jenson, "The Church and the Sacraments," in *The Cambridge Companion to Christian Doctrine*, ed. Colin E. Gunton (Cambridge, UK: Cambridge University Press, 1997), 210.

55. So John of Damascus exegetes Paul by writing that "since we partake of the one bread, we all become one body of Christ and one blood, and members of one another, being of one body with (*sussomoi*) Christ." John of Damascus, *Exposition of the Orthodox Faith*, XIII, in *Hilary of Poitiers, John of Damascus*, vol. 9 of *Nicene and Post-Nicene Fathers*, Second Series, ed. Philip Schaff and Henry Wace (Boston: Hendrickson, 1995), 84.

8. Seeing the Divine Image

1. Ephraim Radner, *The End of the Church: A Pneumatology of Christian Division in the West* (Grand Rapids, Mich.: Eerdmans, 1998). Radner organizes the book as a series of studies focusing on the impact of division on the exercise of authority in the church, the identification of saints, ordained ministry, the Eucharist, and penance.

2. Ibid., 57.

3. See Radner's discussion of the Catholic response to Jansenist miracles in ibid., 116–18.

4. "The actual pneumatic force of (true) martyrdom . . . is necessarily transferred from the individual life and death itself and its specific contours to a more formal association of that life to certain institutional [or, among Protestants,

doctrinal] claims. As with miracle, martyrdom as a pneumatic event becomes clear only retrospectively, through the authoritative confirmation of institutional loyalty." Ibid., 126.

5. Ibid., 307–8; cf. the discussion of the relationship between the Eucharist and the ecclesial "body" offered by the Protestant Jean Claude and the Catholic Fénélon on 252–54 and 264–65.

6. See the discussion of the history of interpretation of this passage in ibid., 316–19.

7. He speaks of using "Scripture itself to bring into relief a proper pneumatology of absence" in ibid., 27–28.

8. In support of the contention that the divided Israel was bereft of the Spirit, Radner cites Stephen's speech in Acts 7, as well as texts like Psalm 106 and Isa. 29:9-16; 63:10-19.

9. Radner, *The End of the Church*, 37, 39.

10. "The restoration of the remnant is not the unveiling, let alone the vindication, of the 'true church' from amid its travails, but rather the gracious action of recreating a united people out of the dust of their past obliteration." Ibid., 36.

11. Ibid., 171.

12. Radner views as especially distressing the degree to which this incapacity extends even to the discernment of division as an occasion for repentance. See ibid., 276–79; cf. 25, where he laments the way in which the enthusiasm for diversity in much contemporary ecumenical discussion makes the work of the Spirit "almost synonymous with scriptural and ecclesial disintegration."

13. Ibid., 195.

14. Ibid., 200–203.

15. This is because "'head' and 'body', that is, Christ and the Church, we know are grasped by us as a single person . . . and so let us not hesitate when we move from 'head' to the 'body', or vice versa, even while we are speaking of one and the same person." Augustine, *De Doctrina Christiana*, III.44; cited in Radner, *The End of the Church*, 217.

16. Following George Lindbeck, Radner identifies the Spirit as a "relational attribute" rather than an "inherent property" of the church. Radner, *The End of the Church*, 34.

17. Of course, Paul also speaks of the Spirit dwelling in Christians (Rom. 8:9, 11; 1 Cor. 3:16; cf. John 14:17), but insofar as he is here drawing an analogy with the temple, the point seems to be more a matter of divine claim *on* the members of the community than a temporally extended presence of the Spirit *in* them (cf. Deut. 14:24; 2 Chron. 6:20 and 1 Kings 8:27; 2 Chron. 2:6; 6:18; but see 2 Tim. 1:14, which does seem to suggest a more "static" sense of presence).

18. Radner argues that the rhetoric of earlier divisions did not reflect the lack of confidence in the integrity of the church that is found in post-Reformation Europe (see especially the discussion of Athanasius in *The End of the Church*, 70n27), but surely here, too, one might query whether this confidence was justified. Indeed, over against Radner's nostalgia for the spirit of the medieval and patristic churches, it

is worth asking whether it might not be possible to interpret the divisions of the Reformation as the judgment of God on a church that was all too confident of its capacity to discern the Spirit's presence or absence in the world. Radner himself notes that such sentiments were mooted by the Jansenist Abbé de Saint-Cyran (*The End of the Church*, 353).

19. Ibid., 133.

20. Urban VIII's reforms to the canonization process were in no small part a response to Protestant attacks on the cult of the saints and, as such, were characterized by a decreasing emphasis on miracles in favor of "heroic virtue"—the latter strongly correlated with "subordination to the guidance of ecclesiastical hierarchy and observance of the sacraments" (Kathleen Ann Myers, "Redeemer of the Americas: Rosa de Lima, the Dynamics of Identity, and Canonization," in *Colonial Saints: Discovering the Holy in the Americas*, ed. Allan Greer and Jodi Blinkoff [New York: Routledge, 2003], 261; cf. 258). While this focus on submission to authority doubtless reflects the kind of rigidification Radner laments, it is important to remember that the practice of canonization has always been colored by the particular, temporally circumscribed interpretations of saintly behavior (e.g., the large number of warrior-kings canonized in the early Middle Ages).

21. Radner, *The End of the Church*, 350.

22. Hütter specifies that catechetical theology "is concerned with gradually accommodating a person to the faith praxis," while intratextual theology "is concerned with maintaining the praxis of Christian faith in the most varied life situations and with interpreting these situations within the context of faith praxis." Reinhard Hütter, *Suffering Divine Things: Theology as Church Practice* (Grand Rapids, Mich.: Eerdmans, 2000), 50–51.

23. Creaturely predicates could, of course, truly be applied to God in the form of *denial*; but since all possible predicates (including the predicate of transcendence insofar as it, too, can be known and used by creatures only within a distinctly inner-worldly, creaturely context) would be equally subject to denial, it would be impossible to use this kind of radical apophaticism as a means for acquiring the kind of precise delimitation of divinity over against the nondivine that is necessary to qualify as knowledge.

24. "The economy of grace is a work of *grace*, the pure and uncaused turning of God to that which is not himself . . . a genuine turning *toward* . . . which has as its end the creation and maintenance of another reality with its own substance and dignity. It is a turning, in other words, which bestows life. And what is manifest in that turning is not a mere accidental or fleeting episode in the divine being, but its deep, constant character: to be for the creature is who God *is*." John Webster, "The Human Person," in *The Cambridge Companion to Postmodern Theology*, ed. Kevin J. Vanhoozer (Cambridge, UK: Cambridge University Press, 2003), 224.

25. This point was affirmed at the Second Council of Constantinople in the following terms: "If anyone shall say that the wonder-working Word of God is one [Person] and the Christ that suffered another . . . and that his miracles and the

sufferings which of his own will he endured in the flesh were not of the same [Person]: let him be anathema." *The Capitula of the Council*, III, in *The Seven Ecumenical Councils*, vol. 14 of *Nicene and Post-Nicene Fathers*, Second Series, ed. Philip Schaff and Henry Wace (Boston: Hendrickson, 1900), 312.

26. Karl Barth, *Church Dogmatics*, 13 vols., ed. G. W. Bromiley and T. F. Torrance (Edinburgh: T. & T. Clark, 1956–1974), II/1, 16; cf. 52.

27. At the same time, the fact that Jesus is the image of Israel's God in particular meant that early Christians acknowledged a responsibility to square their claims about his status with knowledge about God already disclosed in Israel's history, whether by appeal to the fulfilment of prophecy in, e.g., Matthew 1–2, or in terms of more extended arguments regarding the divine character of the sort developed by Paul in Romans 9–11. In this respect, while it remains the case that Jesus defines the content of the divine image, he does not do so (*contra* Marcion) from an epistemological *Stunde nul.*

28. Again, other people can be said to disclose the meaning of the divine image only indirectly, by virtue of their relationship to Jesus: it is Jesus who, by calling them to a place in his body, *defines* their identity, while they merely *illustrate* Jesus' identity.

29. It may seem odd at first glance to view the books of the Old Testament as telling Jesus' story, but this is certainly the understanding of the New Testament writers themselves (see, e.g., Matt. 26:56; Luke 24:27; Acts 18:28; Rom. 3:21-22a) and represents is the decisive reason why the Old Testament remains (*contra* both Marcion and Schleiermacher) indispensable for Christian proclamation.

30. The clearest statement of this principle of sufficiency within the Bible is John 20:30-31: "Now Jesus did many other signs in the presence of his disciples, which are not written in this book. But these are written so that you may come to believe that Jesus is the Messiah, the Son of God, and that through believing you may have life in his name."

31. "Vision . . . is one thing and theology is another, because it is not the same to say something about God as it is to gain and see God." Gregory Palamas, *Defence of the Holy Hesychasts* 2.3.49, ed. Christou, vol. 1, 582.3–6; cited in Dumitru Staniloae, *Revelation and Knowledge of the Triune God*, vol. 1 of *The Experience of God: Orthodox Dogmatic Theology*, ed. Ioan Ionita and Robert Barringer (Brookline, Mass.: Holy Cross Orthodox Press, 1994), 115.

32. Thus, in line with the material presented at the beginning of chapter 7, it is important to keep in mind the distinction between baptism and Eucharist as direct address to the baptizand or communicant on the one hand (where the focus is that person's relationship to God) and as protocol of discernment on the other (where the focus is on the communal discernment of Christ's body in those being baptized or communicated).

33. "The gospel should really not be something written, but a spoken word which brought forth the [Old Testament] Scriptures, as Christ and the apostles have done. This is why Christ himself did not write anything but only spoke. He called his teaching not Scripture but gospel, meaning good news or a proclamation that

is spread by word of mouth." Martin Luther, "A Brief Instruction on What to Look For and Expect in the Gospels," in *Word and Sacrament I*, vol. 35 of *Luther's Works*, American ed., ed. E. Theodore Bachmann (Philadelphia: Fortress Press, 1960), 123; cf. 119–21 for the contrast Luther draws between amassing information about Christ and actually encountering Christ in the gospel.

34. Dietrich Bonhoeffer, *Life Together and Prayerbook of the Bible*, vol. 5 of *Dietrich Bonhoeffer Works*, ed. Geffrey B. Kelly (Minneapolis: Fortress Press, 1996), 113. This is not to deny (as Bonhoeffer himself notes on the very next page) that "by God's grace a person may break through to assurance, new life, the cross and community" without any human intermediary, only that this divine possibility should not be used as an occasion for human presumption. For a similar perspective from a different confessional tradition, see Staniloae, *Revelation and Knowledge of the Triune God*, 42.

35. One might classify such reading, along with prayer, as what Hütter calls an "*active waiting* for God's activity" that looks "to the point that it is engaged publicly, that is, audibly" in the ministry of the church. See Hütter, *Suffering Divine Things*, 72–73.

36. This is true even of baptism and Eucharist, insofar as they function as protocols of discernment.

37. Martin Luther, *D. Martin Luthers Werke, Briefwechsel*, 18 vols. (Weimar, 1930–), 3:81-82; cited in George Hunsinger, *Disruptive Grace: Studies in the Theology of Karl Barth* (Grand Rapids, Mich.: Eerdmans, 2000), 89.

38. Feuerbach, *The Essence of Christianity* (New York: Harper & Row, 1957), 268.

39. "The other person is only a 'You' insofar as God brings it about. . . . *The claim of the other rests in God alone; for this very reason, it remains the claim of the other.*" Dietrich Bonhoeffer, *Sanctorum Communio: A Theological Study of the Sociology of the Church*, vol. 1 of *Dietrich Bonhoeffer Works*, ed. Clifford J. Green (Minneapolis: Fortress Press, 1998), 55. This christological mediation of the other establishes a more positive perspective on interhuman relations than the ultimately tragic vision of Levinas, in which the unmediated otherness of the other can be experienced only as a burden. See the penetrating (if perhaps ungenerous) critique of Levinas's thought in David Bentley Hart, *The Beauty of the Infinite: The Aesthetics of Christian Truth* (Grand Rapids, Mich.: Eerdmans, 2003), 75–82.

40. In this way, black theologians' insistence on the blackness of Christ is fully justified on the grounds that in a North American context the bodies of black women and men are those which society is most unwilling to see as bearers of the divine image.

41. John Webster sounds a salutary warning when he notes that "'skills' and 'roles' are always ambiguous. They do not exist without social frameworks, and such frameworks are notoriously protective against critique, even repressive. Furthermore, skills and roles can rather easily become reliable routines at our disposal. There are no infallible safeguards here." John Webster, *Word and Church: Essays in Christian Dogmatics* (Edinburgh: T. & T. Clark, 2001), 84.

Index